HOUSTON PUB

ADULTS AND CHILDREN
IN THE ROMAN EMPIRE

ADULTS AND CHILDREN IN THE ROMAN EMPIRE

THOMAS WIEDEMANN

YALE UNIVERSITY PRESS

NEW HAVEN AND LONDON

Published in the United Kingdom 1989 by Routledge.
Published in the United States 1989 by Yale University Press.

Copyright © 1989 by Thomas Wiedemann

Typeset by Columns of Reading
and printed in Great Britain by T.J. Press, Padstow

Library of Congress catalog card number: 88–51383

International standard book number: 0–300–04380–5

10 9 8 7 6 5 4 3 2 1

For my son
Richard
*6.2.1987

and in memory of my mother
Johanna Wiedemann
†10.4.1987

CONTENTS

LIST OF ILLUSTRATIONS

LIST OF ABBREVIATIONS

ANRW | H. Temporini & W. Haase (eds.), *Aufstieg und Niedergang der römischen Welt*, many vols. (Berlin/New York, 1972 on).

Bücheler, *CLE* | F. Bücheler, *Carmina Latina Epigraphica* (Leipzig, 1921).

CIL | *Corpus Inscriptionum Latinarum*, many vols. (Berlin, 1869 on).

CJ | The *Codex Justinianus*, ed. P. Krueger (1877: reprint Dublin/Zürich, 1967).

CSEL | The *Corpus Scriptorum Ecclesiasticorum Latinorum*, many vols. (Vienna, 1866 on).

Daremberg-Saglio | C. Daremberg & E. Saglio (eds.), *Dictionnaire des antiquités grecques et romaines*, 5 vols. (Paris, 1877 on).

Digest | Justinian's *Digest* of Roman law; the standard text is that of Th. Mommsen & P. Krueger, available with an English translation by A. Watson; 4 vols. (Philadelphia, 1985).

IG | *Inscriptiones Graecae*, many vols. (Berlin, 1873 on).

ILCV | E. Diehl (ed.), *Inscriptiones Latinae Christianae Veteres*, 3 vols. (reprint Berlin, 1961).

ILS | H. Dessau (ed.), *Inscriptiones Latinae selectae*, 3 vols. (Berlin, 1892–1914).

JRS	The *Journal of Roman Studies* (1910 on).
Mansi	J. D. Mansi, *Sacrorum Conciliorum Nova et Amplissima Collectio*, 52 vols. (reprints Paris, 1901, and Graz, 1960).
MGHAA	*Monumenta Germaniae Historica, Auctores Antiquissimi*, many vols. (Berlin, 1878 on).
Pauly-Wissowa	G. Wissowa (ed.), *Paulys Real-encyclopädie der classischen Altertumswissenschaft*, many vols. (Stuttgart, 1894 on).
PG	J. P. Migne, *Patrologiae Cursus Completus, Series Graeca*, many vols. (Paris, 1886 on).
PL	J. P. Migne, *Patrologiae Cursus Completus, Series Latina*, many vols. (Paris, 1878 on).
Pliny, *NH*	Pliny the Elder's encyclopaedia, the *Naturalis Historia*; text with English translation in 10 volumes by H. Rackham, H. H. S. Jones & D. E. Eichholz (Loeb, 1944–63).
RIB	L. R. Collingwood & R. P. Wright (eds.), *The Roman Inscriptions of Britain*, vol. I (Oxford, 1965).
TAPhA	*Transactions of the American Philological Association*, (1869 on).

INTRODUCTION

It almost seems as if the relationship between parents and children in antiquity had a tenderness often missing in modern times, when families drift apart and their members lose touch with one another.[1]

The history of childhood is a nightmare from which we have only recently begun to awake.[2]

These contradictory estimates of the ancients' attitudes to their children illustrate the very different approaches and concerns which modern scholars have brought to the subject. The roots of their interest have been various, as will be the reasons for the interest of the readers of this book. One of the earliest approaches came from educational psychologists developing the theories of Piaget and others; another from social anthropology, following on descriptions of childhood in non-western societies such as Margaret Mead's *Growing up in Samoa*. The Frankfurt School's belief that historical events needed to be explained in terms of the traumatic childhoods suffered by historical figures such as Martin Luther or Adolf Hitler led from 'psychobiography' to the 'psychohistory' of which Lloyd de Mause's *History of Childhood* is an example.

Another line of approach has come from the development of interest in social and economic history during this century. The so-called Annales School in France has been particularly influential here. This approach stresses that particular historical events, especially political choices, can only be understood within the context of climate and physical geography, factors which are relatively permanent, while human institutions such as states and religious systems come and go. Philippe Ariès suggested that a similar uniform picture could be drawn of the way in which small children were treated in many pre-industrial societies.[3] He argued that pre-bourgeois societies, both Muslim and Christian, did not share our own clear distinction between adult and child. His interpretation requires considerable qualification even for Christian late antiquity, and can hardly be applied at all to classical antiquity. For the city-states of the ancient Mediterranean, including republican Rome, the distinction between the free adult, who was at the centre of civic activity, and his children (together with his wife and his slaves) was basic to the proper ordering of civilisation.

Approaches such as these are stimulating, but they have their weaknesses. There is a tendency to look for evidence that might support a particular theory, and to ignore evidence that does not. What is exceptional may be interpreted as though it were the norm. This is an inevitable risk with a subject like the ancients' attitude to childhood, since there are no systematic accounts from antiquity itself; the modern scholar has to rely on odd references or anecdotes which he extracts from literature, or he has to interpret inscriptions or reliefs. Historical understanding requires generalisations: and it is inevitable that that process results in theories or 'models' which emphasise only a part of the wide range of cultural attitudes to be found in any society. Thus Alan Macfarlane's distinction between the attitudes towards children of 'peasant' societies as opposed to 'market' societies such as England is extremely valuable; but we cannot apply it to those exceptionally rich Romans whose attitudes were in many respects like those of propertied Englishmen. On the other hand Paul Veyne has argued that the alleged sexual licence of a minority of this same group of aristocratic Romans was 'normal' in the classical period.[4] Scholars have not always found it easy to avoid the temptation to draw wide-ranging conclusions that ignore distinctions of chronological period, geographical area, social class, and perhaps especially gender.

The evidence that we have is insufficient to allow us to reconstruct the Roman child's view of the world. (The same is unfortunately true of Roman slaves, and even of Roman women.) It does allow a fairly full picture of some aspects of children's life in antiquity, most obviously education and schooling, on which many excellent monographs have been written. But it also allows a general picture of the place which adults assigned to children in their – adult – picture of the social world. This book attempts to trace changes in those adult attitudes to childhood. It is not intended to be a comprehensive collection of the evidence, literary, legal, epigraphical, or archaeological, about children in the Roman empire.[5] Most of my examples are drawn from Latin sources, from the western part of the empire; I suspect that a very similar book could be written about the Greek world, where there is in fact a great deal more evidence.

The theme is one of change: changing attitudes towards the place of children during the first four centuries AD. These changes were connected with, if not entirely the result of, wider changes in Mediterranean society which were themselves caused by the *Pax Romana*, the unification of the Mediterranean lands within the Roman empire. No attempt is made here to narrate the political background, or to explain the social changes that led from the autonomous city-states of the classical period to the world-state of the Christian emperors of the fourth century.[6]

I began to collect the material which has gone into this book fifteen years ago; the unfulfilled intention was to submit it as an Oxford thesis. What strengths my interpretation of that evidence may have are due not only to my supervisors then, Dr Oswyn Murray and the Revd Dr Henry Chadwick, but also to Mr B. H. Warmington and the many other colleagues in Bristol and elsewhere with whom I have had the pleasure of discussing issues of Roman history. The judges of the 1987 Croom Helm Ancient History Prize made many helpful suggestions for improvements to the first draft. As always, my thanks are due to my wife Margaret for her advice on how to make my English prose more comprehensible than it would otherwise have been.

Bristol, May 1988

NOTES

1 G. M. Lee, 'Coptic Christianity in a changing world', *Studies in Church History 18: Religion and National Identity* (Oxford, 1982), 43.
2 L. de Mause, *The History of Childhood* (Chicago, 1974), 1.
3 P. Ariès, *Centuries of Childhood* (Eng.trans., London/New York, 1962).
4 A. Macfarlane, *Marriage and Love in England: Modes of Reproduction 1300–1840* (Oxford, 1986), section II: 'The value of children'. P. Veyne's

views – intended to be controversial – were first published in 'La Famille et l'amour sous le haut-empire romaine', *Annales* 33.1 (1978), 35 ff.

5 E.g. J. P. Neraudau, *Etre enfant à Rome* (Paris, 1984).

6 Introductions to the history of this period include M. Grant, *A History of Rome* (London, 1982); C. Wells, *The Roman Empire* (Fontana, 1984). For the social changes affecting the Mediterranean city during this period, cf. A. H. M. Jones, *The Greek City* (Oxford, 1940; paperback reprint, 1981). On the religious background to this period, see R. Lane Fox, *Pagans and Christians* (London, 1986).

Chapter One

THE CHILD IN THE CLASSICAL CITY

As the Roman empire developed from a collection of city communities in the classical period to the court-centred Christian world of late antiquity, we would expect changes to have taken place in popular, intellectual, and institutional perceptions of childhood and of the place of children in the community. It goes without saying that there will have been much continuity of attitude between these two periods, in both of which elite culture depended upon a peasantry whose existence was itself circumscribed by the climate, the soil, and the seasons.

Traces of any changes might be most apparent in the writings of the elite. A good place to begin our search would be the *Reflections* or *Meditations* of the Stoic philosopher Marcus Aurelius, who ruled the Roman world from AD 161 to 180.[1] It was Marcus' reign that was acclaimed by Edward Gibbon as the period when – before his own enlightened age – 'the condition of the human race was most happy and prosperous'. As a pre-Christian document, the *Reflections* is unique. Its format is that of a series of moralising meditations on issues which concerned the emperor, not in his official capacity, but simply as a human being confronting the world; the theme that worries him most is human mortality. The work's literary format inhibits the development of consistent lines of thought, and the *Reflections* is more free from theoretical speculation than any other type of Stoic writing. That does not make it more 'genuine' or 'authentic'. People may feel as well as think the way they do because that is the conventional way. But such conventions are the very substance of social history. We may be disappointed that the views the emperor sets down in his address whose Greek title is *To Himself*, are unoriginal, and that he fails to perceive contradictions between the different conventional standpoints he expresses. Classical writing (prose as much as verse) was normally intended not for private reading, but public recitation before a critical audience which expected adherence to the conventions of a genre. Where such philosophical or literary writings were intended for publication, the authors tried to avoid contradicting themselves; Marcus' *Reflections* are uniquely valuable precisely because they were not aimed at any audience other than the writer himself, so that contradictory feelings are candidly expressed.

Marcus' age – like every age – was an age of transition: and some of the contradictions in the *Reflections* may be explained in terms of that transition from the classical to the late antique world, with a court and a Senate whose members no longer came just from the landed Latin-speaking elite of Italy and the Italian-colonised areas of the west, but also from the Greek-speaking and even Punic-speaking areas of the eastern Mediterranean.[2] Although the direction in which these tendencies were leading may have been far from obvious to Marcus Aurelius, his world had already travelled a long way from the 'restored Roman republic' of Augustus, or even the Latin-speaking Italian state of Vespasian or Trajan, the emperors to whom he looked as his paradigms. On the one hand the *Reflections* looks back to the traditions of the individual Greek city and of the Roman republic. But at the same time the very facts that Marcus was a Roman emperor who saw himself as having an obligation to serve the universe, and that he needed to express his feelings in a notebook intended only for his own eyes, point forward to the feelings both of belonging to a universal community, and that one was an individual who stood apart from the community of one's birth, feelings that in late antiquity were to to be articulated so successfully by Christianity. Radical Christians were to go so far as to reject the civic society of this secular world entirely; for Marcus, the moral requirements of membership of the cosmopolis were paramount, but he could never forget that he was a Roman. The question that interests us here is whether Marcus' Stoicism led him to a view of childhood and of children – including his own childhood, and his own children, four of whom died as youngsters – in any way different from that which had been dominant in the classical world of autonomous citizen-communities.

Stoic cosmopolitanism committed the emperor to the view that all men without exception had the potential to share in the divine reason of the universe. In theory, this might lead him to the view – later universalised by Christian infant baptism – that even the youngest infant's life was worth as much as that of any adult. On three separate occasions, meditating on death as the great leveller, the emperor expresses just that opinion: 'What then will be the difference between the most advanced in age, and the one who has died before his time?'; 'What advantage did those who clung greedily to their lives have over those who died young? . . . Consider the infinity of future time: what is the difference in that context between a three-day-old child and a man who has lived for three generations?' 'The only life which a man has to lose is that which he is living at the moment . . . this means that he who lives longest and he who dies soonest come off the same.'[3]

In the face of eternity, then, the child and the adult are equals. Yet if that idea looks forward to late antiquity's view that children are just younger than, not different from, adults, Marcus Aurelius draws no practical consequences from the theory. There is indeed one point where he reflects upon the fact that all 'natural' things are beautiful, and that every stage of human life is 'natural'. 'The sensitive eye will recognise that a certain power and beauty belongs to an old woman or an old man, as well as the grace of a youth.' Yet if the old are, in this sense, the equals of young adults, it did not occur to Marcus to take the further step of saying that childhood had the same natural beauty as adulthood. In his very last 'Reflection', he says that five years as a citizen of this great city (the world) are the equal of one hundred. We must understand this precisely: he is not referring to the first five years of a man's life as a child, but five years exercising the privileges of a citizen of the world-community.[4]

Stoic equality did not extend to those who only imperfectly shared in the rational order of nature. For all that he deeply loved his wife and children, it did not occur to Marcus that women and children were included. Their spirits are simply insufficiently human. When he is worried about being dominated by the less rational element in his soul, he asks himself: 'Whose soul inhabits me at the moment? Is it a little child's, a youngster's (MEIPAKIOY), a woman's, a tyrant's, that of a beast of burden or of a wild animal?' What is the soul of an evil man? 'A black, feminine heart; the heart of a wild beast, a beast of the field, that of a child, lazy and unreliable, stupid and deceitful; the heart of a tyrant.'[5]

The child occurs in association with animals, women, and tyrants – all four symbolise behaviour opposed to that of the adult male citizen. This conventional pattern was entirely appropriate to the classical city-state ruled by the adult male hoplites and legionaries who fought its battles. Marcus does not question the ideal of the community of formally equal adult male citizens. He does not question the stock theme of Greek philosophy and rhetoric that the tyrant has no place in a just political, and therefore human, society. In the same way, it never occurs to him that children have a place in human society. The man who does not follow the precepts of philosophy is no better than a child. Politics are just 'the arguments of children and their games'; the unphilosophical who concern themselves only with achieving honour and status in this life are 'like puppies fighting, or children who love quarrelling, who laugh at one moment and then cry the next'. Marcus shares the beliefs held by philosophers six or seven centuries before him that those adults who do not think philosophically must be dismissed as irrational, like children: he cites Heraclitus' criticism of men who rely blindly on traditional beliefs as 'like children obeying their parents', and similarly Socrates' dictum that the beliefs of the average man were like 'Lamiae', the story-time witches used to scare children. What is appropriate to children is not appropriate to the rational adult. In none of these passages is there any interest in children as being different from adults; the concept of childhood occurs only so that adults who fail to live up to the dictates of reason can be condemned. It is adults who share in reason, and hence can act as nature intended them to act – for instance, by accepting the naturalness of dying: 'If anyone is scared of a work of nature, that is the mark of a child.'[6]

It is not surprising, then, that Marcus Aurelius should have been unable to see childhood from a child's point of view. There are odd references to the things that happened to children: they are all described from the viewpoint of parent or adult. Children are born, children fall ill, and children die. As far as Marcus' interests go, the important thing about a child is that it is a gift from the divine intelligence. When a child falls ill, the philosopher must accept his child's illness as a natural event, while the average unphilosophical parent will pray that his sick child will not die: 'Where another man prays, "Spare me the loss of my little child", you should

rather pray, "May I have no fear of losing him"'. One of Marcus'
purposes in writing the *Reflections* was to come to terms with his
own fears and experiences; it is not reprehensible that he was
concerned with how the death of his children affected himself.
Nevertheless there is no hint that he felt that premature death was
regrettable because it was a tragedy for the children. When he
thinks of his dead children, he quotes Homer's *Iliad* (6,147 f.):

> Like leaves which the wind blows to the ground,
> Such are the generations of men.

He twice cites a fragment from Euripides' *Antiope*:

> If I and my pair of children are forgotten by the gods,
> Then even this must have a reason.

He finds solace in a story told about Epictetus:

> Epictetus once said that when you kiss your child, you should
> say to yourself, 'Perhaps it will be dead in the morning'. 'Words
> of ill-omen', they told him. Not ill-omened, but referring to a
> process of nature. Otherwise it would also be ill-omened to speak
> of the corn being harvested.

For Marcus, his children are like the corn crop: one of the
conventional ways in which classical Greeks and Romans had been
used to perceiving their children.[7]

For the ancients more than for modern westerners, child
mortality was a fact that required coming to terms with. It is
significant that it is one of the few contexts in which Marcus feels
that children need to be meditated upon. One of the others is the
role of a child's *paedagogus*, 'childminder'. (There are no references
to formal schools in the *Reflections*; the ΣΧΩΛΗ of 11,18.18 is not a
classroom, but a public disputation.) Marcus takes it for granted
that children hate authority, and that the normal way of teaching
is by forcing the child to learn against his will. The student of
philosophy must be quite different in his approach: 'If practice falls
short of precept, return to the attack after each failure . . . love that
to which you return, and do not return to philosophy as though it
were a *paedagogus*.' The *paedagogus*' tongue symbolises criticism
(Athenian Old Comedy shares 'the *paedagogus*' freedom of speech').
When the *paedagogus* is away, one can breathe freely again. Here
too Marcus is expressing commonplace views about the relationship

between teacher and child that were normally if not universally taken for granted in antiquity.[8]

Not only was Marcus uninterested in seeing the world through the eyes of a child: more surprisingly, he seems to have had little interest in his own childhood. Leaving aside the first, introductory, book of the *Reflections*, the one possible indication of what his own childhood was like is a reference to the earth as not just his father and mother, but his father, mother, and *nurse*: at death, he will 'sink down upon that from which my father derived the seed, my mother the blood, and my nurse the milk that formed me' – indicative of one major difference between the experiences of children (not just those of the elite) in the ancient world and our own.[9]

In Book 1, there is a list of individuals to whom Marcus gives thanks for making him the person he has turned out to be. Very little emerges about his childhood. He mentions the virtues he learnt from his grandfather, father and, mother. His great-grandfather was responsible for having him educated at home rather than at a public school (a theme which recurs in ancient discussions on education). Only then is there a more personal reminiscence:

> It was my *tropheus* ['he who brought me up'] who dissuaded me from supporting either the Greens or the Blues in the Circus races, or the *Palmularii* or the *Scutarii* in the arena; who encouraged me to put up with hard work, to be limited in my desires, to look after my own needs, to mind my own affairs and to be unwilling to listen to slander.[10]

After that, Marcus' list is simply of the teachers and philosophers to whom he thought that as a precocious teenager he had owed the development of whatever virtue and reason he had; and the book ends with two exceptionally long chapters, the first thanking his adoptive father and predecessor as emperor, Antoninus Pius, the second (just a little shorter) thanking the gods for their respective contributions.

This first book cannot be classified as 'reminiscences', and there is certainly no material here suggesting what we would classify as an 'autobiography'. Yet Marcus' attitude to his own childhood reflects classical antiquity's view of childhood in general. What mattered was his place in his natural family, a family which included nurse and *paedagogus* as much as parents and grand-parents, his education (in Marcus' case, unusually, in philosophy as well as literature), and his induction into his role as a citizen: for Marcus, very exceptionally, the role of Antoninus' successor. That was all. Yet this should not lead us to assume that men like Marcus did not love their children. Nor were they incapable of seeing how children perceive the world. One of his anecdotes concerns an old man who played with a female slave-child: he asked her to give him her top as a leave-taking present, since he saw that in the child's eyes that top was the most precious thing in the world. Marcus' purpose in telling the story is to condemn the unphilosophical: their wants are no different from the irrational child's top.[11] The assumption that childhood is imperfect remains. But the anecdote shows that adults in antiquity were as capable as we are of trying to imagine the world from a child's point of view – if only they thought that there was some point to the exercise.

CHANCES OF SURVIVAL

Marcus' attitudes may have been conventional, but many of those conventions were rooted in the realities of ancient childhood. The most important reality of child life then, as in most human societies until a few generations ago, was high infant mortality. Every age-group and every status-group was of course liable to succumb to sudden epidemics to an extent which the development of better water supply, sanitation, and pharmaceuticals in the last two centuries has made it difficult for us today to imagine. But when a Roman listed the characteristics of different age-groups, it was vulnerability – *infirmitas* – that was characteristic of children.[12]

In industrialised countries today it can be assumed that, when there are no perinatal complications, a child will survive to adulthood, and have a life expectancy of over seventy years. Infant mortality has not been eradicated, but it is so slight that most parents need not, or can choose not to, take it into account. Recent figures for infant mortality and life expectancy at birth in industrialised countries as are shown in Table 1. The definition of 'infant mortality' employed here is the number of babies out of every thousand live births who die before their first birthday. Different countries' statistical offices have slightly different

11

definitions. The Registrar-General for England and Wales publishes a separate figure for stillbirths; in 1985, 5.22 stillbirths per thousand were recorded (the figure for infant mortality in that year was 9.36). It will occasion no surprise that the most dangerous period for a baby is the week after birth; the mortality rate recorded for the first 24 hours was 2.49 in 1985, for the following six days 1.86, and for the rest of the first year only 5.00. After that, survival is relatively well assured; of 8,675 children who died before having reached their fifteenth birthday in England and Wales in 1985, 6,141 were infants.[13]

Table 1 Infant mortality and life expectancy in industrialised countries

	Infant mortality (per thousand)	Life expectancy (years)	
		Males	Females
England and Wales (1978–80)	10.8	70.4	76.6
United States (1982)	10.9	70.8	78.2
West Germany (1980–2)	10.9	70.2	76.9

But our modern assumption that a child, once born, can look forward to becoming a septuagenarian is very different from the experience of other countries and ages. The information on population and mortality given by the United Nations *Statistical Yearbooks* is not always based on uniform criteria and frequently depends upon unreliable estimates. Nevertheless it gives some idea of how exceptional the industrialised west is in this respect. Even some European countries report significantly higher infant mortality rates, and lower life expectancy (see Table 2).

Where reasonably reliable estimates for infant mortality are available for 'Third World' countries, they are of a quite different

Table 2 European countries with higher infant mortality and lower life expectancy rates

	Infant mortality (per thousand)	Life expectancy (years)	
		Males	Females
Portugal (1975)	26.0	65.09	72.86
Romania (1976–8)	28.0	67.42	72.18
Yugoslavia (1979–80)	29.9	67.72	73.15
Soviet Union (1971–2)	27.7	64.00	74.00

order. The Turkish Demographic Survey estimated that in Turkey in 1966, 153 out of every 1,000 children died before reaching the age of 1; life expectancy was calculated to be 53.7 years. In 1967, infant mortality in Tanzania was estimated at 160–5 per thousand; in 1960–1 in Gabon, 229; and in Zambia in 1960, 259. And it is worth noting that even countries which had industrialised in the nineteenth century had significantly higher rates only a generation ago. While the infant mortality rate for the United States was only 11.9 per thousand in 1981, in 1940 it had been 47.0 (and 72.9 amongst black Americans). In the Federal Republic of Germany in 1983–5, 98.9 per cent of male babies and 99.2 per cent of females could expect to survive their first year, and 98.5 per cent of boys and 98.8 per cent of girls could expect to reach the age of 15. But at the beginning of the century (1901–10), the comparable figures for the first year of life were 79.8 and 82.9 per cent, and for the fifteenth only 72.0 and 74.9 per cent. Over a quarter of boys died before they were 5; almost a quarter of girls died before they were 10. Infant mortality rates of between 150 and 200 per thousand were the norm in industrialised European countries at the beginning of this century.[14]

Statistical information about contemporary under-industrialised societies is unreliable enough; we simply do not have the equivalent sources of information to reconstruct mortality or life expectancy rates for the Roman world. This lies in the nature of our evidence. Literary texts select anecdotes about people's ages not for being typical or 'average', but for being remarkable or exceptional, and even where the evidence is reliable, they make no attempt at being comprehensive. Pliny the Elder's encyclopaedia contains a discussion on the subject of longevity. Some of the material is dismissed as fabulous by Pliny himself, but he also makes use of the results of an official census held three years before the time of writing, in AD 72/4. Pliny chooses to select only one region of Italy (Aemilia), and while he tells us that seventy-seven persons claimed to be over 100 years old in this region, he gives us no information about younger age-groups, nor about the size of the population as a whole. Being a centenarian was remarkable; dying as an infant was not, and information about that can be extracted from Pliny only incidentally. This applies to fertility as well as mortality: we learn that Cornelia, the mother of the Gracchi, had twelve children, and the elder Agrippina nine, only because the

children were alternately male and female. There is no parallel to
the information offered about an ordinary citizen of Fiesole named
Gaius Crispinius Hilarus: on 11 April 4 BC, he offered sacrifice on
the Capitol accompanied by his six sons, two daughters, twenty-
seven grandchildren (eight of them with their wives) and eighteen
great-grandchildren.[15]

Since the nineteenth century, scholars have turned to inscriptions for information on which to base calculations of life
expectancy. There are several thousand inscriptions, many of them
from Rome itself or from North Africa, which record the age of the
deceased. But the problems involved in interpreting such evidence
were pointed out a long time ago.[16] The older individuals became,
the greater the tendency to claim even greater seniority, and add
another decade or two to their lives. Nor are those recorded in this
way a typical sample of the population. A tombstone is relatively
expensive to set up, and those commemorated belonged to the
more substantial households. That means that while the statistical
evidence may not have been slanted away from children towards
adults, or away from slaves towards richer citizens, it is slanted
away from the slaves and children of the poor, and towards those
children and slaves who belonged to the households of the rich.

Perhaps more importantly, we just cannot be at all certain what
proportion of infants and children were honoured with a formal
tombstone, and for what reasons some parents chose to honour
some children in this way. There is no way of knowing how many
infants died before they were 40 days old, and consequently (at
least in the classical period) may have been subject to different
forms of burial (see Chapter 6). And statistics based on epigraphy
can take no account of two other facts of ancient child life,
infanticide and the exposition of the new-born.

Both literary and epigraphical evidence reveal another problem
about statistics of this sort in antiquity: there was a surprising
degree of uncertainty about just when a person had been born. It
seems astonishing that there should be controversy about (for
example) the date of birth of the later emperor Tiberius; but some
thought that he had been born in 43 or 41 BC rather than in 42.
Nor was there unanimity about where he was born. The likelihood
of such uncertainty decreased substantially with Augustus' intro-
duction of birth registers,[17] and Tiberius' case is perhaps
exceptional; but it is an indication that people were much more

interested in knowing the exact hour and day of birth (in order to be able to cast an effective horoscope) than in the year. It did not matter all that much how many years old a child was. Many inscriptions, particularly from late antiquity, state that a person had lived for more or less, 'P[lus] M[inus]', a number of years. Romans were satisfied to count their age in terms of *lustra*, periods of five years which had their origins in the republican censuses. But these censuses were not always held exactly every five years. The effect seems to have been that people's perception of their own age tended to be approximate, something that is confirmed by the statistically improbable frequency with which literary and epigraphical evidence gives people's ages as some number divisible by five. Thus of Pliny's seventy-seven Aemilian centenarians recorded in the census of AD 74, only one declared an age not divisible by five. To refer to someone's age in terms of *lustra* was not just a poetic conceit: 'Her playful boy had added two years to two *lustra*', or, 'He who seals his first *quinquennium* with a new *lustrum*'.[18]

For these and other reasons, we should have a number of reservations about the reliability of figures based on the evidence of inscriptions. For what they are worth, assessments of inscriptions on Roman tombs have concluded that about one-third of the population was dead by the age of 10; average life expectancy for men may have been 22 years, for women below 20 years. A study of similar information from a first and second century AD cemetery at Carthage has revealed that here only one fifth of the population was recorded as having died by the age of 10. These estimates have to be seen as highly approximate, and there is no need to speculate about possible medical or social reasons for the differences between them.[19]

Rather than construct a picture upon unreliable and problematical empirical evidence, it is more sensible to make assumptions by analogy with comparative evidence from other pre-industrial societies. Allowance must of course be made for differences in social practices such as the forms of marriage, or the acceptability of infanticide, as well as the availability of food and medical help to different status-groups in a population. Nevertheless theoretical 'population pyramids' can give a very general impression of the level of infant and child mortality in a pre-industrial society, an impression not contradicted by the scattered pieces of empirical evidence which literature and epigraphy provide us with for the ancient world.

One interesting piece of evidence is a 'life table' which the jurist Ulpian says was used by the imperial taxation officials to calculate life expectancy at different ages (infant mortality was not of course of interest to such officials). While some scholars have expressed extreme scepticism about the applicability of this text, Professor Bruce Frier has suggested that it corresponds to the 'model' of the population of Mauritius in the 1940s, and has proposed a life table for the Roman citizen population in which the infant mortality rate was 350 per thousand, only 49 per cent of children saw their fifth birthday, and just 40 per cent of the population survived to the age of 20. In other words, every couple needed to have five children if two of them were to reach the age where they would have children themselves. Such a conclusion would in general terms not be contradicted by our literary, epigraphical, and archaeological evidence.[20]

Such tables do not claim to be more than an approximate guide. There will have been different figures for different social groups and in different parts of the empire as a result of different marriage patterns, birth control, exposition, and infanticide; and there may have been changes over time, as a result of the 'individualism' or of the development of Christian attitudes which some scholars have postulated.[21] It is enough of an insight into the ancient world if we note that where life expectancy lies between 20 and 25 years, any parent must expect there to be only a fifty–fifty chance that a particular child will survive to the age of 10, and therefore a less than one-in-two chance that he or she will survive to become an adult. That applied to families of all social classes: no doubt the children of the poor were more likely to succumb to illnesses as a result of undernourishment, particularly during the one year in three which followed an under-average harvest, but the children of the rich were not immune. Only three of the twelve children of Cornelia recorded by Pliny are known to have survived into adulthood; three of Agrippina's nine died as children. Even in the imperial family, there were numerous children who died before being of an age where they might play the sort of political or social role that leaves a trace in our literary sources.[22]

That circumstance makes it easier to understand why parents seem to have been less willing to invest emotionally in their children, and especially in babies, than in a modern industrial family where there are fewer children, but all of them are expected to survive to adulthood. If the first year of life in particular was a time that a child might not survive, then the extent to which parents gave their children to nurses to be looked after can be seen not just as a refusal to commit themselves to the unpleasant work of changing nappies and being kept awake at night by the need to breast-feed, but perhaps more as a refusal to invest unnecessary emotions in a child who might not survive. It is noteworthy that the word for 'baby' originates in the culture of north-western Europe, where for some centuries a child's chances of surviving into adulthood have been exceptionally good. Romans, Greeks, and most European peasant cultures, in which there were actually far more babies (proportionally), did not allow themselves to feel enough affection for the young child to need a specific word for him.

The week immediately after birth, when a baby will actually be losing weight until it learns to suck properly, is the most critical; by the end of that week it will be clear whether it is feeding well enough to have a chance of survival. Girls tend to have a better chance of survival than boys. It was appropriate that the *dies lustricus*, the day on which the Romans gave a child its name, should have been the eighth for girls, and the ninth for boys. There was no point in ascribing individuality to a baby in its first week.[23]

INFIRMITAS PUERORUM: CHILDREN AS PHYSICALLY AND MENTALLY WEAK

The Romans perceived children as particularly vulnerable. There is a considerable number of occasions where children's illnesses appear in literature: Ovid's account of Ceres' miraculous healing of the little boy Triptolemus at Eleusis may be taken as an example.[24] Lists of medical and magical household remedies for use in cases of illness in infants and children survive from antiquity. Cato the Elder in the second century BC had recommended bathing young children in the warmed-up urine of cabbage eaters, on the grounds that this would make them strong.[25] Pliny refers to children suffering from infantile convulsions if their nurses have been eating parsley. In an account of the efficacy of spittle, he recommends that a nurse should protect a baby against danger by spitting at it three times if a stranger comes into the room, or if the child is looked at by someone (i.e. a stranger) while asleep. Not that Pliny is prepared to believe in any old charm: he vehemently denies Democritus' account of the efficacy of various parts of the anatomy of the chameleon, including its tongue and eye, at childbirth. But there is a whole chapter on remedies for infants: butter is recommended for teething troubles or ulcers of the mouth; a wolf's tooth or piece of skin from a wolf may help too. Against diarrhoea, he recommends smearing the mother's or nurse's breast with hare's rennet. Goat's milk or hare's brains are useful during teething. Children who do not quieten down can be restrained by putting some goat's dung in their nappies; this is said to work particularly well with little girls.[26]

In his account of the magical lore ascribed to the Persians (but practised throughout the Roman world), Pliny lists further purported cures, in which he does not himself believe. Whatever the efficacy of the charms, the illnesses were real enough, and most of them will be readily identifiable to the parents of young children today. The list includes problems with drinking curdled milk, teething, inflammation, hernia, digestive problems, coughing, and incontinence. Some of the problems are psychological rather than physiological: teething is said to make children scared (*pavidos*); an ass's hide will make them free from fears.[27]

Children were not just more liable to sickness than adults, they were also more likely to be frightened. Consequently the ancient world saw them not just as examples, but – like women – as symbols of human fear as well as physical frailty. When, for example, after the destruction of Varus' legions in Germany in AD 9, some Roman units tried to break through to the safety of the Rhineland, their plan was betrayed: 'This was because the women and children, who were both frightened and exhausted, and troubled too by the darkness and the cold, kept calling to the soldiers to come back.' Philosophers like to develop the theme of the weakness of the new-born child. When Pliny describes how the animal world is subject to man, he begins with a description of man's weakness as a new-born baby.

On the day of his birth, Nature throws a naked human-being down on the naked earth to cry and wail; of all the other animals, none is so prone to cry, and to cry right from the start of its life. The idea that a baby soon smiles is a poetic fiction; that happens on the fortieth day at the earliest. After that first experience of daylight, children have all their limbs swaddled, a severer bondage than that of any domestic animal. Once successfully born, there he lies crying, with his hands and feet tied, the creature who is going to govern the rest, and because of the one fault of having been born, he begins his life with punishment. What madness, that some should think they are born to nobility from such beginnings.[28]

Consequently the appearance of a child in a dream was thought by professional dream interpreters to portend that the dreamer would become as helpless as a child, or perhaps even die. The best-known surviving handbook of dream interpretation is the *Oneiro-critica* of Artemidorus of Daldis in the second century AD, but his explanations seem to have been as acceptable to westerners as to Greeks. There were other respects in which children appeared on the dividing line between life and death: in magic, and in public executions (see Chapter 6, p. 179 below). These apparent peculiar-ities may be explained in terms of the Structuralist contrast between a society's 'central' and 'marginal' figures. In the Mediterranean city of the classical period – republican Rome as well as Greece – the adult male citizen was at the centre of activity. Hence those who were not adult male citizens were in various respects 'marginal'. Sometimes these groups are discussed by intellectuals who are interested in objectively describing them; but far more frequently they are mentioned, not for their own qualities (positive or negative), but because they symbolise the absence of certain qualities thought to be typical of the adult male citizen. Children frequently appear as one such symbol; others are the old, women, and slaves.[29]

The first function of the citizen was to fight to protect his community in war. Isidore, Bishop of Seville in Visigothic Spain in the seventh century AD, writing at the very end of antiquity to explain the language and customs of the classical age, notes that the *iuvenis* (young adult) 'is so-called because he begins to be able to help, *iuvare*': it is military help that is meant primarily. Children, women, and old men are different because they are not capable of joining in the fighting, while slaves are forbidden to do so, at least in normal circumstances. Warfare is the major theme of epic, and of its parallel prose form, historiography, and the largest single category of references to children in classical literature is as typical non-combatants. As fighting is a primary duty of the citizen, the virtue of courage in the face of the enemy plays an important role in rhetorical as well as other literary character descriptions. We have seen in Dio's account of the aftermath of Varus' disaster one of many instances where children share the absence of this virtue with women.[30]

In monumental representations, as well as literary accounts of warfare, children, women, and old men figure together as a group of the weak, in contrast to the men under arms who do the fighting; the groups of Dacian and Germanic civilians represented on Trajan's Column or on the Antonine Column are examples. One implication was that the victorious side in battle ought to spare the children of the defeated since, like the women and old men, they had not actively taken up arms: but once a boy had formally joined the ranks of adult citizens, then he could be considered an enemy whatever his actual age – like Cleopatra's son Caesarion, and Antony's son Antyllus after the battle of Actium: 'This enrolment [as adults] was to bring about their destruction. Octavian spared neither, but treated them as grown men, who had been vested with some semblance of authority.'[31]

In epic literature, this distinction between the child and the fighting man was a theme that can be traced back to Homer. Some of the most vivid descriptions of infant behaviour anywhere in ancient literature are to be found in the *Iliad*: but often they appear precisely to highlight the physical powerlessness of the child. When Ajax challenges Hector to battle, the Trojan hero replies that he is not going to be frightened 'like a feeble child, or like a woman, who know nothing of fighting'. The powerlessness of children is indicated by the parallel between the Trojans and children in a famous simile where Ajax retreats unwillingly, but at his own pace, in the face of a Trojan onslaught: 'He is like a stubborn donkey which refuses to be driven on until it has finished its meal, in spite of the feeble cudgelling it is given by the boys who are meant to be in charge of it.'[32]

By the nature of their subject matter, epic and historiography describe largely the affairs of fighting men; in some writers, such as Thucydides, women and children appear almost exclusively as victims. If war is normally an activity for men, then the appearance of such 'marginal' groups in the pages of history is a sign that warfare had become particularly brutal, as in the story of the massacre of a class of schoolchildren by Thracian (i.e. barbarian) mercenaries at Mycalessus during the Peloponnesian war. In Latin historiography, too, it is as symbols of war's victims that we find them, particularly as the victims of enslavement. Caesar's account of his conquest of Gaul is an example.[33]

All women and children are potential victims of enslavement at the hands of an enemy, but they may be the victims of enemies within as well as without the community. Ancient rhetoric makes the widow and orphan the extreme cases of those within the community liable to be exploited by the unscrupulous, and therefore the most deserving of support. Quintilian, in his textbook on oratory, refers to the frequency with which accused persons bring their children into court in order to excite the pity of the jury – he cites the example of an uncomprehending infant who when his father was in danger of conviction was asked by the defence counsel why he was crying, only to reply truthfully that it was because he had just been pinched by his *paedagogus*.[34] In that role the figures of widow and orphan appear in pagan, Jewish, and Christian moral tracts in antiquity and since. A good political leader – and specifically, in the period under discussion, the emperor – had an obligation to protect the weak, and in particular those women and children who had no one else to turn to. Women and children thus appear as symbolic figures on reliefs portraying *congiaria*, distributions of money, food, or clothing.[35]

But the child suffered from more than just a weak and undeveloped body. Greek thinkers had been in general agreement that what held the classical city-state together despite the conflicts of interest and sentiment of its members was the application of reason (*logos*) to the problems dividing them, and the avoidance of violence (*bia*) as a solution. Since the fifth century BC at least, intellectuals had assumed that there was some connection between the *logos* which corresponds to the English word 'reason', the *logos* which corresponds to the English idea of 'speech-making', and the *logos* which we translate as a 'word'. Women and old men had some share, if only potentially, in the *logos* of the adult male citizen; barbarians and slaves (at least 'true' slaves) had none. The child too symbolised the absence of *logos*. That was implicit in the words used to describe them; like barbarians, they were non-speakers – NHΠIOI in Greek, *in-fantes* in Latin. The child's inability to communicate in the way adults do made him a symbol of non-participation in the rational world of the adult citizen. That is another of the attitudes which can be found as early as Homer. When King Menelaus of Sparta wishes to criticise his retainer Eteoneus for making a rather silly suggestion (that Telemachus should be sent away from his palace), he says that 'He is talking nonsense: like a child'.[36]

The child's failure to think or plan rationally is taken for granted in Athenian tragedy. In Sophocles' *Ajax*, the hero is amazed to see that his son Eurysakes is able to sleep peacefully in spite of the dreadful dangers that are hovering over him. But then, as a child, he is just not capable of grasping what is going on. When Plato wished to draw attention to the Greeks' ignorance of their place in the universe, he told the story of how Solon was said to have visited Egypt and was told by the priests there, 'You Greeks are all children – there is no such thing as a Greek of mature years'. Latin philosophers such as Lucretius take over as axiomatic the view that no child can be intelligent. Dramatists share this view. A character in Terence says that it is the incompletely rational mind of a child which explains its propensity to quarrel for no reason at all: silly old women are just like children. Just occasionally the descriptions of childish or irrational behaviour are more vivid. In an Atellan farce a foolish person is compared to a child that stuffs anything it can lay its hands on into its mouth.[37]

In rhetoric, to call someone a boy is one of the ultimate insults. During the civil war of 43 BC, that was what Antony called Octavian during the period when the latter was fighting on the Senate's side, and since he was only 19 at the time, the insult rankled. Octavian went so far as to issue a formal decree that no one was to refer to him in this way. When Cicero defended Octavian against this and other of Antony's accusations in the Thirteenth *Philippic*, he had to admit, 'That is certainly a word which we apply to a particular age-group, but hardly to be used by someone who makes a boy a present of his own stupidity as a source of glory'. That childishness is foolishness, *pueritia amentia*, is common ground. These are the qualities of non-adults: and we may note that, in both Greece and Rome, 'child' was the standard way of addressing a slave, another individual who could not share in the community of adult citizens. In similar terms, children may be coupled with the aged: when Cicero wishes to denigrate an opponent by accusing him of being unable to act as a political leader should, he compares him 'To a little child or a foolish and powerless old man'.[38]

Intellectuals made attempts to explain this absence of adult rationality in children, as they tried to do for women and for barbarians; the rationality of adults was assumed to be the norm, and required no explanation. The Epicureans came up with an answer which might be sympathetically received today: children behaved in the irrational way that had once been common to all humanity in its beastly, pre-socialised state. Alternatively, children could be thought to have within them 'sparks of manliness', seeds of the virtues of liberality, gratitude, intelligence, wisdom, and bravery.[39]

Much more generally accepted was the view that the child's lack of rationality had something to do with an imbalance in the four humours. It was in fact analogous to an illness. The pre-Socratic physicist Diogenes of Apollonia in the fifth century BC had suggested that irrationality was due to an excess of the wet humour; that was the standard explanation for the inability of women, too, to share adult male rationality. Plato thought that children under 18, like women, had too much heat: hence it was a good idea for both groups to have their intake of wine strictly controlled.[40] Like women, slaves also had their wine apportioned by the master of their household in the ancient world. But while women and slaves are frequently accused of being secret or immoderate drinkers, there seem to be no discussions of alcohol problems amongst children.

Drinking wine – or rather, wine mixed with water – was one of the specific ways in which Mediterranean man distinguished himself not just from his women, children, and slaves, but also from those barbarians who lived to the north or the south of him. For the Stoics, who thought that all human beings were potentially rational, one way of explaining the absence of rational customs in actual human populations was by blaming different diets. Stoic ethnographers like Posidonius in the first half of the first century BC remarked upon the fact that northern Europeans (Celts and Germans) ate meat and drank milk; and they downed their imported wine without mixing it with water. No wonder their minds were less philosophical than those of Greeks or Romans. The slave herdsmen who rose in revolt against their owners in Sicily in 134 BC had been reduced to eating meat and drinking milk from the flocks in their charge; no wonder they behaved with such brutality. Was it a coincidence that young children drank milk? The fact that, before their first teeth appeared, they were unable to swallow anything more substantial than milk might be an explanation for their lack of reason.[41]

That Marcus Aurelius or Seneca should so frequently use the figure of the child as a symbol for irrationality – especially for the irrationality of an unphilosophical adult – was a natural consequence of their Stoicism. Children cannot think out their moral obligations: the best they can do is learn moral maxims off by heart. 'We give children proverbs – what the Greeks call *chriai* – to learn off by heart, since a childish mind which cannot yet comprehend anything more can nevertheless grasp such proverbs.' Seneca can use the difference between the human child and the human adult to illustrate the difference between natural things that are *adiaphora*, neither morally good nor morally bad, and natural things that are positively virtuous: 'He used to be a child: he has become adult. That is a difference of quality. For the child is irrational, the adult rational.'[42]

Lack of judgement, the inability to distinguish right from wrong or to follow duty rather than pleasure, are the salient marks of a child. Puberty brings with it not just physical growth, but also the ability to reason: a literary theme which we still find being used by poets in the fourth century AD. Congratulating his grandson on the birthday which makes him a *iuvenis*,[43] Ausonius says, 'This is the time when you are active with the strength of youth, and are able to distinguish brave deeds from weak deeds, and appear as your own adviser in behaviour and in speech'. It is difficult, says Cicero, to praise a child (in a rhetorical performance): childhood is of interest only because it precedes adult life: 'The thing itself cannot be praised, only its potential.'[44] It was all too well understood that one aspect of children's irrationality was that they were no respecters of social conventions. They would make rude noises at passers-by; they would chase peculiar adults, like Horace's poet, along the streets; they would pluck the beard of a venerable philosopher; and a favourite game would be to stick a coin firmly in the mud, and then wait to see if an adult would try to pick it up.[45] To the wide range of literary passages which take the non-rationality of children for granted, we may add some examples from the *Digest*, the sixth-century AD compilation of classical Roman law, where infants (here formally children below the age of 7) are coupled with lunatics. Neither is liable for homicide under the late republican *Lex Cornelia de Sicariis et Veneficiis*.[46]

Like women and slaves, the marginality of children occasionally gives them certain advantages. We have seen that they should not normally be killed in warfare, and generally have a claim to protection and respect from those more fortunate than themselves: in Juvenal's words, 'A boy is owed the greatest respect'. In a first-century AD school declamatory exercise ascribed to Quintilian, a child is 'sacred and venerable'. As a marginal being, the child is only partially a member of citizen society; but that implies that he is nearer to the world of the gods than the adult male. Hence the presence of young children as acolytes at religious ceremonies, both pagan and, later, Christian. The fortuitous utterances of children might be regarded as particularly ominous, since the very young, like the old, are nearer to the divine world (see Chapter 6).[47]

AFFECTION AND 'DISCIPLINE'

It was certainly not the case that Roman adults could see nothing positive or lovable in their children. Classical writers are quite capable of recording parents' pleasure in the company of their children; Vergil and Catullus both insist that it is a matter of fact that a new-born infant will smile at its father,[48] though we have seen that Pliny the Elder was well aware that the apparent smile of a very small baby with wind was not a real smile at all. Where appropriate, an ancient writer could marshal suitable rhetorical arguments in favour of bringing up children:

> Is it not a joy to acknowledge a child who possesses the qualities of both parents, to tend and educate a person who is both the physical and the mental mirror of yourself, so that, as he grows up, another self is created? Is it not a blessing, when we leave this life, to leave behind as our successor an heir both to our family and to our property, one that is our own, born of our own essence, so that only the mortal part of us passes away, while we live on in the child who succeeds us?

This speech was attributed by Cassius Dio to Augustus, trying to persuade wealthy Romans to take on the responsibilities of parenthood.[49]

Augustus' worries about childlessness in senatorial and equestrian families suggest that a considerable number of wealthier Romans saw children as a luxury rather than a necessity, a luxury which some preferred not to afford. But their attitude was by no means the social norm. In a pre-industrial world, children are the only relatively safe insurance against illness or the incapacity of old age available to those living at or near subsistence level. But the wealthy do not need children to provide them with economic security: they can buy that security, when the need arises, with their reserves of property. This has important consequences for attitudes towards children: in a 'market' society such as England has been at least since the later Middle Ages, well-off parents will not perceive children as an economic investment for their old age. Consequently there is no feeling that children should start working to earn their keep as soon as possible. Parents see their property as security for their own old age, rather than as a trust on behalf of their 'family' which should be passed on to their children. On the other hand parents feel no great need to control their children's labour or income. When children grow up, they will not remain on the estate under the father's authority, but earn their living elsewhere. Parents do not need to see their children as a costly necessity, but rather as 'pets' they have chosen to have.[50]

Such attitudes are not characteristic of a peasant society such as that of ancient Italy; but there were Romans wealthy enough to share them. While Roman law assumed that a man's sons (and daughters) had a right to inherit his property, it also gave a testator remarkably extensive rights to leave his property to whomever he pleased. Legacy hunting looms large in Latin literature: in other words, the rich could buy themselves security in their old age by promising to leave their property to those who were prepared to look after them. They did not need children of their own to provide them with security. Consequently rich men could treat children who were not their heirs – often very young slave boys or girls – as 'pets' (Lat. *deliciae*) in whose company and antics they took pleasure and delight.[51]

But such experiences were restricted to the elite. The overall picture is a negative one. Old age may be respected for its experience and intelligence, even when it is accompanied by physical decrepitude; but the dream of rejuvenation looks back to youth (Greek HBH), to being a vigorous young adult, not to

26

reliving the experience of childhood. In his dialogue *On Old Age*, Cicero illustrates his willingness to face the experience of death by ascribing to Cato the Elder the view that, if the gods were to offer him the gift of returning to the cradle and starting life over again as a child, he would categorically refuse. It would be like having to go back to the starting point again when one had almost finished the race.[52] The ancient world's worst fears about the physical and mental helplessness of old age were encapsulated in the proverb 'Old men are children twice over' (ΔΙΣ ΠΑΙΔΕΣ ΟΙ ΓΕΡΟΝΤΕΣ).

The incapacity of the child to participate in the rational world of the adult male citizen had one striking implication. For Greeks, perhaps more than for Romans, the appropriate way for citizens to resolve differences and disputes amongst themselves was through *logos*, rational discourse. But for those who had no share in *logos*, another means was required: force, *bia*. The universality of violence in the ancient world, as in most pre-industrial societies, is well attested; the gladiatorial games of the Romans glorified violence to the point where these games became the central ritual of civic life.[53] Modern scholars agree in expressing their revulsion at the frequency of beating in the ancient world, but they are divided in their attempts to provide an explanation. We may dismiss the view that it was a mark of psychological insecurity, particularly in the supposedly uncertain social world of late antiquity. Rather, socially recognised violence can be seen as an institutionalised symbol of an unequal relationship. It was considered entirely normal for adult Greeks or Romans to beat those whom they could not control through rational discourse, namely children and slaves – slaves, whatever their age, being in a sense children who had not been allowed to grow up. The wise man, says Seneca, will admonish those who have done him harm

> just as he admonishes children, with pain and ill, not because he has been wronged, but because they have done wrong, so that they should stop doing wrong; for that is how beasts are controlled by being beaten. We are not angry with them when they throw their riders, but we restrain them so that the pain overcomes their obstinacy.

The child's lack of reason made it appropriate to use physical pain to force him to do right.[54]

Roman law gave enormous prominence to the rights of the head of the household, the *paterfamilias*, to chastise his dependants. As late as the fourth century AD, he was held to have the 'right of life or death' over his children; although there is no reliable evidence that any Roman father ever executed a son or daughter, other than as a result of a decision to expose him or her at birth, the principle illustrated the very real coercive powers of fathers, e.g. to order errant sons to live on a particular country estate ('rustication'), and in particular to beat them. That applied equally to toddlers and teenagers: the later emperor Otho, as a teenager, was said to have been thrashed repeatedly and to no good effect by his father for night-time hooliganism. The *Rule* of St Benedict, although composed at the end of antiquity, can be taken to describe the normal practice of a Roman household:

> Every age and state of intelligence ought to be controlled in the manner appropriate to it. Therefore the faults of children or youths, or of anyone who is incapable of understanding the force of the penalty of excommunication, must be punished either by strict fasting, or by a severe thrashing.[55]

Just as the whip was a symbol of the master's superiority over his slave (and the question of how often masters made use of their whips does not affect its efficacy as a symbol), so the schoolteacher's rod came to symbolise the master's authority over his irrational child pupils. That association between beating and schooling, taken for granted by Marcus Aurelius (see p. 9 above) remained constant throughout antiquity, and some traces of it remain even in contemporary arguments about the rights of English secondary school headmasters to 'cane' their pupils.

Hence the Latin word for teaching, *disciplina*, also has the standard meaning of 'punishment'. The Silver Age satirist Juvenal, as well as St Jerome in the fourth century, can use the phrase 'to subject your hand to the rod' as the equivalent of 'to learn'. But it was nothing peculiar to Rome, as Menander's line 'The man who has not been beaten is uneducated' suggests. References to beating by schoolteachers in classical and late antique literature are legion (we will find that St Augustine develops this theme). Two Roman poets, Horace and Domitius Marsus, celebrated the first century BC schoolmaster Orbilius Pupillus for his beatings. In prose and in poetry, school means beating. Ovid complains to Aurora the dawn-goddess that when the day dawns, 'You defraud boys of their sleep and hand them over to their teachers, so that their tender hands should suffer savage blows'. Those who had not been brought up to respect the Graeco-Roman school found this aspect of ancient culture positively repellent; the Ostrogothic king Theoderic thought it explained the servility of adult Romans. It is hardly surprising that we should find occasional references to children physically attacking their teachers in return.[56]

In the late fourth century AD, the Gallic professor of rhetoric Ausonius wrote a poem to give to his grandson, who was about to start school. He tells the 5- or 6-year-old what an excellent thing education is. In the covering letter to the little boy's father, he expressly states that he means his *Protrepticus*, his poem of encouragement, 'to be attractive rather than forceful'. To attract the child, he explains that apart from the time to be spent under the supervision of the schoolteacher, he will continue to enjoy periods of leisure. Games and play are not forbidden; they are a necessary relaxation between periods of work. But he takes it for granted that the little boy will be terrified of the teacher whose authority he will have to accept:

> Learn willingly, dear grandson, do not curse the control of that grim teacher. Never shudder at the teacher's appearance. His age may make him frightening, and his harsh words and frowning brows may lead you to think that he wants to pick a quarrel with you – but once you've trained your face to remain impassive, he will never seem an ogre.[57]

Ausonius refers to the myths of the schooling of Achilles and of Hercules to argue that there is no need for the boy to be afraid: in spite (he says) of the noise of pupils being flogged, 'You should not be afraid even though the school resounds to the sound of beating, and the ancient teacher's face is angry'. Citing Vergil's line, 'Fear reveals cowardly minds', Ausonius tells him that the fact that he was sure to be thrashed should not worry him. In any case, both his father and his mother had survived the same system. In fact, the illustrious status that his father and his uncle had attained by going through this same violent system of schooling was an additional reason why the child had a duty to do well. We should not be surprised that one of the few pictures of school scenes surviving from antiquity, found at Herculaneum, should depict a flogging, or that adults who had passed through this education like Marcus Aurelius should have taken it for granted that school-teachers were unsympathetic beings and that children hated being taught.[58]

The frequency and acceptability of child beating should not persuade us to accept the wilder flights of fancy of some modern psychoanalytic interpretations of the ancient attitude to childhood as symptomatic of a social death-wish, a lack of interest or even hostility towards the community's future for which contraceptive practices on the part of the rich, abortion, and the exposition of new-born children have also all been adduced as evidence. The beating of children is characteristic of a peasant society in which the nuclear family constitutes the workforce; sons have to co-operate with their father until he dies, daughters until they marry into another household. Given the high mortality rate in antiquity, a large proportion of sons would in fact have been released from *patriapotestas* by the time they reached adulthood because their fathers would no longer be alive: but it was essential for the functioning of the household as an economic unit that, where a father survived, his authority be respected. The beating of children does not imply that parents rejected their offspring, let alone that there was some sort of widespread social 'death-wish'.[59]

Nor for that matter do the occasional references to the sexual exploitation of children by perverts prove that Roman society as a whole was imbued either with a psychotic hatred of childhood, or with a degree of sexual freedom to put modern California to shame. The stories told of the emperor Tiberius' sexual depravity while at Capri, whether based on fact or merely expressing that ruler's unpopularity, are evidence of widespread horror at the idea of such behaviour. Such stories should be seen as part of a literary tradition of describing the tyrant-figure's lack of self-control, including self-control in matters of sex. Similar stories circulated about Nero and Hadrian. Hadrian's infatuation with the adolescent Antinous, to the extent of declaring him a god after he had drowned in the Nile, was not a case of child abuse but rather an aspect of his love of Greek culture. Pederasty had been a recognised element of that culture in the classical period.[60]

In contrast, pederasty was not acceptable to Romans, and if it involved a boy of citizen status it was apparently a criminal offence. References to homosexual affairs in Latin literature have to be explained as a result of the Roman elite's adoption of both the literature and other cultural practices of the Greek world. In Latin poetry on homosexual themes, the characters frequently have Greek names, and the object of the poet's love is not a respectable boy of citizen status but a *declassé* or a slave. That is an indication of the unacceptability of pederasty to Romans in general, even if some wealthy aristocrats expressed their elite position by adopting this particular Greek custom. But it was offensive to society in general: Nero's relationship with Sporus may be taken as an example. The accusation that a particularly evil emperor had castrated his slave catamites to prevent them from ever growing up is meant to illustrate how tyrants had the power to live out their fantasies.[61]

Latin pederastic poetry ought to be distinguished from poems in praise of *deliciae*, the slave 'darlings' or 'pets' to whom wealthy Romans, whether or not they had children of their own, often became emotionally attached (see note 51). Many such poems occur in Martial's collection, written towards the end of the first century AD. The sentiment that such a slave should remain a child (i.e. young and beautiful) for ever does not necessarily have sexual overtones. Rather than an indication of the supposed sexual freedom of the classical period, such sentiments should be seen as an illustration of how different the concerns of the rich might be from those of ordinary smallholders. While the Roman elite shared the cultural assumption that it was good to be survived by someone to whom they could pass on their property, they were much less dependent on children for economic security. Instead of maximising the number of children, they could be highly selective in their choice of heirs, by limiting the number of their children and through legal processes such as adoption and the disposal of their property by will. Such people did not need to control children by beating them, and they did not need their labour. For them, they might be sheer delight.

Nevertheless the literature of the classical period, both prose and verse, is not rich in expressions of sentiment on the part of adults towards children. A fragment of Varro, cited by the grammarian Nonius Marcellinus in the fifth century AD, states that infants are sometimes fun to watch, while older children are not worth turning one's head to look at.[62] As we saw, Catullus in his wedding-poem to Torquatus and Vergil in his fourth *Eclogue* referred to the expectation that an aristocrat's new-born child would smile at his father; it is interesting that ancient manuscripts of Vergil unanimously preferred to read the text as saying that parents smile upon their new-born child. The context of Catullus' remark – like the speech Cassius Dio attributes to Augustus – shows what it was that adults in the classical period were really interested in: while they might well appreciate having a child as an object of their love and affection, they also wanted to be certain that they had an heir who reproduced the father's characteristics.[63]

SECURITY FOR THE COMMUNITY

That this was the, rather than just 'a', major concern of Roman parents in the late republic is confirmed by the vocabulary of the classical period. Children are the 'successors' of the present generation in two senses. First, as the individual heirs of particular households. Obviously, the attitudes of the very wealthy were not the same as those of ordinary peasant smallholders. Peasants needed successors to look after them in their own old age; an important public figure needed a successor to ensure that his *virtus* and the *gloria* he achieved would be handed down to future generations. Children were also 'successors' in a communal sense: as a new generation of citizens, capable of taking over responsibility for protecting the community in warfare. 'It is good that you have given the country and the Roman people a citizen, if you make sure that he is suitable material for the country, useful in the fields, useful in all the activities of war and peace.'[64] Analysis of the Latin vocabulary found in republican literature suggests that this was indeed largely how Romans – rich and poor alike – of the second and first centuries BC perceived their children.[65] The most common word, *liberi*, is associated with the concept of *libertas*, 'freedom', not in our western liberal sense of being independent of others, but in the sense of being a member of the (free) community; it is philologically cognate with the Greek word for freedom, *eleutheria*, but also with the German word for 'people', *Leute*. The *liberi* were on the one hand those junior members of a household who were free, as opposed to the slaves, *servi*; and on the other a collective group of free-born Roman boys and girls, contrasted with adults of citizen status. They were the future citizen community.

The other common word for child, *puer*, refers to the junior members of the family or household; in the classical period, the same word is used for the free-born children of the *paterfamilias*, and for his slaves, whatever their age. Romans thought that this indicated the *paterfamilias'* supreme power over all the dependent members of his household, free or slave, in the archaic age. We may note that originally the word was used without distinction of gender: as late as the first century BC, grammarians still argued over which innovative form would be suitable as a feminine, *puera* or *puella*.[66] *Puella* eventually won acceptance and became the classical word for 'girl'. In ordinary speech it came to replace *virgo* as the word for an unmarried girl, and in erotic poetry came to be used for the object of the poet's desires whatever her actual age or status; as a diminutive form, the word *puella* indicated affection on the part of the speaker, rather than an indication of female weakness.

There is no conclusive evidence that *puer/puella* replaced the word *liberi*, or that such a development reflected less emphasis on the distinction between free children and slave dependants which some have associated with the greater individualism which Hellenism is supposed to have brought to Rome in the second century BC.[67] Rather, *puer/puella* refers to children (and slaves) as members of the household community, while *liberi* refers to free children as potential members of the citizen community. Both these concepts were required in the late republic; but as we shall see, it was the concept of the citizen that gradually became less and less important over the course of the next few centuries, and along with that development the word *liberi* ceased to become central.

Other words which might refer to children within the family structure were *filius/filia* or *natus/nata* (son/daughter), the first formal, the second rather more affectionate. But these words would be applied to children of any age; they did not refer to an age-grade, but to the parent/child relationship. The idea that children represented the next generation of the family or the community was also expressed by a group of less frequently used, more poetic words. *Propago*, *stirps*, and *fetus* (offspring) are metaphors taken from agriculture, and – like Marcus Aurelius' references to children who die as being akin to harvested corn (see p. 9 above) – suggest that a household's children could be envisaged in terms of an investment in the future, much as the young of animals were. If this was a way of looking at one's own children, then we should not be shocked to find Romans discussing female slaves as a source of further slave children (though Roman jurists were careful to point out that 'female slaves cannot properly be bought for the purpose of producing offspring').[68] Romans were well aware that using words like *fetus* did not mean that they could see no difference between the young of animals and human children, slave or free.

The words *progenies* and *posteritas* again refer to a man's children or descendants as a collective group, rather than as individuals. A man's *progenies* is the sum of all his *progeniti*, all those who can trace their descent back to him, however many generations lie between. The *posteritas* is the future population of the community as a whole. For the great political families of the republic like Catullus' Manlii Torquati, children are valuable and deserve to be cherished because the future of the family rests with them. When Mercury in Vergil's *Aeneid* wishes to remind the hero, dallying at Carthage with Dido, of his future Roman destiny, he refers to 'growing Ascanius and the hopes of Iulus your heir'.[69]

The need for a public figure to hand on his *gloria* makes it less surprising that noble Romans were so frequently happy to adopt someone from a different household to be their heir, and appear to have been relatively happy to hand over their sons to be adopted by someone else so long as they were left with an heir themselves. Adoption was acceptable to the wealthy because the absence of primogeniture meant that the wealth and influence of a household would be dissipated if there were more than one child at the father's death, yet the high rate of infant mortality meant that families who restricted the number of potential heirs to one (male) child often found that that child did not survive into adulthood.[70] The practice will have been easier for those who saw children not so much as companions upon whom to bestow affection, as potential heirs. There is no reason to suppose that the great families of the classical period were any more affectionate towards their own children than towards the sons they adopted from other families in order to have an heir. There are of course stories accusing political figures of preferring their own children to adopted ones, an accusation levelled at Tiberius by Tacitus for preferring his son Drusus to Germanicus, whom Augustus had forced him to adopt; that accusation does not seem to be substantiated by the facts, and in any case shows that Romans did ιdopted son to be treated with any less affection than

... of the principate the existence of an heir to the famil... ...sars guaranteed the stability, not just of that househ... the whole empire. Imperial heirs, like other imperial ... ...ions, were widely advertised on coins. Twins, like Tiberiu... ...erius Gemellus and his brother, were thought to be a partic... ...sign of good fortune.[71]

Consequently the cost of that investment in future security was a matter of concern to Romans. Men as well as women were well aware of the high risk to mothers of death in childbirth. Men thought that their women-folk were likely to try to avoid conception, or to use magical or medical means to induce abortions, in order to avoid that risk, despite the high value that men placed on children as heirs. Men also thought it likely that women would avoid the wider responsibilities of motherhood, irksome even for the wealthy whose children would in practice have been looked after by nurses and childminders. The theme occurs in Latin love poetry, in moralistic ethnography, and in satire: 'Childbirth hardly ever occurs in a gold-embroidered bed [i.e. in a wealthy household], since abortionists have such skills and so many potions, and can bring about the death of children in the womb.'[72]

Roman law treats abortion as a crime against the father, not against the mother or the child.[73] This confirms that law-makers assumed that it was the mother-to-be who might have an interest in avoiding giving birth, often against the wishes of the father. The males' concern that their wives might not wish to provide them with children was even expressed by a myth to the effect that Roman matrons had as a class once refused to bear children, in protest against a decree of the Senate banning them from riding around in carriages: 'When this honour was taken from them, each matron decided not to renew her ungrateful husband's progeny, and not to give birth; with a courageous strike against her own womb, she aborted the growing burden.'[74]

While men condemned their women if they suspected that they were unwilling to have children because it might spoil their appearance, they insisted on the legal right of a father to decide whether the child to whom his wife (or his slave) had given birth was to be allowed to live or not. If the child's principal role was to

35

be his parents' successor as a citizen, as *paterfamilias* or as a *matrona*, then there was no point in allowing a deformed child to live. That has been common practice in many societies less prosperous than our own.[75]

Ancient writers assumed that belief in the exposition of unwanted babies was widespread. The plots of many of Plautus' and Terence's comedies depend upon one of the characters – almost always a female – having been either exposed or kidnapped as a child, and brought up as a slave far from home. A letter of Pliny the Younger written by him as governor of Bithynia in AD 109 asks the emperor Trajan for advice about the status of persons of free parentage who had been exposed at birth and brought up as slaves.[76] Plautus and Terence of course borrowed their plots from Greek predecessors, and Pliny's query also refers to the Greek-speaking part of the empire. But Suetonius' series of short biographies of *Grammarians and Rhetors* – almost the only biographical notes we have about persons who did not win more than average fame in either the political or the literary world – confirm that exposition, often resulting in enslavement, also occurred in Italy. It was taken for granted in the rhetorical school exercises of the elder Seneca, though here too we are concerned with an artificial Graeco-Roman world, and not the real Italy of the first century AD.[77] It is the fulminations of Stoic moralists, Jews, and Christians that suggest that infanticide and exposition were sufficiently widespread for these groups to need to express their moral outrage.[78] And there are occasional indications that, as in rural China in the recent past, infanticide and exposition were aimed at female rather than male children: we are told that Augustus allowed any citizen who was not a senator to marry freedwomen 'Because the free-born population contained far more males than females'.[79]

This is an area where there appears to be a major difference between the beliefs of the classical period and the beliefs, if not necessarily the practice, of late antiquity. Pagan philosophers had not been worried about the morality of infanticide or exposition. Democritus noted with approval that while other living creatures instinctively try to raise their offspring, it is accepted among human beings that the purpose of raising children is, consciously, to gain certain material advantages.[80]

Greek and Roman writers noted that it was a peculiarity of the

Jews that infanticide and exposition were frowned upon, and all children born were accepted as members of the community. Every Jewish child was included in the covenant between God and his people, and the rabbis insisted that this included those still in the womb.[81]

Christians inherited this view that infanticide was murder. On 7 February 374, the Christian emperors Valentinian, Valens, and Gratian decreed, 'If anyone, man or woman, should commit the sin of killing an infant, that crime should be punishable with death'. That was the position taken up by Justinian's jurists when they came to compile the *Digest* in AD 538. Only those passages by earlier legal writers which supported this Christian view were selected for inclusion. They cite the *Sententiae* attributed to the third-century lawyer Paulus to the effect that

> It seems that murder is committed not just by a person who induces an abortion, but by those who throw a child away, those who deny it sustenance, and those who expose it in a public place in order to elicit from others that sympathy for the child which they themselves do not have.[82]

That, interestingly enough, is all that the *Digest* has to say on the subject; it is very different from the law that Cicero ascribed to the traditional Roman law code of the Twelve Tables, that any child which is obviously deformed should quickly be killed. That this was believed to be the ancient practice is confirmed by Dionysius of Halicarnassus, who says that Romulus decreed that all male children, and the first female child to be born, had to be raised, and that no child under the age of 3 should be destroyed unless it was seen to be deformed or monstrous right at the moment of birth. Such a child could only be exposed if the parents first showed it to a council of five neighbours. Dionysius treats this provision as peculiar, connected with the Romans' constant need to find manpower for their wars; for Dionysius, it is a specifically Roman peculiarity, like the practice of accepting immigrants and freed slaves as citizens. The story does not prove that the Romans were any less keen than the Greeks to kill off any children surplus to requirements; but it suggests that the needs of the Roman state for more citizens to serve as soldiers actually meant that fewer male children were liable to be killed at birth. We may note that not even the 'Romulus' to whom the law is ascribed saw any need for more than one girl per family. If this was a genuine republican law, it was no longer enforced in the Augustan period when Dionysius was writing.[83]

The fact that a monstrous birth which occurred during the Second Punic War with Hannibal is reported to have been disposed of at sea by order of the Senate after the advice of Etruscan soothsayers had been taken shows that even such unfortunates were sometimes not immediately left to die by their parents. There was always a chance that such monsters might be brought up for display purposes in the households of the rich; not a pleasant existence, but at least an existence.[84] Other anecdotal evidence, however, confirms the acceptability, if not the frequency, of exposition: Augustus forbade the raising of the illegitimate child of his granddaughter Julia; Claudius had a daughter by his wife Urgulanilla exposed although he had at first actually recognised her as his child – he subsequently suspected that she was in fact the child of a freedman.[85]

The continuing concern of the Roman government about Italy's manpower resources also suggests a widespread desire on the part of Italian parents to limit the number of their children. Even in the republic, the Roman leadership had been worried about any decline in the number of potential soldiers that might be available for fighting. When Augustus became emperor, he thought it was part of his duties to encourage an increase in the number of children that Romans, especially those of high status, were prepared to bring up. He may not have been very successful in finding appropriate methods to achieve this aim, as Roman historians agree in pointing out.[86] The fact that he thought that legislation would have some effect does show that he believed that the infertility of the elite was not natural, but induced.

The same assumption lies behind later emperors' encouragement of schemes giving financial support to poor families in return for raising children they would otherwise have left to die. These *alimenta*-schemes were first introduced in the time of Trajan, and continued up to the time of Septimius Severus (the time when the special status of citizen children as potential legionaries ceased to be relevant). Epigraphical as well as literary evidence shows that more than forty Italian cities had such a scheme at some point during the second century AD.[87]

The motives of different emperors in encouraging these alimentary schemes are not always explicitly stated, but we may be sure that the perceived need for more soldiers to fight in the legions, and possibly for more free workers to help with the harvests on the estates of the rich, was as important as abstract humanitarian concern to protect the lives of unborn or new-born infants, or look after the material well-being of their parents. Ideology was of course involved; as we have seen, the emperor as 'head of the community' (*Pater Patriae*) saw himself as having a special concern for the welfare of the weak – old men, women, and children. We have referred to monumental representations of Trajan and Marcus Aurelius distributing largesse. Marcus expressed his concern for the good of the *iuvenes* of the cities of Italy in an edict reported by Fronto. Christian emperors continued this tradition. Two edicts of Constantine's time order the public authorities to give food and clothes to needy parents, explicitly so that such parents can raise their children instead of having to expose them. Constantine's biographer Eusebius confirms his liberality towards widows and orphans. This will have been as much an expression of a good emperor's traditional concern for the weak, and for the state's manpower requirements, as a consciously Christian attempt to stop people from committing the sin of infanticide.[88]

SECURITY FOR PARENTS

As individuals as well as as a community, classical Romans saw their children primarily as an investment in future security; and they had a realistic, and materialistic, idea of the cost of that investment. Greek texts had already referred to the unpleasantness of bringing up a child. An inscription of the second century BC from Cyzicus talks of the ΜΟΧΘΟΣ ΤΡΟΦΗΣ, the 'hard work of bringing up a child'.[89] Two ideas were paramount: that children had the function of looking after their parents in old age in return for the sustenance that their parents had given them as infants; and that the child (normally the son) would bury his parents just as his parents had brought him to life. This idea of reciprocity or repayment can already be found in Homer. When Ajax butchers Simoisios, son of Anthemion,[90] we are told that Simoisios 'Was not able to repay his dear parents for having brought him up'. The same assumption appears in Hesiod's *Works and Days*, where one of the dreadful things about the Age of Iron is said to be that children no longer automatically fulfil this obligation laid upon them by nature.[91] At Athens, a law ascribed to Solon imposed on children the duty of ΓΗΡΟΒΟΣΚΕΙΝ, looking after parents; the need for a law suggests that reality did not always correspond to the social ideal. Plato makes a similar provision for the need for legal coercion in Book 11 of the *Laws*. The twin ideas of the funeral as a recompense for life, and help for the parents in old age as recompense for the parents' help in childhood, are to be found in Euripides' *Medea*. When Medea sends her two children away finally to their death, she expresses her regret:

> It was all for nothing – those years in which I reared you, my cares, my aches and exhaustion, and the sharp pain when I gave you birth. I once built many hopes on you. I imagined that you would care for me in my old age, and that you yourselves would prepare my body for burial when I was dead.[92]

These ideals were not restricted to poets or law-makers. Both Greek and Latin inscriptions contain expressions of disappointment on the part of parents whose children have predeceased them: the parents have been cheated of the return that was due to them. A child may be said to have been raised in order to be 'an anchor for his parents in their old age', according to a first century BC epitaph from Amorgos. An inscription from Caesarea in Mauretania refers to the deceased son as a staff of support which the father now lacks in his old age. There are Greek inscriptions from the second century AD which, like Marcus Aurelius who was writing at that time, refer to the dead child as a 'lost harvest'. Another north African inscription in Latin expressed the idea that children had an obligation to bury their parents as recompense for having given them birth: 'The son set up this altar to his dear parent, and returned the honour that was due, even if late.' The same idea occurs in an Italian inscription: 'Your son Eutychius paid you these honours, as is fitting.'[93]

These inscriptions suggest that it was not just the very rich, or the very literate, who thought that if a child died before either of its parents, this was more than just an unnatural tragedy for the child and for its parents. The parents were entitled to feel that they had been defrauded. The Fates, or the Underworld, had stolen from them the harvest they had worked to prepare, or had prevented the repayment of a due debt of piety: 'What great hopes would there have been, if the fates had allowed it; when I was a boy, the Muses gave me the gift of eloquence. But Lachesis was jealous, savage Clotho killed me, and the third fate did not allow me to repay my mother her piety.' A prose epitaph from Trebiati in Umbria tells us that a child 'died before he was able to reciprocate his well-deserving parents'.[94]

These are more than just general complaints about the cruelty of the gods and the fickleness of fortune. When a son or daughter dies before his or her parents, at whatever age, then quite apart from the dead child's claim to a complete life, the parents can feel that they too have been cheated of something they had a right to. The parents of Caius Licinius Torax at Cartagena in Spain warn the passer-by: 'Let parents fear the future, and mothers not be too pleased to give birth';[95] and a Dalmatian inscription refers to a woman who had died at the age of 25, predeceasing her parents: 'She teaches wretched mothers that they should not raise children.' The idea that those who have no children to lose ought to consider themselves happy occurs in literary consolations as well as on inscriptions; an example is to be found in a letter by Cicero to an otherwise unknown Titius. Even where epitaphs express sorrow at an early or unexpected death, rather than just protesting that the parents' efforts had been wasted, it is sympathy with the parents (who of course paid to set up the inscription) rather than with the child that is expressed. A 20-year-old soldier is represented as saying that he is 'wretched not just because this fate tore me away; what makes me even more wretched is that my mother and father grieve'.[96]

Apart from this parent-centred view that there can have been no point in struggling to raise a child only to see it die before it was able to repay them for their trouble, inscriptions also express the idea that the child itself could not have got anything worthwhile out of life if it died before reaching adult status. This theme of *mors immatura*, 'premature death', has been examined in detail for the Greek world by Ewald Griessmair. In philosophical terms it was expressed by the Aristotelian notion that there was a natural end, a *telos*, to human life. That *telos* normally included marriage; Greek epitaphs mourning girls who had died before marriage particularly emphasise that they had lived to no purpose. Some Latin epitaphs also articulate this view that a girl ought to have been married if her life was to have had any value. Inscriptions may metaphorically describe Hades as 'stealing the child away to be his bride'. It was taken for granted that a dead child would lament the fact that it had never become a complete adult. A first- or second-century AD inscription makes a 7-year-old boy lament 'I did not know what it is to enjoy the life of a man', and a third-century inscription states that a child 'was not capable of knowing the good or the bad that life brings' (cf. the remarks about the 'irrationality' of children which we have seen to be widespread in classical literature).[97]

The evidence of inscriptions is far too scanty and too atypical to function as some sort of opinion poll of what parents thought about their children. But it confirms the largely negative picture which emerges from literature and philosophy: pagan Romans had a substantially less romantic view of bringing up children than recent generations of Europeans. Before condemning the Romans for failing to see the world from a child's point of view, we should recall that the very fact that some of them bothered to spend considerable sums of money on a tombstone shows that they considered it quite as important to make public statements about their children as about their parents, their spouses, or themselves. Like all funeral ceremonies, one reason for that was to assert the status of their family; but this does not mean that all their love for their children was in our terms purely 'selfish'. Above all, we must bear in mind that physical survival was a constant source of concern to parents and children alike. In the absence of effective community care for the elderly, the death of one's children – particularly of an adult child already capable of working – was a very real loss.

These factors have been constantly present in societies whose economies have been pre-industrial or not geared to production for the market. But not all such societies have tried to come to terms with them in the same ways. Between the classical period and late antiquity, there were a number of considerable changes in the ways in which Mediterranean men and women tried to make sense of childhood. Some attitudes of course remained constant. It continued to be assumed, by adult males, that what gave a girl importance and a personality of her own was marriage and motherhood: the Christian poet Ausonius in the fourth century can say, just as a classical pagan might have, that the 16-year-old

Anicia 'had enjoyed everything that can be wished for in a long life-span . . . as a child she gave suck to her baby, as a girl she was already an adult. She married, conceived a child, gave birth, she was already a mother when she died. Who can blame death?'.[98] But the evidence suggests that teenage parenthood was not the only way in which children began to be able to transcend the limitations with which the ideology of the classical city had dismissed them.

NOTES

1 A. Birley, *Marcus Aurelius* (London, 2nd edn, 1987); P.A. Brunt, 'Marcus Aurelius in his *Reflections*', *JRS* 64 (1974), 1 ff.

2 H. Halfmann, *Die Senatoren aus dem östlichen Teil des Imperium Romanum* (Göttingen, 1979); M. Hammond, 'The composition of the Senate', *JRS* 47 (1957), 74 ff., is still useful.

3 The quotations are from the *Reflections* or *Meditations*: 9,33; 4,50; 2,14. The references which follow are to the same work.

4 3,2; 12,36. We may note that the period between one census (*lustrum*) and another was theoretically (not always in practice) five years (see p. 15).

5 5,11; 4,28.

6 9,24; 5,33; 4,46; 11,23; 2,12.

7 12,26; 8,49; 9,40; cf. 10,35; 10,34; Euripides' *Antiope* 207 Nauck: 7,41 and 11,6, where the lines are described as 'helpful', ΧΡΗΣΙΜΩΣ; 11,34.

8 5,9; 11,6; 10,36.

9 5,4.

10 1,5.

11 5,36.

12 *Infirmitas*: Cicero, *On Old Age* 10,33.

13 United Nations, *Statistical Yearbook 1982* (New York, 1985), 79; Office of Population Censuses and Surveys, Series DM3 No.19, 1985: *Mortality Statistics: Childhood* (London, 1987), 5.

14 United Nations, *Statistical Yearbook 1982* (New York, 1985), 79; *Statistical Abstract of the United States 1985* (Washington, 1984), Table 104, p.70; *Statistisches Jahrbuch 1987 für die Bundesrepublik Deutschland* (Wiesbaden, 1987), 76. G. Newman, *Infant Mortality* (London, 1906).

15 Pliny, *NH* 7,48/153 ff. The *Statistical Yearbook of China 1986* (Oxford, 1986) interestingly includes the information that of the 1,008,152,137 persons registered in the third national census on 1 July 1982, 3,851 claimed to be over 100 (Table 18, p.88). The same rate of 3.85 centenarians per million would give us a population of 20 million for first-century Aemilia; its present population is actually just under 4 million. Fertility: Pliny, *NH* 7,13/57 f.

16 M. Clauss, 'Probleme der Lebensalterstatistiken aufgrund römischer Grabinschriften', *Chiron* 3 (1973), 395–427.

17 J. F. Gardner, *Women in Roman Law and Society* (London, 1986), 144 ff.

18 Suetonius, *Tiberius* 5; Ovid, *Fasti*, 4,702; Martial 4,45.3.

19 L. Moreti, 'Statistica demografica ed epigrafica', *Epigrafica* 21 (Milan, 1959); R. Etienne and G. Fabre, 'Démographie et classe sociale. L'exemple du cimetière des *officiales* de Carthage', *Colloques nationaux du CNRS* (Paris, 1970).

20 B. Frier, 'Roman life expectancy: Ulpian's evidence', *Harvard Studies in Classical Philology* 86 (1982), 213 ff.; 'Roman life expectancy: the Pannonian evidence', *Phoenix* 37 (1983), 328 ff. Cf. T. H. Hollingsworth, *Historical Demography* (Ithaca, NY, 1969); E. A. Wrigley, *Population and History* (London, 1969), 171.

21 J. P. Neraudau, *Etre enfant à Rome* (Paris, 1984), 395; K. Hopkins, *Death and Renewal* (Cambridge, 1983), esp. Chapter 2, written in association with G. Burton.

22 R. Syme, 'Neglected children on the *Ara Pacis*', *American Journal of Archaeology* 88 (1984), 583 ff. Cf. plate no. 2.

23 Macrobius, Saturnalia 1,16.36: 'est autem dies lustricus quo infantes lustrantur et nomen accipiunt; sed is maribus nonus, octavus est feminis'. Cf. L. and P. Brind'Amour, 'La deuxième Satire de Perse', *Latomus* 30 (1971), 999–1024, and 'Le dies lustricus', *Latomus* 34 (1975), 17–58.

24 Ovid, *Fasti* 4,529 ff.

25 Cato, *Res Rustica* 157 = Pliny, *NH* 20,83.

26 Pliny, *NH* 20,114 and 191 f.; 28,39; 28,114; 28,257–9.

27 Pliny, *NH* 30,135 ff.; 28,257–9.

28 Cassius Dio 56,22; Lucretius, 5,222 ff.; Pliny, *NH* 7,2 f.

29 On the 'marginality' of slaves, cf. T. E. J. Wiedemann, *Slavery* (Greece and Rome New Surveys in the Classics No. 19, 1987); R. Just, 'Freedom, slavery, and the female psyche', *CRUX* (Exeter, 1985), 169–88.

30 Isidore, *Etymologies* 11,2.16; Cicero, *Pro Sestio* 24: L. Calpurnius Piso, the consul of 58 BC – 'parvo puero aut imbecillo seni ac debili'. R. Kassel, *Quomodo quibus locis apud veteres scriptores Graecos infantes atque parvuli pueri inducantur describantur commemorentur* (Würzburg, 1954).

31 L. Rossi, *Trajan's Column and the Dacian Wars* (London, 1971); E. Nash, *Pictorial Dictionary of Ancient Rome* I (Tübingen/London, 1961); Cassius Dio 51,6.

32 *Iliad* 7,234 f.; *Iliad* 11,558 ff.

33 Thucydides 7,29.5; T. E. J. Wiedemann, 'Thucydides, women, and the limits of rational analysis', *Greece and Rome* 30.2 (1983), 163 ff. Three examples of references to children in Caesar's *Gallic War*: as prisoners of war (*BG* 1,11.3); as hostages (*BG* 1,31.8); and as one of the categories incapable of fighting – Caesar discovers two census lists: 'eorum qui arma ferre possunt et item separatim pueri senes mulieresque' (*BG* 1,29.2).

34 Quintilian 6,1.41.

35 A panel re-used on the Arch of Constantine shows Marcus Aurelius distributing largesse to women, children, and a bearded old man: E. Nash, *Pictorial Dictionary of Ancient Rome* I. There are several similar scenes. Cf. p. 38 on *alimenta*.

36 *Odyssey* 4,32.

37 Sophocles, *Ajax* 552 ff.; Plato, *Timaeus* 22b; Lucretius, *De Rerum Natura* 3,762; Parmeno in Terence, *Hecyra* 310 ff.; O. Ribbeck, *Comicorum Romanorum Fragmenta* II (Leipzig, 1873), 264: Novius, *Milites Pometinenses* fg.3: 'Tu pueri pausilli simil es, quia enim ad os fers quicquid nanctus'.

38 Cicero, *Philippics* 13,24. Cf. *Ad Fam.* 12,25.4.

39 Lucretius 5,1028 ff.; Cicero, *De Finibus* 5,42.

40 Diels-Kranz, *Vorsokratiker* 64 A 19; Plato, *Laws* 2,666a; Seneca, *De Ira* 2,20.2–5.

41 J. Malitz, *Die Historien des Poseidonios* (Munich, 1983). Cf. Diodorus Siculus 5,26.2; 34,2.30; Athenaeus, *Deipnosophiston* 152 C.

42 Seneca, *Letters* 33,7; 118,14.

43 Presumably the fifteenth, if that is what 1.20, 'Sexta tibi haec primo remeat trieteris ab anno', means.

44 Cicero, *De Republica* p.137.3 ed. Ziegler frag. incert.5. (cf. Aristotle, *Ethics* 1100A).

45 Persius, *Satires* 5,13 (with Scholiast's comment: 'stloppo dixit ΜΕΤΑΦΟΡΙΚΩΣ, ludentibus pueris, qui buccas inflatas subito aperiunt, et totum simul inflatum cum sonitu fundunt'). Horace's poet: *Ars Poetica*, 455 f. The philosopher: Horace, *Satires* 1,3.133 ff. Coin trick: Horace, *Epistles* 1,16.63 ff.; and Persius, *Satires* 5,111 f. (with Scholiast's comment: 'quia solent pueri, ut ridendi causam habeant, assem in silice plumbatum infigere, ut qui viderint se ad tollendum eum inclinent nec tamen possint evellere. quo facto pueri etiam acclamare solent'). For the kinds of graffiti scrawled by children and adolescents at Pompeii, cf. J. Kepartova, 'Kinder in Pompeii', *Klio* 66 (1984), 207 ff.

46 *Digest* 48,8.12; *Digest* 4,4,7.5; 4,4,18.1, and elsewhere.

47 Juvenal, *Satires* 14,47: 'maxima debetur puero reverentia'. Quintilian, *Declamations* 340.

48 Catullus 61; Vergil, *Eclogue* 4,60.

49 Cassius Dio 56.3. The proposition that 'Certainly the most striking feature of classical literature's attitude toward children is the thundrous silence that envelops the idea of childhood' is an overstatement: R. Pattison, *The Child Figure in English Literature* (Athens, Ga., 1978), 5.

50 For the history of the peculiar English attitude to children, cf. A. Macfarlane, *Marriage and Love in England 1300–1840* (Oxford, 1986); P. Laslett and R. Wall (eds), *Household and Family in Past Time* (Cambridge, 1972).

51 Naked slave children as companions: Cassius Dio 48,44.3 (Livia); 67,15.3 (Domitian); Herodian 1,17.3 (Commodus); perhaps Suetonius, *Tiberius* 42.2.

52 Cicero, *Or Old Age* 83.

53 K. Hopkins, *Death and Renewal*, ch. 1.

54 Seneca, *De Constantia Sapientis* (= *Dial.*2) 12.3.
55 W. V. Harris, 'The Roman father's power of life and death', in
    R. S. Bagnell and W. V. Harris (eds), *Studies in Roman Law in Memory of
    A. Arthur Schiller* (Leiden, 1986), 81 ff.; Suetonius, *Otho* 2.1; *Rule of St
    Benedict* c.30, cf. 2, 45, 70.
56 'Manum ferulae subducere': Juvenal, *Satires* 1,15; Jerome, *Epistles*
    32,33. Menander, 573. Orbilius: Horace, *Epistles* 2,1.70, and Suetonius,
    De Grammaticis 9,3. Ovid: *Amores* 1,13.17 f. Theoderic: Procopius
    5,11.14 f. Cato the Elder is reported to have been critical of those who
    beat their children (and wives), but the context is unclear: Plutarch,
    Cato 20. Cf. also Juvenal, *Satires* 7,213 f.; Plautus, *Bacchides* 440 f.
57 Ausonius, *Letters* 22.
58 Ausonius, *Letters* 22, 24 f., quoting *Aeneid* 4,13. Pictures: Daremberg-
    Saglio, *Dictionnaire des antiquités* III, 2.1380, fig. 4647.
59 L. de Mause's 'infanticidal' stage: *The History of Childhood* (Chicago,
    1974), 51, with table on p. 53. On *patriapotestas*, cf. R. P. Saller,
    '*Familia, domus*, and the Roman conception of the family', *Phoenix* 38
    (1984), 336–55. S. Dixon, *The Roman Mother* (London, 1988), argues
    that mothers as well as fathers were (in comparison with today)
    relatively distant authority figures.
60 P. Veyne, 'La Famille et l'amour sous le haut-empire romain', *Annales*
    33.1 (1978), 35–63. Suetonius, *Tiberius* 43; *Nero* 28f. – Sporus; cf.
    Commodus in Herodian, 1,17.3; Tacitus, *Annals*, 5,9.3; *SHA, Hadrian.*
61 R. MacMullen, 'Roman attitudes to Greek love', *Historia* 31 (1982),
    484 ff. Poems: Valerius Aedituus; Lutatius Catulus; Martial 4,42;
    Anthologia Palatina 12,4.39, 191. Cf. K. Dover, *Greek Homosexuality*
    (London, 1978).
62 Nonius p.141,15 ed. Mueller.
63 Catullus 61,216–25; cf. Cicero, *De Finibus* 3,7.9. Juvenal's fourteenth
    satire develops the idea that children mirror their parents.
64 Juvenal, *Satire* 14,70–2
65 W. Heimbecher, 'Begriff und literarische Darstellung des Kindes im
    republikanischen Rom' (diss. Freiburg, 1958).
66 This increasing emphasis on gender differentiation may have reflected
    the paramount importance of military service. From the time of the
    Second Punic War on, Roman males were increasingly spending much
    of their youth away from home as soldiers: cf. P. Brunt, *Italian
    Manpower* (Oxford, 1971), esp. Table XI.
67 J.P. Neraudau, *Etre enfant à Rome*, p. 395 ff.
68 *Digest* 5,3.27.
69 *Aeneid* 4,274.
70 K. Hopkins, *Death and Renewal*, on succession in Roman political
    families.
71 Tacitus, *Annals* 2,84.1. Cf. plate 5.
72 Juvenal 6,593 ff.; cf. Ovid, *Amores* 2,13; Tacitus, *Germania* 19.5.
    K. Hopkins, 'Contraception in the Roman Empire', *Comparative Studies
    in Society and History* 8 (1965), 124–51, shows that knowledge of
    contraceptive methods was widespread amongst (mainly Greek)
    physicians. S. K. Dickison, 'Abortion in antiquity', *Arethusa* 6 (1973),

159 ff., reviews E. Nardi's *Procurato aborto nel mondo Greco-Romano* (Milan, 1971), which I have not been able to see.

73 *Digest* 47,11.4; 48,19.38.5. J. F. Gardner, *Women in Roman Law and Society*, 158 f.

74 Ovid, *Fasti* 1,621 ff.: describing the festival of Carmenta on 15 January.

75 S. B. Pomeroy, 'Infanticide in Hellenistic Greece', in A. M. Cameron and A. Kuhrt (eds), *Images of Women in Antiquity* (London, 1983), 207 ff.; J. F. Gardner, *Women in Roman Law and Society*, 154 ff.
D. Engels's scepticism about the possibility of widespread infanticide (*Classical Philology* 75 (1980), 112–20) was countered by W. V. Harris, *Classical Quarterly* 32 (1982), 114 ff. See M. Golden, *Phoenix* 35 (1981), 316 ff.
Only eleven homicides of infants were reported in England and Wales in 1985; on the other hand there were 171,873 legal abortions compared with 656,417 live births, i.e. 26.2 per cent of reported conceptions. In the United States the proportion of abortions was 29.9 per cent of reported conceptions. Cf. G. H. Payne, *The Child in Human Progress* (New York, 1916), for other cultures earlier this century, esp. China (there is an illustration of a 'repository for the bodies of neglected babies' opposite p. 56).

76 Pliny, *Letters* 10,65 f.;

77 Seneca, *Controversiae*, e.g. 10,4.2; 15–18.

78 Philo, *De Specialibus Legibus* 3,114 f. For references to condemnation by Christians, cf. H. Leclerc, 'Alumni', *Dictionnaire d'archéologie chrétienne et de liturgie* I (Paris, 1907), 1288–1306. One of the earliest condemnations appears in the *Epistles of Barnabas*, §19, *c*. AD 130.

79 Cassius Dio 54,16.

80 Diels-Kranz, *Vorsokratiker* 68 B 278.

81 Hecataeus of Abdera, ap. Diodorus Siculus 40,3.8; Tacitus, *Histories* 5,5; cf. Josephus, *Against Apion* 1,60.

82 *Theodosian Code*, 9,14.1; *Digest* 25,3.4.

83 Cicero, *De Legibus* 3,19; Dionysius of Halicarnassus 2,15.

84 Livy 27,37.5–7. At 31,12.6 f., he tells of a hermaphrodite who was drowned although already 16 years old. Cassius Dio mentions a child without arms who could shoot with his feet: 54.9. Cf. Suetonius, *Dom.* 4.2.

85 Suetonius, *Augustus* 65,4; Suetonius, *Claudius* 27; cf. Cassius Dio 62,16.2.

86 Cassius Dio 56,10.3. Suetonius, *Augustus* 41, 46. Cf. S. Dixon, *The Roman Mother*, ch. 4.

87 R. J. A. Talbert (ed), *Atlas of Classical History* (London, 1985), x; P. Garnsey, 'Trajan's Alimenta', *Historia* 17 (1968), 367 ff.; A. R. Hands, *Charities and Social Aid* (London, 1968), 108 ff.

88 Marcus: Haines II, 112. Constantine: *Theodosian Code* 11,27.1 (13 May 315) and 2 (6 July 322); Eusebius, *Vita Constantini* 1,43 = *PL* 20.957.

89 E. Griessmair, *Das Motiv der Mors Immatura in den griechischen metrischen Grabinschriften* (Innsbruck, 1966). Cf. also R. Lattimore, *Themes in Greek and Latin Epitaphs* (Urbana, Ill., 1962).

90 *Iliad* 4,477 f.

91 Hesiod, *Erga* 187 f.

92 Euripides, *Medea* 1032; 432 BC.

93 W. Peek, *Griechische Versinschriften* I (Berlin, 1955), No. 1097, 1 f.; Cf. 635, 3 f., a second century BC inscription from Pagos, near Smyrna: 'Old age, devoid of its support, has orphaned a father'; *Carmina Latina Epigraphica* (= *CLE*), ed. Buecheler (Leipzig, 1921), 526, l.9. Peek 1934, l.3 f. and 1162, l.8. Buecheler, *CLE* 157, from Thubursicum in Numidia: 'meritumque honorem sero quamvis reddidit'. Buecheler, *CLE* 380 = *CIL* VIII suppl. 15361, from Città di Castello: 'Eutychius, ut par est, tribuit tibi natus honores'. On the 'costs' of raising a child, cf. G. Clark, 'Roman women', *Greece and Rome* 28 (1981), 193 ff.

94 Rome, *c.* AD 120, Buecheler, *CLE* 422.10 = *CIL* VI,7578; Trebiati: Buecheler, *CLE* 93.

95 Buecheler, *CLE* 980 = *CIL* II,3475.

96 Buecheler, *CLE* 382 = *CIL* III,3196; Cicero, *Ad Fam.* 5,16.3; Buecheler, *CLE* 409 = *CIL* IX,4756.

97 E. Griessmair, *Das Motiv der Mors Immatura*; W. Peek, *Griechische Versinschriften* I 1680, cf. 1507; R. Lattimore, *Themes in Greek and Latin Epitaphs*. In some parts of Greece girls who died before being married were buried in their 'wedding' dresses even in this century: L. M. Danforth, *The Death Rituals of Rural Greece* (Princeton, NJ, 1982), 13.

98 Ausonius, *Epitaph* 35:

> infans lactavit, pubes et virgo adolevit.
> nupsit, concepit, peperit, iam mater obivit.
> quis mortem accuset? . . .

Chapter Two

IMPERIAL CHILDREN IN BIOGRAPHY AND PANEGYRIC

We might expect to find the best evidence for changes in the Romans' attitudes towards childhood over the centuries in literary descriptions of the birth and upbringing of particular individuals. The Romans, unlike the Greeks, clearly distinguished between the sphere of the community and that of the individual. There is no shortage of descriptions of individuals in Latin literature – law-court speeches, poems of praise, obituary notices in historical texts, and the separate literary genres of imperial biography and Christian hagiography.

Yet we shall be disappointed. Most of the anecdotes which appear in these texts are repetitive and predictable, and only rarely do they give the slightest indication that any changes were going on in perceptions of the place of children in the community. One reason for this is purely literary. In antiquity, literature had to be 'classical', i.e. to adhere to traditional vocabulary, themes, and forms of exposition. 'New' institutions and beliefs could only be accommodated into classical forms of writing with the utmost difficulty: we can see this with the problems that historians had in describing Christian rituals in classical vocabulary, even centuries after the Mediterranean world had become Christian, or in the survival of themes from pagan mythology in poets like Claudian who wrote for a Christian court.[1]

Like other types of classical literature, biography had its own rules, and both writer and audience had certain definite expecta-tions of what would be said about the subject's childhood and upbringing. As with many other Latin literary genres, these expectations can only be understood in the context of the Greek literary background. We are used to biography as an account of the development of a person's life over time: in its most basic form, a sequence of the things he did. 'Development' implies an account of how a person changes over time. This idea that personality can change was almost completely alien to Greek and Latin biography. The Latin *vita* and the Greek *bios* do not refer to 'life' in the sense of 'the series of events that a person experienced during the course of his life', but 'life-style': a *vita* is an account of what sort of person he was, throughout his life. A *bios* or *vita* need not even give an account of the character of one individual: thus we have a *bios Hellados*, a description of how Greeks live, and Varro wrote a description of Roman customs entitled *De Vita Populi Romani*, 'the way of life of the Roman people'.

Indeed much Greek biography is not primarily about individuals at all: it is about character-types. This goes against the modern assumption that the only really interesting subject for human interest is not *man*, but *individual* men. Nineteenth-century scholars had noted that archaic and fifth-century Greeks had little interest in individuals: the heroes of Thucydides' history, for example, are not individual leaders but 'The Athenians' or 'The Lacedaemonians'. These scholars were unhappy about this, and they applauded the development of interest in particular individuals in fourth-century literature. One great German scholar, Friedrich Leo, noted that Plato and Xenophon both wrote about Socrates: and he concluded that it was the individual personality of Socrates that was at the root of Greek biography.[2]

Leo was right in seeing that in the context of the Greek city only an exceptional type of person could be the subject of a biography. The city-states of the Mediterranean world – republican Rome as much as Greece – were torn by a constant tension between two conflicting principles: on the one hand the competition between individual citizens to prove that they were supreme in virtue, on the other the belief that all those who took part in public life were fundamentally equal, and that no one should be able to build up his wealth, power, or reputation to such an extent that fair competition with his peer-group was no longer possible. Such an individual was labelled a 'tyrant', and much of Greek literature from the archaic to the Roman period is concerned with proving that no tyrant will ultimately escape punishment for having more good fortune than any human being deserves.[3] The individual who was perceived as setting himself above his community was a threat, and tended to be dealt with severely; Socrates, we recall, was executed for 'not believing in the gods in whom the city believes'. Those who did break free from the equality and uniformity imposed by the classical city-state were those who would become the subject of biography and panegyric; but precisely such persons were *not* normal citizens, and the accounts which were given of their childhood do not tell us about the childhood of the normal citizen, but rather pick out abnormal, superhuman traits.

The earliest subjects of formal, ceremonial praise giving were indeed superhuman: gods and heroes. Where childhood events appeared in such poems of praise, their purpose was to illustrate the permanently divine nature of the god. Poets were not interested in the behaviour of children, but used the behaviour of children in the anthropomorphic setting of a myth to underline the fact that gods and heroes already had the plenitude of their powers from the moment they first existed – in anthropomorphic terms, from 'birth'. Typical stories such as those of Heracles in his cradle strangling the serpents sent by Hera throw as little light on the sort of behaviour that Greeks expected from their children as the story of the 'birth' of a fully adult Athena from the head of Zeus. In myth, child god and adult god are not two chronologically sequent stages.

It follows that chronology need not be the crucial factor in arranging the material of a life. Indeed rhetoricians' textbooks make it clear that an individual's 'life', i.e. character, can be dealt with either chronologically (Lat. *per tempora*) or by topics (*per species*). The latter requires a series of illustrations – anecdotes – for which chronological sequence is irrelevant. The twelve labours of Heracles are an example: each illustrates Heracles' power, but it is of no consequence that they fail to fit together to create a chronological sequence. We may consider the Homeric *Hymn to Hermes* as another instance; it tells us about the newly born infant god's thefts. This does not show that the ancient world was unable to distinguish between adults and children: rather, it is a statement that even from the very moment of his birth, the god Hermes had certain characteristics which were to be his throughout his divine 'life'. That is the literary background to the childhood miracles which are to be found in a number of lives dating to the Roman period: the Alexander of the *Alexander-Romance*, Homer, Apollonius of Tyana, a number of neo-Platonist teachers, as well as the child

51

Jesus of the so-called Apocryphal Gospels (e.g. the 'Gospel of Thomas').[4]

By the fifth century BC, this biographical 'form' was being used to praise not just gods and heroes, but also outstanding human beings such as the Olympic and Pythian victors whom Pindar honoured in his *Odes*, or cities such as Athens, honoured by Thucydides in Pericles' famous Funeral Speech. The prose *epitaphios* or funeral speech was a recognised rhetorical genre, and came to be the main example of epideictic oratory, one of the three types into which oratory was formally divided by theorists. By the fourth century BC, there were many examples of such formal speeches of praise, delivered on ceremonial occasions. This led directly to the next stage, the first formal 'biography' in Xenophon's *Agesilaus*.[5]

There were other elements that went to make up Greek biography, and when Roman writers began to produce lives, yet other, typically Roman, traditions such as the funeral laudation contributed as well. But the most important influence on ancient biography was rhetoric, and the rules prescribed by teachers of rhetoric can help us to understand not just the ancient attitude to character in general, but also the reasons why certain material about childhood was chosen by biographers for inclusion in the lives of outstanding political, military, and religious figures.

Towards the end of the first century AD, Quintilian discussed the topic in his treatise, the *Institutio Oratoriae*.[6] He is careful to stress that the remarks he makes are relevant to the requirements of the Roman situation: we are not entitled to argue that he had merely copied his precepts uncritically from those of Greek teachers, as Cicero (for example) seems to have done. For Quintilian, the panegyric was a serious institution of Roman public life: he begins by criticising Aristotle's and Theophrastus' view that it was primarily meant to entertain. On the contrary, panegyric and invective are the tools used to praise one's own witnesses in a court of law, and to denigrate those of one's opponents. It is also required in the specifically Roman custom of the funeral laudation, and, in the context of Roman politics, in order to attack political rivals and electoral competitors.

Quintilian begins his discussion with some remarks about *probatio*, the kinds of arguments that will be recognised as valid proof, when a speaker praises someone. The example he uses is interesting: because Romulus, although abandoned as an infant, did not die, the story that he was the son of a god and brought up by a she-wolf is at least *possible*. The *probatio* lies in using something within the experience of the audience (the exposition of new-born children) to persuade them of the truth of something that is not within their experience (divine affiliation). Immediately we are confronted with the fact that, for Quintilian and his readers, birth and infancy anecdotes are a fundamental feature of the description of character – not just in panegyric, but in many other types of literature.

After some remarks about panegyrics in honour of gods (only to be expected, if we are right in seeing the origin of the rhetorical panegyric in hymns of praise of Greek divinities), he goes on to say that panegyrics honouring mortals are more varied. The first arrangement is chronological: what happened before the subject's time, how the subject himself lived, and (in the case of those who have already died) what happened after their death.[7] In greater detail,

> we must describe, before a man was born, his city, parents, and ancestors [*patria, parentes et maiores*]. These can be treated in two ways: if the man's background was noble, he will gain credit from this, but if not, then he will be judged to have ennobled a poor background through his own particular achievement.

Any oracles that foretold the subject's birth should be included at this stage: Quintilian's example is the oracle that Thetis' son (Achilles) was fated to be more powerful than his father.

The next section is praise of the man himself, divided into 'spirit', 'physique', and 'external (fortuitous) advantages'.[8] Mention should of course be made of physical strength and beauty, though if these are notoriously absent the orator must point out what a great achievement it was for the hero to have attained his position in spite of physical defects. As regards the external advantages which a capricious fortune allots to some people but not to others – for instance, wealth – Quintilian says that what ought to be praised here is not so much the possession of such advantages, as their virtuous use.

But it is his discussion of the *laus animi* that concerns us most. There are two ways of dealing with it:

> For on some occasions it has been better to speak according to
> different stages in life, and follow the chronological order of
> events . . . so that inherited traits are praised first, then learning,
> after that his acts in due order (that is, his deeds and his words)

and alternatively, 'divide up the praise according to categories of
virtues – courage, justice, self-control etc. – and list those events
that are appropriate under each category'.[9] These rules are not of
course rigidly obeyed by the writers of all surviving prose
panegyrics in either Greek or Latin, let alone on any and every
occasion when a Roman lawyer or historian describes the character
of a man he wishes to praise or blame. But the fact that they were
academic – intended to teach young men how to make speeches –
does not make them divorced from reality. They give us a good
idea of the kinds of things which anyone who had himself gone
through the Greek or Roman tertiary education – effectively, any
educated Greek or Roman – would assume were worth saying
about any particular individual. Anecdotes associated with birth
and childhood play a vital role in this view of character. Character
is inherited, and that inherited character is revealed through a
child's behaviour: 'natural genius must be praised, as revealed in
his earliest years'. In addition, a man may be praised or blamed for
the way in which as a child he learnt the skills necessary for his
adult role (*disciplinae*).

This approach to describing character had the effect of making
the orator or biographer seek to push any evidence of his subject's
virtues – or vices – as far back into his childhood as possible. But
there was a further result which seriously affects the light which
such literary accounts of childhood can throw on ancient attitudes
towards 'normal' children. The tradition of panegyric meant that
praise was something bestowed on abnormal, and often on
superhuman, beings. Omens and miracles were assumed to be a
normal element of panegyric, not because they were a normal
element of ancient childhood, but because the subjects of
panegyrics and biographies were not normal men. The most
obvious instance of this is what is undoubtedly the most popular
work of literature to survive from antiquity, the *Alexander-Romance*
ascribed to Callisthenes. It contains all the elements of a divine
childhood: suspected filiation from a god; miracles at the time of
Alexander's birth; games which reveal the boy as a natural ruler;

acclamation by a wise man (in Alexander's case, Aristotle); and great learning at school. The childhood of Christ, as described in the canonical as well as the Apocryphal Gospels, contains similar material.[10]

It is not therefore surprising that, even from an early date, there should have been an infusion of divine elements into Latin accounts of birth and childhood. This is only to be expected in the case of mythical figures such as Romulus and Remus or Servius Tullius. But such stories could also be encouraged as an element of policy by powerful individuals who wanted to escape the limitations which the republican constitution imposed upon their peer-group – those who, in Greek terms, were seeking tyrannical powers. During the Hannibalic War, Scipio Africanus was elected, at an extremely early age, to take command of the Roman army fighting the Carthaginians in Spain. Livy explains how 'from his youth Scipio had consciously nurtured the impression that he was inspired by the gods through dreams and visions'. Scipio's behaviour

> confirmed the belief that he was a person of divine origin,
> reviving the story which had previously been told of Alexander
> the Great: that he had been conceived as a result of intercourse
> with a huge snake. This prodigy had often been seen in his
> mother's bedroom, and had immediately glided away and
> disappeared whenever anyone entered.

Needless to say, citizens who believed this story would be more likely to entrust the difficult task of the Spanish war 'to a young man who had not yet grown up'.[11]

Livy was clearly sceptical: such claims to a special, semi-divine status do not accord well with the ideology of a republic in which, although some citizens may be 'better', have more *virtus*, than others, nevertheless the rules must apply to all equally. Nothing miraculous is reported in the lives written by Nepos in the first century BC, the first surviving Latin collection of literary biographies of individuals from the worlds of politics and literature. Nepos was a younger contemporary of the wealthy and influential equestrian Caecilius Atticus (Cicero's correspondent). His account of Atticus' schooldays shows us what sort of characteristics a Roman writer considered typical of the childhood of a friend who was intelligent, eloquent, popular, and recognised as deserving his exceptional social status:

In addition to his capacity for learning, the boy had an extremely pleasant voice and pronunciation, so that he was not only able to learn quickly the passages he had been set, but could also declaim them faultlessly. For this reason he became conspicuous among those of his own age even as a child: in fact he was so outstanding that his nobly born school-fellows were in no position to ignore this.

Thus he inspired them all to emulate him, including Lucius Torquatus, Gaius Marius the Younger, and Marcus Cicero. 'With all of them he became such good friends that no one ever became dearer to them than he.'[12] The qualities which Nepos chose to recall about this boy were precisely those which were important for life as an adult male citizen: rhetorical excellence, and the ability to make friendships, so crucial to Roman public as well as private life.

It seems that this Roman republican resistance to the intrusion of miraculous childhood elements extended to panegyrics, even those praising the emperors of the first century AD. Unfortunately, only one such speech has survived, that delivered by Pliny the Younger in AD 100, thanking the emperor Trajan for having promoted him to the high honour of the consulship. Pliny's speech deviates markedly from the recommendations made by his contemporary Quintilian: not only are there no miracles, there are no references of any kind to Trajan's childhood or to his place of origin. The only omen Pliny refers to is the crowd's acclamation on the occasion when Trajan's predecessor Nerva had succumbed to the pressure to adopt him. Pliny mentions that Trajan's qualities were such that it was clear that he would have become emperor even if Nerva had not adopted him: but there are no childhood presages of kingship. Trajan's military service is praised; in his first campaign, serving under his father in Syria (where he was governor between AD 73/4 and 75/6), his virtues are said to have deserved glory even though he was 'still a boy' (*puer admodum*). This is rhetorical exaggeration; Trajan will have been 20 to 22 at the time. Again, no details are given or invented to illustrate this assertion. Although there is praise for Trajan's support of the liberal arts, contrasted with Domitian's persecution of philosophers, it is striking that not a word is said about Trajan's own education or upbringing. In spite of Quintilian's remarks about introducing birth and infancy anecdotes, we are almost entitled to deduce that for Pliny – and for Trajan – the birth and childhood of an emperor were of no significance.[13]

Pliny's panegyric may not have been entirely typical of the speeches of thanks which incoming consuls gave year by year in honour of the emperor. Pliny made a great deal of the contrast between Trajan, a citizen-emperor (*civilis princeps*), and his predecessor Domitian, condemned by the Senate after his death as a 'tyrant'. Childhood miracles were associated in the literary tradition with those who were claimed to be superhuman; what we are entitled to deduce from Pliny's panegyric is that childhood had no place in the praise of an emperor who claimed to be, not a king, but the first of citizens.

Notwithstanding the egalitarian ideology of the republic, emperors were not normal citizens; and it is not surprising that when writers came to describe their lives, there was a strong tendency to assign a prominent role both to childhood miracles and to precocious achievement in academic studies. These elements are prominent both in Suetonius' *Lives of the Caesars* and the much later *Augustan History*.[14] To some extent this may be ascribed to the Hellenistic background of particular biographers, but that is not the whole explanation. It is noteworthy that the earliest (Greek) account of the life of Augustus of which considerable portions survive, by Nicolaus of Damascus, is in fact extremely factual. He says that it is his intention to describe Augustus' ΠΕΠΡΑΓΜΕΝΗ ('deeds', translating the Latin *res gestae*), and explains that to do this successfully he must first 'describe his ancestry and his nature and the parents from whom he came, as well as his upbringing from childhood and the life-style as a result of which he became such a great man'. He ignores the birth miracles recorded by other writers: the first episode of which he has knowledge occurred at the funeral of Augustus' grandmother, Julius Caesar's sister Julia. While Suetonius mentions this in a short aside – 'At the age of twelve he made a public speech in praise of his deceased grandmother Julia' – Nicolaus gives the episode a special significance: 'At about the age of nine, Caesar became a major source of amazement to the Romans, demonstrating the keenness of his nature even at that age. People applauded him noisily when he spoke before a large crowd. . .'. The confusion about the precocious boy's age is interesting (see pp. 14 f. above): Nicolaus clearly wants to minimise his age, in order to turn the occasion into an omen.[15]

Some of Augustus' other biographers had no scruples about introducing elements which made it easier for the reader to grasp that the hero's nature was above the human norm. Especially in the years following the conquest of Egypt, Octavian/Augustus was keen to be compared with Alexander. Suetonius notes that already at the time of his birth there were omens 'from which his future greatness and eternal good fortune could be clearly seen'. The freedman Julius Marathus (probably from Marathos, near Arados in Phoenicia) recorded a portent presaging the birth of a future king which, he claimed, led the Senate to forbid any male child to be reared for a whole year (the law was technically invalidated by the actions of senators who selfishly hoped that they themselves would be the new king's father, said Julius). Another story suggested that Augustus was the son of a god who appeared to his mother Atia at a nocturnal religious festival in the form of a serpent. This Alexander-like story was recorded in the *Theologoumena* of the Egyptian grammarian Asclepiades of Mende. There were other signs – among them the story that his father received a response from a Thracian oracle which only Alexander the Great had received before. Augustus himself revealed his divine nature as a child: one night he disappeared from his cradle and was found at the top of a tower, facing towards the rising sun. Then, when he was just learning to talk and disturbed by the croaking of frogs at his grandfather's villa, he successfully ordered them to stop (the divine child has power over all aspects of nature). And he is acclaimed by a wise and great man when still only a child: none other than Cicero recognised him as a figure he had seen in a dream, sent by Jupiter to rule Rome.[16]

Similar omens are recorded as having occurred during the early years of other emperors who were expected to bring peace, principally Vespasian and also Galba, who as a child was recognised as a future ruler by Augustus. Titus' beauty 'right from boyhood' foreshadows his later apotheosis; supernatural signs are adduced in support. In the case of the short-lived emperor Vitellius, the omens accompanying birth are, on the contrary, appalling.[17]

The character of evil emperors as well as good ones is represented as present from birth. Even as a teenager at Capri, 'Caligula could not control his brutal and debauched nature'. Otho was 'prodigal and shameless from his teens', so much so that his father frequently had to beat him for his nocturnal escapades. Vitellius' boyhood and youth, spent among Tiberius' assortment of prostitutes at Capri, foreshadows the fact that in later life too his morals were disgusting. Tiberius' savage and dour character did not escape notice even when he was a boy: his rhetoric teacher Theodorus of Gadara is cited in confirmation. 'From his earliest years' there were omens predicting Tiberius' future power – the cock chick which his mother Livia had hatched in order to find out if her child was to be a boy or a girl turned out to have a wonderful crest, and the astrologer Scribonius prophesied monarchy at his birth.[18]

The other category of information which Suetonius was interested in recording about the boyhood of future rulers was also in accordance with Quintilian's recommendations: how well they had done at school. As a boy, Augustus worked eagerly and industriously at his rhetorical and general liberal studies. Tiberius 'studied the liberal arts, Greek and Latin, most attentively: as regards Latin rhetoric, he modelled himself on Messala Corvinus, whom he respected very highly as a young man, when Messala was already very old'. Claudius 'gave no little attention to liberal studies, from his earliest age'. Nero 'studied almost all liberal arts as a boy', except, interestingly, philosophy. Galba was a conscientious law-student, Caligula worked hard at his rhetorical studies, and it is implied that Domitian had studied literature and rhetoric before he neglected these pursuits when he became a bad emperor.[19]

Suetonius' series of imperial lives was continued by the consular biographer Marius Maximus in the first half of the third century AD; Maximus was very probably a major source of the so-called *Augustan History*, a series of biographies of emperors from Trajan to AD 284 written in the late fourth or early fifth century.[20] A comparison between Suetonius and the *Augustan History* shows that literary descriptions of childhood had hardly changed over the intervening three centuries, despite the major changes that had been taking place in Mediterranean society.

We have the expected omens: Marcus Aurelius, as a boy of 8, had been elected to the college of Salii, and when at the end of their ritual banquet all the priests present threw their ceremonial crowns onto the couch on which the idol of Mars had been placed, Marcus' crown landed on the god's head. Frequently omens occur during the pregnancy of the future emperor's mother, or at the actual moment of birth. Commodus' mother Faustina dreamt that she was going to give birth to two serpents, one of them fiercer than the other; in the event, Commodus' twin brother Antoninus died at the age of 4. A black horse climbed onto the roof of Helvius Successus' home at the time of the birth of his son Pertinax. At the birth of Geta, there was the curious incident of the discovery that a purple-coloured egg had just been found somewhere in the palace. Caracalla seized it and smashed it on the floor – 'as children will do' (*quasi parvulus*) – and his mother's joke, that he had symbolically killed his brother, was later seen to be only too true. There was another omen too – when an attendant inadvertently slaughtered the sacrificial victim on Geta's birthday. There was also an ominous outburst by Caracalla when Severus was not yet emperor: they were having a picnic in the garden, and the 5-year-old Caracalla took more than his fair share of the rather meagre portions that had been prepared. Severus castigated his son, telling him that he did not possess the wealth of a king, and the boy replied 'I soon will'.[21]

One theme which had not appeared in Suetonius, but goes back in Greek literary tradition to the story of Cyrus' childhood in Herodotus, was the idea that the future king is made manifest by his role within the hierarchy of children at play. Septimius Severus as a young boy, before he had been sent to school to learn Latin and Greek, 'used to spend all his time with the other boys playing nothing else but "judges": he would come in with fasces and axes borne before him and sit down with the other children standing around in a circle and give judgement'.[22]

The rhetorician Menander, writing about AD 300, advises speakers to include such miracles in their praises of the emperor.

> If there is anything like this in connection with the emperor, develop it; if it is possible to invent, and to do this convincingly, do not hesitate to do so. Your subject allows this, since the audience has no choice but to accept your panegyric without testing it.[23]

Where the author of the *Augustan History* had little or no source material, as for the emperors of the third century AD, he did just that. The very unreliable life of the boy-emperor Diadumenus (Diadumenianus, Macrinus' son and co-emperor in AD 217–18) contains a number of spectacular omens: his father, an inspector of the imperial treasury, filed a report declaring that the supplies of purple were most satisfactory (*claras*) two hours before the birth of the boy. Purple eggs were laid on his father's estate. The astrologers' predictions were so favourable that they led to suspicions that his mother must have committed adultery with an emperor. Later, as a boy, he was playing in the fields with some friends when an eagle snatched his cap from his head and lifted it onto the head of a statue of a king in the nearby villa. The most fantastic of the stories invented by the *Augustan History* is of the lion which mauled Diadumenus' nurse to death, but merely licked the face of the baby lying in the cradle.[24]

The later sections of the *Augustan History* are full of such fictions. In the biography of the two Maximinuses, the writer devotes a special section to presages of empire – including a serpent surrounding the head of the younger Maximinus when he was asleep, and an incident which occurred when he was first sent to the *grammaticus*: a relative gave him a present of the complete works of Homer inscribed on purple vellum in gold lettering. On one occasion the emperor Alexander Severus invited the boy along to a dinner he was giving in honour of his father, and when the little boy arrived at the palace without the proper clothing, he was given something from Alexander's own wardrobe to wear. Earlier, as a toddler, he once climbed onto Caracalla's official carriage as it was being driven along the street, empty; and the grooms could only manage to get him off it with the greatest difficulty. Although Caracalla was warned of the danger presented by this omen, he refused to take any action, since the child was quite unknown and exceedingly young at the time.[25]

The qualities and interests of adult emperors, positive and negative, were manifest in their behaviour as children. Marcus Aurelius 'was serious from earliest childhood'.

He was keenly interested in philosophy even when he was still a small boy. At the age of eleven he assumed the garb of a philosopher, and then a philosopher's endurance too: he took his lessons wrapped in a pallium [the recognised uniform of Greek teachers of philosophy] and slept on the ground – although at his mother's insistence he reluctantly agreed to make his bed on a couch covered with skins.

61

His mother Domitia Lucilla was certainly justified in worrying about Marcus' over-identification with academic studies: while attending lessons on jurisprudence 'he devoted so much work and effort to his studies that he destroyed his health. This was the only respect in which his childhood may be criticised'. As a teenager he was good at gymnastics and hunting, and allowed himself to be taken to the theatre or amphitheatre or on hunting parties, but his interest in philosophy distracted him from all these pastimes (although the *Augustan History* is quick to stress that this did not make him an unpleasant person). Other positive qualities such as a sense of honour which prevented him from accepting unsolicited legacies already showed themselves when he was a *puer* and kept his procurators under tight control.[26]

Marcus' son Commodus was an exemplar of the wicked tyrant. Although his father tried to educate him through his own teaching and that of respected public professors, this was of no effect – 'So great is the power of natural character compared to the tutors that are maintained in a royal palace'. 'From his earliest years' he was base and dishonourable, cruel, sensual, foul-mouthed and debauched. Already he was expert at skills, *artes*, which do not become a future emperor: decorating drinking cups, dancing, singing, whistling; he could play the part of a court fool or a gladiator to perfection. At the age of 11, at Centumcellae, he gave a token of his cruelty:

> When the bath-water happened to be cooler than he wanted, he ordered the man who was responsible to be thrown into the furnace. The *paedagogus* who had been told to do this was so scared to disobey that he had a sheepskin burnt in the fire, so that the stench of the vapour would convince Commodus that the punishment had in fact been carried out.[27]

On the other hand Caracalla's childhood was quite unlike what he later became – his popularity, hard work at school, liberality and clemency were widely respected. He broke down in tears when he saw criminals condemned to the wild beasts in the amphitheatre. When he was 7 and heard that a boy with whom he used to play had been severely beaten because of his association with Jews (*ob Iudaicam religionem* might also refer to Christians), he refused for a long time to look his own father or the boy's father in the eye since he held them responsible for the beating.[28]

As in Nepos' *Life of Atticus*, two elements that are emphasised are friendships made at school, and excellence (or otherwise) at learning. The less successful emperors, like Pescennius Niger and Clodius Albinus, are said not to have done well at school: as a schoolboy in Africa, Clodius Albinus (AD 193–7) used to keep repeating Vergil's line 'Madly I seize my weapons' ('arma amens capio', *Aeneid* 2,314) whenever the class had to chant this section of the epic, 'since even then his spirit was bellicose and proud'.[29]

The stories told of future emperors in the *Augustan History* are so similar to those of Suetonius that we might believe that the world of late antiquity had much the same attitudes as the classical period. But we must remember that this literary tradition dealt with exceptional individuals, those who had risen above the level of the normal citizen. For Pliny, Trajan's childhood had been of no interest; for Nepos, Atticus' had been of interest only as a preparation for his subject's adult life as a citizen. The *Augustan History* develops these traditional themes to a much greater extent than earlier biography. This is a reflection of the fact that, by the time it was written, the classical distinction between child and adult citizen had disappeared to such an extent that we even find children holding the imperial office.

The existence of child-emperors from the third century on also makes its presence felt in surviving panegyrics, both prose and verse. As in biography, the themes – birth miracles, childhood omens, excellence in literary and rhetorical studies – were generally traditional; what was new was a much greater emphasis on these themes. We have already mentioned the discussion of how to praise emperors (the *Basilikos logos*) which appears in a Greek handbook composed in about AD 300 by the professional rhetorician Menander.[30] Menander advises an introductory passage in which the speaker will note that, if he can demonstrate his ability by praising the emperor's deeds, he himself will win reflected glory because of the excellence of his subject matter; and the speech itself is a solemn, almost a religious, occasion. Naturally anything negative must be omitted.

The narrative is to begin with a reference to the emperor's town or province of origin, and any notable services it may have rendered the empire. If this line of approach appears to be barren, the speaker should move on to the emperor's family background: either he is glorified by the possession of a long list of ancestors, or his own personal virtues have been so great that they have enabled him to found a new dynasty himself, thus proving that his origins are not really human at all, but that, like Heracles, the gods have sent him to be the salvation of mankind. We have already noted that Menander says that if the speaker has been unable to learn of any good omens having been observed at the time of the emperor's birth, then he must have no hesitation in inventing some.

Already, in the cradle, the future emperor can be easily identified: his beauty is radiant as the brightest star in the sky. Among the points of significance of which the orator should inform his audience is whether the ruler's family was already imperial and, if so, whether he was the eldest son of his father, and whether he had still been a child when first raised to the purple. For all the similarities between Menander's exposition and Quintilian's, it would have been unthinkable two centuries before for a magistracy, including the imperial office, to be held by a child. Of course, even in late antiquity, many emperors were mature adults when they were acclaimed. Menander says that if the emperor had been born into a 'private' family, the orator will have to emphasise his excellence at school. We can see in this the two ways in which a child may be recognised as outstanding: by holding public office, and by precociously assimilating the learning of a free adult, the *artes liberales*. In the latter respect also, Menander warns against hesitation in inventing appropriate anecdotes if they are not already common knowledge. The child's intellectual qualities must be stressed: thirst for knowledge, a keen mind, application to hard work. It is crucial to mention any campaigns on which the child's father may have taken him as a boy. Even as a child, says Menander, the future emperor can be identified as exceptional; he will be outstanding among his peer-group, proving his natural vocation of leadership.

Menander goes on to list the sequence of topics that follow: first, the circumstances of his accession to power, and then the virtues, in proper order: the four moral virtues, fortitude, justice, piety, self-control (with regard to items such as food, drink, sleep, and sex) and then the 'fortuitous' virtues, those over which man has little control: physique, health, good fortune.

A considerable number of Greek and Latin panegyrics in honour of emperors survive from late antiquity, and they show that Menander's rules – while by no means slavishly adhered to – provided a useful framework for those who drew up such speeches. The contrast with Pliny's speech of thanks to Trajan (see p. 56 above) is striking. Pliny's panegyric is preserved in a corpus of twelve such speeches, the *Panegyrici Latini*; the other eleven all date to the late third and fourth centuries. It is a sign of the changes which Roman society had been undergoing in the intervening period that references to birth and childhood are much fuller here. The earliest panegyric was performed at Trier in AD 289 in honour of Maximianus 'Herculius', joint emperor with Diocletian. The orator Mamertinus only refers to his subject's early years in a series of rhetorical questions, asking what the most suitable point is at which to begin the list of the emperor's praises. Yet within this limiting framework, he finds an opportunity to mention 'the outstanding contribution of your native city to the commonwealth', comparing Pannonia favourably with Italy; the divine origin of the emperor's family, to which Maximianus bears witness 'not only by your undying achievements but also by bearing the name [sc. Herculius]'; and the upbringing he received

> in that frontier region, the headquarters of the bravest of our legions, where recruits exercise strenuously and the noise of weapon-training drowned your crying: in the case of Jupiter's childhood, such stories are fictions, in yours, emperor, they are true.[31]

These *topoi* of birth and childhood appear again in other panegyrics. In the latest, presented by Pacatus at Rome in honour of the Christian emperor Theodosius in AD 389, the orator begins by apologising for his 'uncultivated transalpine accents' and assures the audience that he 'will go through everything from the beginning in proper order'. He starts with the wealth of Spain, which has produced so many good soldiers and scholars, including Trajan and Hadrian: 'Crete which glories in having the cot of young Jupiter and Delos where the twin gods [sc. Apollo and Artemis] first learnt to crawl, and Thebes, noted for its infant Hercules, yield precedence to Spain.' There is praise of Theodosius' father and then we come to his own appointment to the imperial office. Theodosius deserved the job because Fortune had trained him for it through wars and political crises 'just as austere fathers treat with particular severity those sons whom they love most': Pacatus mentions winters when Theodosius as a child was wrapped in skins, summers when he sweated, days spent fighting and nights on guard duty, battles by land and sea fought in his father's company. He is favourably compared to the stock exemplars of Scipio Africanus, Hannibal, and Alexander the Great as children: the fathers and teachers of these three would have wished them to have behaved the way Theodosius did. There are no omens accompanying the birth of this very Christian emperor, and Pacatus does not pretend that he did anything particularly outstanding at school; but in other respects he has kept closely to the 'proper order', as promised.[32]

Just as Pacatus chose to omit omens and schooling, so some of the other orators whose panegyrics survive in the collection chose to say nothing at all about birth and childhood. Speakers were free to select only those items which they felt were appropriate to the particular context. Particularly interesting are the remarks about the emperor Constantine's own young children made in AD 321 on the fifteenth anniversary of Constantine's accession, by Nazarius, whom St Jerome in his *Chronicle* acclaims as the most respected orator of his time. Their virtue 'is not just budding under the surface, not merely in bloom, but already in a state of maturity – contary to what one would expect from persons of this age'. Nazarius' language is that used by Quintilian two centuries before in praise of his elder son; that should not be allowed to obscure the fact that we are now in a world where children are 'mature' not just because of their literary precociousness, but because they hold office.[33] The 14-year-old elder son Crispus had celebrated his first consulship in 317 at the age of 9. He had already shown through his military campaigns that he had inherited his father's power over barbarians. The younger, Constantine, born in 317 – so he would have been 3 or 4 at this time – is said already to be conscious of the fact that he holds consular office, and has a high social status inherited from his father. The little boy proclaims (*declarat*) that if there is any territory which his father and brother are going to leave unconquered, he will conquer it himself, since, says Nazarius, 'He has already conquered the childishness of his years through his own willpower'.[34] Nazarius explains how this can be: any outstanding person will inevitably 'fulfil the potential of his own nature', and this happens very quickly 'since a lively nature will soon break the swaddling-bands of childhood'. Crispus and

Constantine had certainly done that: they both held the consulship before they were 10. In the fourth century, an imperial child no longer suffered from the limitations which being a child imposed upon ordinary mortals. This was quite unlike the childhood of Trajan, which Pliny had not even mentioned.

Quintus Aurelius Symmachus (*c.* AD 340–402) was recognised by his contemporaries as one of the greatest orators in the Latin language. The only complete writings of his which survive are his letters, which we will look at in the next chapter; but fragments of eight speeches have been recovered from a palimpsest originating from the monastery of Bobbio in northern Italy which contains some other important texts, including the letters of Fronto.[35] On 25 February 369, Symmachus recited two panegyrics in honour of the emperors, one for Valentinian I and the other for his son Gratian, who would have been a child of about 2 years at the time. The beginning of the first speech is lost. Where the surviving text begins, Symmachus is telling the audience about Valentinian's upbringing in his father's company in Africa (this would have been in the 320s). Here, says Symmachus, he was taught what sort of emperor he should become, as well as how to suffer heat and dust; previously his cradle had been covered by the snows of Illyria. 'Shortly before, you had drunk water melted from blocks of ice; then, as if born to different elements, your patience had to learn to overcome the thirst which parched Libya inflicts.' The fact that Valentinian had got to know all parts of the empire as a child would ensure that no part would ever suffer as a result of his inevitable temporary absence as emperor. 'Born among the frosts, brought up beneath the sun', he would be in a position to conquer Scythians (representing the peoples of the North) as well as Indians and Ethiopians (in the South, here as so often in antiquity assumed to be the same people). Valentinian's father Gratianus is praised for the upbringing he arranged for his sons, since this *institutio privata*, education suitable for a private citizen, showed the army that Valentinian was indeed worthy of the imperial dignity.

As for the baby Gratian, 'his first spell of military service was in the rank of emperor'. His consulship, as a constitutional office handed down from the days of the republic, has guaranteed an auspicious start to his rule, since the rule of law and freedom of speech will be respected. Symmachus seems to go on to counter possible objections to having an emperor-consul of such tender years (the text is not easy to reconstruct at this point): 'Those who would assess you only by your years would be making a great mistake. You are fighting on behalf of old men although only a boy, you are sweating in defence of our children although you are their equal in age.' The 2-year-old's literary studies in his father's camp are said to parallel Accius' presence among the legionary eagles and blasts of the trumpets in Fulvius' army, or Panaetius with Africanus and the philosopher-companions of Alexander the Great: 'these ancient fables may now be believed, since books as well as weapons are handled in your tents'. Whatever unease Symmachus may have detected among some members of the Roman aristocracy or court at a 2-year-old in command, it was certainly a fact: the child Gratian had transcended the age-grades of the classical period.

When Gratian was 11, he appointed his literature teacher Ausonius to the consulship for 379. Ausonius' speech of thanks survives. As might be expected, it refers to the 'scholarly' and 'erudite language' of the imperial decree conferring the appointment; but Ausonius explicitly says that he wants to avoid in his speech the commonplaces of panegyric (*laudes regiae*): 'I shall deal not with outstanding, but with everyday aspects of my theme.' So there are no birth or childhood omens, and no references to a precocious military upbringing. Instead, Gratian's habit of regular prayer since childhood (*ab adulescentia*) is noted, and his lack of ostentation and extravagance, his excellence at athletics, jumping, throwing the javelin and horsemanship – so much so, says Ausonius, that the roles of pupil and instructor are reversed. And with respect to the oratorical skills required of an emperor, we are told that the boy was like Xenophon's Cyrus – 'not the real Cyrus, but the ideal'. Ausonius' description is not of course devoid of flattery and exaggeration; but it is the most authentic account in a panegyric of a young noble's real interests and activities.[36] We sense that it describes a world in which much is seemingly as it had been in the classical period – the rules applying to *laudes regiae*, and the importance of rhetorical erudition. But some things have changed. The 11-year-old emperor is interested in hunting rather than gladiatorial contests; and he says his daily prayers as a Christian.

By contrast, the descriptions of young princes and princesses in the verse panegyrics of the poet Claudian seem highly artificial, and many of them keep close to the recommendations of Menander Rhetor; perhaps Claudian had had to learn them as a student in Egypt. Claudian's invectives attacking those imperial officials opposed to his patron Stilicho also seem to make use of the same standard scheme for describing a person's birth and childhood. It is very noticeable that Claudian distinguishes clearly between the rubrics *infantia* (infancy, babyhood) and *pueritia* (childhood).[37]

This can be seen in two panegyrics from 396 and 398 celebrating the third and fourth consulships respectively of Theodosius' son, the young emperor Honorius, who had been born on 9 September, 384. The earlier one describes the boy as having been born to the purple, son of a king, surrounded by soldiers and military eagles. Germany, the Caucasus, and Meroe (symbols of North, East, and South) trembled in recognition of his charismatic power. As a baby, he crawled among the soldiers' armour, and played with battle-spoils newly captured from barbarian kings; he was always the first to greet his father on his victorious return from the battlefields on the Danube frontier, and would demand some item of booty as his share of the spoils. Claudian stresses that the boy was not frightened by his father's armour or the light reflected from his helmet (unlike Homer's Astyanax, *Iliad* 6,466 ff.), but actually 'stretched out your hands towards the lofty plumes'. In his joy, his father Theodosius is then said to have uttered a prayer to Jupiter (based on Hector's prayer for Astyanax at *Iliad* 6,476 ff.) that his son be blessed with similar success on the battlefield. The scene is an instance of how Claudian couples an outstanding awareness of how babies actually behave, and what attracts their interest, with literary artifice: the 'real' Theodosius was of course a convinced Christian, and his prayer to Jupiter is invented in emulation of Homer's Hector. The realities of the turn of the fourth century are expressed in the language of a literary tradition that goes back more than a thousand years.[38]

Later, when the child had attained *pueritia* and was able to stand up and walk, his father undertook his training. Sleep, luxury and sloth were discouraged, and the boy's young limbs were strengthened by exercise and inured to pain. He is said

> to suffer the keen frost, not to shrink from a violent rainstorm, to bear the heat of summer, to swim across the roaring fury of a torrent, to conquer mountains by climbing them, plains by

running across them, and valleys and hollows by leaping over them; to spend sleepless nights on guard-duty; to drink melted snow out of your helmet; to shoot arrows from your bow and stones from a Balearic sling.

Claudian also says that Theodosius told his son many stories about his grandfather's military conquests in Mauretania and Britain

to enkindle an even greater love of fighting . . . these were the stimuli he gave to your *virtutes*, the seeds of fame, ideals to follow. Achilles did not drink in the teaching of the old centaur Chiron any more quickly when he was learning the arts of fighting, the lyre's tunes or the medicinal properties of plants.[39]

When Theodosius led his army to the west in 394 to overthrow the usurper Eugenius and his generalissimo the Frankish *magister militum* Arbogast, the 9-year-old Honorius gave evidence of his warlike character by demanding to accompany his father – 'like a young lion who, when his claws and teeth begin to grow, decides that he prefers to leave his mother and burns to join his father in raiding the local cattle-herds'. Claudian's lion-cub never actually managed to get out on the hunt: and Theodosius, instead of letting Honorius accompany him, 'entrusted the government into your hands' (this means that the younger son was proclaimed *Augustus* on 20 November 393: as throughout this poem, Claudian makes no reference to the elder son, Arcadius). The public was so impressed by the young boy's precocious *pietas*, 'by the extent to which his spirit was ahead of his years', that there was a general complaint that he should actually have been raised to the imperial office sooner.[40]

In the panegyric recited two years later to honour Honorius' fourth consulship, Claudian begins according to form with references to the emperor's family background: from Trajan's Spain, with a conqueror of Africa and Caledonia as his grandfather, and a father whose rule ran from Gades to the Tigris, the Tanais to the Nile, won by his own military ability and neither by birth nor by political intrigue. After a short résumé of Theodosius' reign, Claudian returns to Honorius: 'Ennobled by this background, you were a king immediately that you were born and never suffered the blemish of being a private person' (perhaps a subtle way of down-grading Honorius' elder brother, Arcadius).

Claudian mentions that he had been brought up in a palace, dressed in purple like his father; there is praise of Constantinople as his birthplace, which is compared with Spain as his *origo*, and with Thebes, Delos, and Crete as the birthplaces of Hercules and Bacchus, Apollo and Zeus. (We have seen a similar comparison in Pacatus' panegyric, p. 65 above.) But the circumstances of Honorius' birth were preferable to those of these divinities – maternity arrangements at Constantinople were much more comfortable for his mother Flaccilla than Mount Cynthus on Delos had been for Leto. The reverential acclamations of the palace servants are noted. Then – Christianity notwithstanding – there are the omens of future prosperity: the songs of birds and their flight-path through the heavens; soothsayers are said to have flocked to the palace; the oracles at the oasis of Ammon in the Libyan desert and at Delphi broke their long silence, as did the Sibyl at Cumae, and Persian, Etruscan, and Mesopotamian clairvoyants all recognised that a powerful person had been born into the world. Honorius' cradle was not surrounded by noisy Corybantes as Zeus' had been (cf. Mamertinus in AD 289: *Panegyrici Latini* 2/10, 2.4, p. 65 above), but by a glittering army – the infant was made more imperial by the standards which surrounded him, and he recognised the helmets of the respectful soldiery, while the trumpet sounded in answer to his ferocious howling.[41]

Here too Claudian stresses that the first day of Honorius' life (9 September, 384) immediately brought him *imperium*, in that he was appointed to his first consulship (*proveheris*, l. 155; this was in fact the consulate of 386). 'Your mother herself when you were small wrapped you in the consular robe and encouraged you to crawl towards your first consular throne.' Fantasy takes over completely when Claudian describes how the child was nursed by the goddesses Diana and Minerva, with whose shield and aegis he played fearlessly. His mother, in anticipation of a positive answer to her prayer that her younger son become emperor, often placed the diadem on his head when she handed him to his father to be kissed. When, aged 9, he was proclaimed Augustus, the favour of heaven manifested itself in meteorological omens, which Claudian compares with the fire which played around the young Ascanius' locks in Vergil's *Aeneid* (2,682; but Honorius' future was guaranteed by flames which appeared in heaven itself), and also with the child Jupiter's receiving the homage of the weather-gods when he was a boy on Mount Ida and still 'learning to cleave the clouds and hurl his thunderbolts with unpractised hand'.[42]

Theodosius is said to have been pleased at the omens, and proud of his two sons, now equal as Augusti – the trio is compared with Jupiter and the twin sons of Leda, Castor and Pollux. There follows a lengthy speech put into the mouth of Theodosius, in which he tells the new Augustus that unlike oriental despots, Roman emperors are constitutional rulers whose legitimacy ought to come from ability and not heredity alone. Rather cleverly, Claudian does not ascribe all imperial virtues directly to the young Honorius: instead, he puts an analysis of their importance into the mouth of his father Theodosius. They are the Platonic virtues of self-control, reliability, justice (and in particular the readiness to obey one's own rules), and preparedness in war. Little Honorius impatiently interrupts his father's lecture, promising to obey, but at the same time demanding that his father take him with him on the wars against the pagan usurper, Eugenius – is he still such a child that he is thought incapable of fighting? He is, he claims, as old as Pyrrhus had been when he showed himself a worthy son of Achilles and overthrew Troy. Theodosius is delighted by this outburst and kisses his son: but although praiseworthy, his desire to perform heroic deeds is premature (*festinus*). The little boy must be patient, since he will become physically stronger in due course. The emperor compares his son with Alexander, who wept to hear of Philip's conquests on the grounds that there would be no one left for him to fight himself (a theme we have already found in connection with Crispus and Constantine, see p. 66 above). Theodosius acclaims his son: 'You will be as great' (sc. as Alexander). But Honorius' future kingship is not a father's gift, it is nature's. The reader suspects that after all this, it must have come as something of a disappointment that the two brothers had to remain behind at Constantinople until Theodosius had won his victory over the usurper. Even for a fourth-century emperor, it was not possible for nature to overcome all the weaknesses of childhood.[43]

Theodosius' address ends with advice on how the boy is to spend his time while his father is away: Honorius' mind is to apply itself to literature while it is still impressionable, and read about things which it may soon imitate. He should unravel the scroll containing the stories of the commanders of antiquity, thereby accustoming himself to his own future campaigning by projecting himself into the early age of Latium. As regards his attitude towards the ideal of liberty, his hero should be Brutus (a remarkable indication of how Roman emperors continued to pay lip-service to the republican tradition even at the end of antiquity). If he hates treachery, he should gain satisfaction from reading of the punishment of Mettius Fufetius.[44] Claudian compares Theodosius providing his son with a reading list to an old helmsman giving his son advice about the weather, and congratulates him on having a son (Honorius would have been 13 in January 398) who equals or surpasses him, thanks to his father's foresight in entrusting his boy to Stilicho, Claudian's patron, whom the poet goes on to praise at some length.

Elsewhere in his poetry, Claudian's references to children are not markedly different from what we would have expected to find in classical literature four centuries earlier. They symbolise physical weakness: in the second book of his invective against Eutropius, he compares the Romans calling desperately on Stilicho to come to their help to

children whose father is transporting merchandise across the seas – they are intent on their play and have forgotten about schoolwork, and with their guardian away, they roam further than they should – yet when a powerful neighbour and his supporters take over the empty property and drive them unprotected from their home, then at last they will beg their father's help, hopelessly call out his name, and pointlessly gaze at the shore for his return.[45]

There are a number of passages which suggest that Claudian was very much aware of the contradiction between the inherited theme of the weak and thoughtless child and the glory accorded to the child emperors of his own time. That theme can be exploited to add to the praise of a young emperor's guardian. We have already seen how he emphasises that Theodosius did not think that Honorius at the age of 9 had the physical stamina to take part in the campaigns of 394. In Claudian's short epic poem on the war against Gildo, the deceased emperor Theodosius appears to his son in a vision to tell him how dangerous the political situation had been at the moment of his death – there was rebellion in northern Italy, and it is implied that the courtier Eutropius was trying to bring about civil war between the brother-emperors. 'Such madness could hardly have been overcome by my own vigilance, much less by a boy's rule.' Honorius should be thankful that Stilicho was there to take Theodosius' place as his guardian, 'looking after you, young and immature, and bringing you to the real age of a prince'.[46]

Claudian's ability to use authentic elements of child behaviour in his poetry extends to the princesses of the imperial family. Thoughts of marriage and school loom large – and sometimes exclude one another: in the *Epithalamium* in honour of the marriage of Honorius to Stilicho's daughter Maria, Claudian tells us that the girl had had no thoughts about marriage, since she was too interested in what her mother was teaching her, and busy reading Greek and Latin literature; Claudian specifies Homer, 'Orpheus', and Sappho.[47]

In his panegyric on Serena, Stilicho's wife and Theodosius' niece and, after the death of her own father, adopted daughter, Claudian tells us about a series of birth miracles conventionally associated with the coming of the Golden Age – the gold-bearing Spanish river Tagus overflows its banks, there is a rich harvest along the banks of the Douro in Galicia. Sheep spontaneously don purple fleeces, as in Vergil's *Fourth Eclogue*. The Nereids acclaim the newborn baby as their future queen. Instead of an ordinary, mortal nurse, the Nymphs give her suck, and the three Graces hold her in their arms and teach her to speak. When the baby crawls about in the grass, roses and white lilies immediately spring up; when she falls asleep, purple violets suddenly appear, surrounding the baby with imperial splendour. 'Your mother has not the courage to tell anyone about these great omens, and – conscious of the secret which she eagerly hopes for – she keeps its outcome to herself.' Claudian gives us an anecdote about the child in her innocence complaining about her uncle Theodosius taking her away from her mother, thereby acclaiming him as a future emperor – 'he always orders everyone about'.

In another realistic passage, Claudian describes how when the emperor came home in a temper, depressed by the weight of public affairs, so that his sons fled his presence and not even Flaccilla would go near him, it was Serena who would overcome her adoptive father's anger and bring him round by her conversation. Claudian praises the girl's modesty (*reverentia*), and again her study of Homer and Vergil, Greek mythology and Roman history.[48]

Royal children had always been exceptions in demonstrating their superhuman characters from the moment of birth. More remarkable is that at the end of the fourth century, even youths belonging to a non-imperial family were on one exceptional occasion granted the highest republican office, the consulship. After the defeat of his rival Eugenius at the battle of the Frigidus in September 394, Theodosius thought it advisable to conciliate the leading senatorial families of Rome, many of them pagans who had supported Eugenius, by appointing the two teenage sons of the leading pagan Sextus Anicius Petronius Probus as consuls together for 395.[49]

Claudian's description of the boyhood of the two youths Olybrius and Probinus is very similar to that of the Augustus Honorius. In accordance with the rules of panegyric, he begins with a reference to the fact that their ancestors (Auchenii and Anniadae) had held consulships over the generations. Their father Probus, unlike an emperor or *magister militum*, had no military achievements to his credit for which he could be praised. Instead, Claudian has to lay much emphasis on the virtue of generosity (a comment on the urban aristocracy's major function). His sons appear to have been even more successful as adolescents: 'Few old men have merited the honours with which you have begun. You have attained the finishing-post before the full flower of youth has cast a shadow on your smooth cheeks and maturity clothed your faces in its smiling down.' Rome is depicted as imploring Theodosius to grant the two boys the consular honour: 'I myself gave the little ones their cradles when Lucina freed their mother's happy burden and the stars brought forth her glorious children'. They are favourably compared with the heroes of the Roman republic, the Decii, Metelli, Scipiones, and Camilli. 'They are endowed with all the qualities of the Muses, and their eloquence is more than sufficient.' Their virtue is not subject to the vagaries of 'playful years': 'Because their grave obligations have burdened them with an old man's mind, their fiery youth has been restrained by an old man's heart'. Claudian mentions that it is their 'respected mother' Proba who will prepare the gold-embroidered consular gowns; the two young men are still living in their parents' household. It was not just in the case of emperors that, by the late fourth century, the shortcomings characteristic of a particular age-grade were being overcome by high office. It has become acceptable for a young man to hold positions of responsibility, so long as he shows that he also has the virtues of an old man – an instance of the *puer senex* motif which occurs in another panegyric in honour of a consul, Flavius Manlius Theodorus.[50]

In invective as well as in panegyric, a political figure's character is described by Claudian as having been foreshadowed in childhood. Flavius Rufinus was Praetorian Prefect of the East from 391 until his assassination with the connivance of the emperor Arcadius in November 395. In his attack on him, Claudian puts a description of his birth and upbringing into the mouth of the Fury Megaera:

> As soon as his mother gave birth to him, I took him to my
> breast. Often the little boy crept into my arms, and with a flood
> of childish tears demanded to be fed as he hung about my neck.
> My horned serpents licked his pliant limbs into shape with their
> three-pronged tongues. And I was his teacher when he learnt the
> skills of harming others and deceiving them – I myself admit
> that I am surpassed, that by his quick genius he has outstripped
> his teacher.

With typical artifice, Claudian inverts the *topos* of the ideal pupil who learns quickly – and also makes use of a realistic decription of a baby demanding to be fed.[51]

In spite of his use of traditional themes taken from the classical, pagan world, Claudian wrote for a Christian court, where we would have expected Christian rituals and attitudes to children to have left much more of a mark on the formal speeches made to honour the imperial family on ceremonial occasions. The *form* of the panegyric continued to be much the same as it had been for 800 years. But the emphasis on omens, miracles, and education masks both changes in the secular world, such as the fact that it was taken for granted that a child could be emperor, and the more positive attitude to children expressed by the Christian practice of infant baptism. Only gradually are such changes explicitly reflected in the literary culture.

Despite its fragmentary condition, the verse panegyric written by Merobaudes in the second quarter of the fifth century in honour of Aëtius shows that his childhood was described in familiar terms. There are fragmentary references to the renown of his great father, and Aëtius' conscious attempt to emulate him. Then we come to his martial skills as a boy (fortunately most of this section survives).

> No sooner had an unfamiliar ability to walk enabled him to raise his face from the ground and to plant his first steps in the snow over which he had hitherto crawled, when his hands itched for something to throw: he played with hailstones, and formed javelins out of icicles. He tried his hand at fighting: the childish games he played were invariably battles, and even then he was on the lookout for real spears to throw.

While he was still a boy, the Romans handed him over to the Goths as a hostage (which enables Merobaudes to say that as an adult Aëtius defeats in war the same barbarians whom as a boy he had pacified by means of a peace treaty). The Goths were suitably impressed by the boy's physical appearance: their king, Alaric, noting his fearsome dignity and the eyes foretelling his destiny, personally gave Aëtius his first quiver and praised the way he held his weapons and spear. Aëtius would have been about 13 at this time.[52]

In another poem, Merobaudes refers back to this time: 'The boy, only just grown up, was already a father.' This poem is based in its metrical form and to some extent its subject matter on Statius' poem in honour of Lucan's birthday; it celebrates the first birthday of a son of Aëtius, probably the same Gaudentius mentioned by Sidonius in his panegyric in honour of Majorian. There is an interesting mixture of classical pagan and Christian symbolism in Merobaudes' account of the boy's baptism at his mother's breast:

> She was not like Thetis, who washed away her anguished fear [sc. that her son Achilles would be killed] beneath the hidden waters of the Styx . . . contrary to the destiny of the gods and out of fear of his death. . . . She wet the young limbs of the new-born boy in the fountain which is filled by divine power, where God, the master of the pure baptismal font, is received by the mystical waves of the water; He drives away our sins, and does not allow their previous existence to stand; He renews life, He removes punishment. You, boy, were consecrated by these initial rites, and Roma received you to her brilliant bosom; her dress was loose, laying bare her breast, and she offered you her nourishing teat.[53]

In a poem honouring the baby daughters of Valentinian III, the classical pagan allusions are replaced by Christian baptism as the salient feature of childhood. Merobaudes apparently describes a mosaic depicting the imperial family: 'Behold a young child, only recently sent into the world; already she carries the mystic rites in her young heart, attesting to God's presence within her by her crying.'[54] No pagan would ever have described the irrational screams and wails of a baby wanting milk or comfort as a sign of its divine nature.

Sidonius Apollinaris' verse panegyric on the second consulship of the emperor Anthemius was recited in the presence of the Roman Senate on 1 January 468. Sidonius praises Constantinople for having sent such an emperor and consul to the west; he notes that the city lies in Thrace, 'a shore fruitful of heroes, where new-born children lie on the ice and the snow hardens the supple limbs of new-born infants'. At the emperor's own birth, there were the usual omens foretelling a Golden Age – rivers flowing with honey, flowers blooming although it was winter. Sidonius mentions the parallel cases of the birth of Ascanius (Vergil, *Aeneid* 2,682), Cyrus (Herodotus 1,108), Romulus being suckled by a wolf, an otherwise unknown episode of a bay tree burning when Julius Caesar was born, the association of a serpent with the birth of Alexander and of Augustus. In Anthemius' case, Sidonius tells the Senate, a severed vine branch in his father's house put out new shoots.[55]

We move on to infancy. 'After the first years of his childhood had passed, he used to crawl over his father's armour, and gripping his father's neck with his forearms he would try to unfasten the helmet to find a way of smothering him with kisses.' As a boy he used to play with arrows his father had captured from the enemy, throw the javelin or ride about in full armour, or go hunting (Sidonius notes the acclamations of his comrades: Achilles and Apollo were less successful horsemen and archers). But at the same time the boy was busy studying the moral maxims of the seven sages, and some other philosophical–ethical textbooks as well, including quotations from the Presocratics as well as Plato and Aristotle (this must surely refer to his learning by rote some compendium like the *Dicta Catonis*). Apart from this the boy studied Roman history: in fact, Vergil's *Aeneid*. Other texts from the school syllabus are Homer, then Cicero and Demosthenes, Livy, Sallust, Varro, Plautus, Quintilian and Tacitus. 'These were the studies by which he was educated, the background from which he came, the habits in which he was nurtured' before he began his administrative career.[56]

There is more in the panegyric for Avitus. Jupiter himself reports on the imperial candidate's curriculum vitae to an assembly of gods summoned to consider Roma's petition for a new Trajan to be sent to rule her. 'I wish to report on the achievements of this great man and say a few words about the earlier part of his life.' As soon as he had been born, Jupiter gave plain signs that he was going to be emperor; his father grumbled at this high destiny, but, conscious of his responsibilities towards Rome rather than personal wishes, he brought his son up in the requisite way:

> First he entrusted the suckling's limbs to the snows, he ordered him to stamp on the ice with his bare feet, he told the little boy to laugh as he trod the frost. As his mind developed, it was nurtured on the Muses, on Cicero who makes Latin speech sound like thunder; and he learnt all about the deeds of earlier Roman leaders. He learnt about battles, and read up in books what he ought to do on the battlefield.

Again a clear distinction is made between infancy and boyhood: 'Hardly had he begun to be a boy instead of a baby' when he killed a hungry she-wolf out foraging for her cubs, with a stone that chanced to be lying nearby. This is said to be like the deed of Hercules in killing the Nemean lion: a small thing, but worthy of being told. Jupiter goes on to praise first his hunting ability, then his falconry, and finally his skill as a public speaker, as evidenced by the impression he made on the later emperor Constantius, who was amazed 'at such great virtue in such boyish years – that the words of an old man should come from a youthful ambassador'.[57]

Even after the collapse of the imperial court in the west in AD 476, panegyrics continued to be addressed to rulers. Latin verse panegyrics survive from Africa (there is one honouring the Vandal king Thrasamund (496–523) in the Codex Salmasianus, ascribed to the poet Florentinus, but it makes no mention of any incidents illustrating the king's childhood). Corippus' eight-book epic in praise of the Byzantine general Johannes includes many elements from panegyric. In general, however, poems of praise from the western 'Dark Ages' make no reference to the birth or upbringing of their heroes. The most that they will say is that they were descended from noble ancestors (e.g. Venantius Fortunatus for Gaul, or Archbishop Eugenius of Toledo for seventh-century Visigothic Spain). This reflects the extent to which classical rhetoric was increasingly giving way to hagiography as the most common form of biographical writing for early medieval Christians. Although saints' lives from (for instance) Merovingian Gaul by no means always ignore the years of childhood, the range of anecdotes selected is much more limited, since hagiography's sole interest is to prove the exceptional holiness of the saint, to the exclusion of secular values.[58]

But while the kings of the Visigoths, Vandals, and Franks had little interest in listening to classical panegyrics, this was not true of the Ostrogoth Theoderic. Ennodius' panegyric in his honour still contains the elements recommended by Menander. Theoderic had been born in 456 and came to the throne over his Ostrogothic people in 471; Ennodius notes that

> It was Greece that brought you up in her bosom, an omen of
> future political skills; Greece taught you in such a way once you
> had entered the threshhold of life that while she maintained your
> boyish affability, soon your tutor brought you imperturbability
> as well.

While he was still a 'beardless youth' in 476, he was responsible for expelling the emperor Basiliscus and restoring Zeno to his rightful throne. And finally there is a reference to the support he has given rhetorical studies simply by performing deeds that are worth praising.[59]

The classical form of the panegyric survived to the end of the western empire, and occasionally beyond. But that only masks the extent to which the political and social and religious world which these panegyrics describe had changed. Old themes such as the acclamation of a new king by the great men of his time survive. Some new themes appear: children achieve a personality by being outstanding at school, they become consuls and emperors, children honour God by crying. But we must look elsewhere to find broader evidence for the changes in attitudes that had been taking place in the Latin-speaking world during these centuries.

NOTES

1 A. and A. M. Cameron, 'Christianity and tradition in the historiography of the Late Empire', *Classical Quarterly* 14 (1964), 316 ff.

2 F. Leo, *Die griechisch-römische Biographie* (Leipzig, 1901); cf. G. Misch, *Geschichte der Autobiographie* (Eng. trans., *A History of Autobiography in Antiquity*, London, 1950); A. Momigliano, *The Development of Greek Biography* (Cambridge, 1971).

3 Such punishment may come from the hands of the gods rather than the men of his community; and it may fall on his descendants rather than himself. Cf. H. Lloyd-Jones, *The Justice of Zeus* (Berkeley, Cal., 1971).

4 *Homeric Hymns* IV; L. Bieler, ΘΕΙΟΣ ΑΝΗΡ (Vienna, 1935/6); Gospel of Thomas: Hennecke-Schneemelcher, *Apocrypha*, esp. §14, where a schoolteacher is punished for daring to beat the child-God.

5 Thucydides 2,35 ff.; cf. Isocrates' *Panathenaikos*, or Gorgias' *Praise of Helen* (ΕΓΚΩΜΙΟΝ ΕΛΗΝΗΣ). Agesilaus lived from 444 to 360 BC, and was king of Sparta from 399.

6 Quintilian, *Institutio Oratoriae* 3,7.

7 'nam primum dividitur in tempora: quodque ante eos fuit, quoque ipsi vixerent, etiam quod est insecutum'.

8 'ex animo et corpore et extra positis'.

9 'namque alias aetatis gradus gestarumque rerum ordinem sequi speciosius fuit – ut in primis laudaretur indoles, tum disciplinae, post hoc operum (id est factorum dictorumque) contextus – alias in species virtutum dividere laudem, fortitudinis iustitiae continentiae ceterarumque, ad singulis adsignare quae secundum quamque earum gesta erunt'.

10 Pseudo-Callisthenes, *Alexander Romance*, ed. J. Kroll (Leipzig, 1956); medieval translations were made into every literary language from Ireland to Indonesia.

11 Livy 26,19.7. Cf. Polybius 10,3.3 on the 18-year-old Scipio's heroism in saving his father's life at the battle of the Ticinus.

12 Nepos, *Atticus* 1,3 f.

13 *Panegyrici Latini* 1; 5,3 f. and 8,1 ff.; 7,6; 14,1; 47.

14 B. Baldwin, *Suetonius* (Amsterdam, 1983); A. Wallace-Hadrill, *Suetonius* (London, 1984); on the *SHA*, R. Syme, *Emperors and Biography* (Oxford, 1971).

15 *Life of Augustus* 3.4 (ed. J. Bellemore, Bristol, 1984); Suetonius, *Augustus* 8.1.

16 E. S. Gruen, 'Augustus and the ideology of war and peace', *The Age of Augustus* (Louvain, 1986), 68–72; Suetonius, *Augustus* 94 f.

17 Suetonius, *Vespasian* 5; *Galba* 4; *Titus* 3; *Vitellius* 3.

18 *Caligula* 11; *Otho* 2: 'prodigus et procax a prima adulescentia'; the same negative picture appears in Tacitus: *Histories* 1,13: 'pueritiam incuriose, adulescentiam petulanter egerat'. *Tiberius* 57: 'ne in puero quidem'; and 14.

19 *Augustus* 84.1; *Tiberius* 70; *Claudius* 3.1: 'ab aetate prima'; *Nero* 52.

Agrippina, like other Roman mothers, thought too much interest in philosophy inadvisable for a young senator: cf. Tacitus, *Agricola* 4; *Galba* 5; *Caligula* 53; *Domitian* 20.

20 But pretending to have been written by six different writers in the time of Diocletian and Constantine at the beginning of the fourth century: cf. R. Syme, *Emperors and Biography*. The writer or compiler was not a Christian.

21 *Scriptores Historiae Augustae (SHA)*, *Marcus* 4.1–3; *Commodus* 1.3; *Pertinax* 1.2; *Geta* 3.2, 3.7 f.; *Severus* 4.6.

22 Herodotus 1.114; *Severus* 1.4. Cf. Chapter 5 below.

23 Menander Rhetor, *Treatise II*, 371.10 ff. = p.83 in D. A. Russell and N. G. Wilson's edition (Oxford, 1981).

24 *Diadumenus* 4.1; 4.5; 5.6.

25 *Maximini duo* 30. 30.5 is lifted from *Severus* 1.7; 30.7, 'inter ignobiles et nimis parvus'.

26 *Marcus* 2; 2.6; 4.10; 7.1.

27 *Commodus*, 1.7 and 10.1.

28 *Caracalla* 1.3–7.

29 *Albinus* 5.1.

30 See pp.60 f., and n.23 above.

31 *Panegyrici Latini*, 10/2,2.2; 2.4 f.: the reference is to the Curetes clashing their weapons to prevent Cronus from hearing the wailing of his new-born son Zeus. Much the same material is repeated in the same orator's speech on Herculius' birthday in AD 291: *Panegyrici Latini* 11/3.

32 *Panegyrici Latini* 2/12,4.1; 4.5; 5.1 ff.; 7 ff.; 8.2.

33 Jerome, *Chronicle*, under the year AD 328; 4/10,3.4: 'contra rationem aetatis'; Quintilian, *Institutio Oratoriae* 6, preface §6 ff.

34 *Panegyrici Latini* 4/10,3.5.

35 Symmachus: ed. Seeck, *MGHAA*, VI (Berlin, 1883), 318 ff.

36 An accessible text and translation of Ausonius' *Gratiarum actio* can be found in H. G. Evelyn White's Loeb edition (1921), II, 218 ff.

37 A. Cameron, *Claudian* (Oxford, 1970). The most accessible, but incomplete, text and translation is M. Platnauer's Loeb (1922).

38 Claudian, 6,13 ff.; 31 f.:

> intrepidum ferri galeae nec triste timentem
> fulgur et ad summas tendentem brachia cristas.
> tum sic laetus ait: 'rex o stellantis Olympi. . .'.

39 6,39–50; 51–62.

40 6,86: 'sic aetas animo cessit'.

41 8,24 ff.; 46: 'non generis dono, non ambitione potitus'; 121 ff.; 149 ff.

42 8,157 f.; 196: 'At tua caelestes inlustrant omina flammae'; 192–202.

43 8,220: 'virtute decet, non sanguine niti'; 362: 'usque adeone puer?'; 371 f.: 'veniet robustior aetas: ne propera'; 379 f.: 'tantus eris. nostro nec debes regna favori/ quae tibi iam natura dedit'.

44 The last ruler of Alba Longa: Livy 1,24 ff. Theodosius' list of *exempla* includes Torquatus, the Decii, Horatius Cocles, Mucius Scaevola,

Fabius Cunctator, Camillus, Regulus, Cato of Utica, Curius, Fabricius, and Serranus.

45 18,509 ff. Cf. the story of the old peasant of Verona, walking with the aid of his stick over the same sand on which he had learnt to crawl as a baby (Platnauer II, 194).

46 15,296 f.: 'nedum puero rectore'; 303: 'in veros principis annos'.

47 10,230 ff.

48 *Laus Serenae*, 70 ff.; 101 f.: 'Quid me de propriis auferre penatibus? imperat hic semper'; 134 ff.:

> Et quoties rerum moles ut publica cogit,
> tristior, aut ira tumidus flagrante redibat,
> cum patrem nati fugerent, atque ipsa timeret
> commotum Flaccilla virum, tu sola frementem
> frangere, tu blando poteras sermone mederi.

The *Laus Serenae* is not included in Platnauer's Loeb.

49 'An unheard-of honour': A. Cameron, *Claudian*, p. 31.

50 1,15: 'per fasces numerantur avi'; 150 f.: 'multo redundant eloquio'; 154 f.: 'Sed gravibus curis animum sortita senilem / ignea longaevo frenatur corde iuventus'. Theodorus, consul 399: 16,18 (an example of the *puer senex* theme): 'his earliest youth outrivalled other people's maturity', 'primaeque senes cessere iuventae'.

51 *In Rufinum*, 1,93 ff. Eutropius' childhood (18,44 ff.) is a less promising subject.

52 *MGHAA* XIV, 11 ff., 1.112f., 121 ff.: 'bella repressit / ignarus, quid bella forent'.

53 42: 'vix puberibus pater sub annis puer'. Cf. Statius, *Silvae* 2,7; Sidonius, *Carmen* v, 203–6; spring 442 is a likely date; 19 ff., followed by a lacuna in the text; 23 ff.

54 1,19:

> En nova iam suboles quae vix modo missa sub {auras}
>   mystica iam tenero pectore sacra gerit,
>   vagitu confessa Deum. . . .

55 Sidonius Apollinaris (Loeb edn, trans. W. B. Anderson) II, 102 ff.; 114 f., 'venisse beatos / sic loquitur natura deos'.

56 Sidonius II, 134 ff.; 181 ff.; 193 f.

57 Sidonius II, 162 ff.; 171 ff.; 177 f.; 187: 'parva quidem, dicenda tamen'; 212 ff. Cf also Sidonius, xxiii, honouring Consentius of Narbonne.

58 P. Cox, *Biography in Late Antiquity: A Quest for the Holy Man* (London, 1983).

59 '*Panegyricus dictus clementissimo regi Theoderico*' (*MGHAA* VII, 203, ed. Vogel, and *CSEL* ed. Hartel (1882), 264, 282.

Chapter Three

THE EVIDENCE OF PAGAN AND CHRISTIAN LETTERS

CICERO

Where birth and childhood appear at all in character descriptions in ancient literature, it is generally the birth and childhood of the great, whether superhumanly good or superhumanly evil. We have seen that the nature of classical literature was such that what references there are – whatever the particular literary *genre* – correspond to a relatively limited range of *topoi* expected by the audience, a range which remained surprisingly constant until the end of antiquity, even if some of the changes that had been going on could not always be masked. We must look elsewhere for more information about these changes, and for a wider range of attitudes than those which Roman adults expected from, and expressed in, literary character sketches. That wider range of attitudes towards children and childhood will not be found in accounts of the childhood of individuals or groups; the evidence has to be anecdotal, and the less 'formal' the source, the less the likelihood that only a very atypical sample of attitudes will have been given expression by the writer.

In Graeco-Roman culture, literary conventions to a very great extent defined what was expressed in public; that holds for inscriptions as well as written records. There was no such thing as 'private' literature (as we have seen, the one exception in classical literature, Marcus Aurelius' *Reflections*, was highly literary). The only type of written evidence available from the Roman world that is in any way comparable to the private diaries and notebooks, or even the 'objective' records of law-courts and accounts of noble and ecclesiastical households which are available to late medieval and early modern social historians, is letters: and even there we find that, for the ancients, the writing of letters – epistolography – could be a stylised literary pursuit.

The nearest to a modern collection of 'private' letters are those of Cicero in the first century BC. These letters were by and large not written with publication in mind (though many are nevertheless highly stylised both in the arrangement of material, sentence structure and phraseology, and the choice of vocabulary). Some were scribbled down or dictated in the heat of the moment. If we have doubts about the 'authenticity' of the attitudes and emotions expressed in high literature, Cicero's letters are both a corrective and a control. The references to children include Cicero's own daughter Tullia, born *c.* 75 BC; his son Marcus, born 65 BC; Tullia's son Publius Lentulus, who died a few months after his birth in January 45 BC; and Cicero's nephew Quintus, born *c.* 67/66, who through his mother Pomponia was also the nephew of Cicero's close friend and correspondent Atticus.[1]

Many of the remarks Cicero makes in his letters accord with the negative picture that we have found to be general in the classical period. There are references to the pregnancies of his wife Terentia, of Atticus' sister Pomponia, and of his daughter Tullia: 'On May 19th, my Tullia gave birth to a seven-months-boy; I should be glad that the birth went well; but what was born was too feeble to survive.' He uses the neuter gender for the baby, and immediately changes the subject.[2] Cicero expresses his worry at his nephew Quintus being ill, and there are seven letters in which he asks Atticus about his little girl's progress through a sickness lasting from March until August 45 BC. Nepos' son is reported to have died: 'I am terribly affected and bear this badly. I had not known that the boy even existed.'[3] The word *puerilis* is contrasted with *virilis* to refer to thoughtless or unplanned behaviour in politics, including the murder of Julius Caesar.[4] And children are listed amongst the material goods that make life tolerable: 'Wealth, ability, children, relatives, friends.' There is a similar list of goods that Cicero lost when he had to go into exile in 58 BC.[5] Conversely, in a letter of consolation written during the civil wars, Cicero feels able to argue that having children is a disaster at a time of political uncertainty.[6]

These outbursts are conventional, but that does not prevent them from being authentic. In a crisis, such as his exile, Cicero's genuine fear and anger at political events takes the form of a stereotyped expression of concern for the conventionally weak members of his family. During his period as governor of Cilicia in 51 BC, he sent the boys to be looked after by king Deiotarus: 'While we are on our summer campaign, I thought that that was the best place for the boys'; and similar concerns surface between January and May 49, after Caesar's invasion of Italy.[7]

The dividing line between child and adult is as sharp as the conventions of the classical city-state require. It is symbolised by the ceremonial donning of the white toga, the *toga pura* or *toga virilis* of the adult male citizen: 'I am thinking of giving Quintus the *toga pura* at the festival of the Liberalia, for that is what his father requested', he wrote in February 50, when his nephew would have been about 16; and after the ceremony, in April, Quintus is no longer a child: 'The boy Cicero, or rather now young man'. (We may recall how incensed the young Octavian was when Cicero called him a *puer*: see p. 22 f. above.) At the end of March 49, it was the turn of young Marcus, and Cicero used the occasion as an excuse for staying in his home town of Arpinum and avoiding seeing the dictator Julius Caesar in Rome: 'Since I did not want to be seen in Rome, I gave my Cicero his *toga pura* at Arpinum, much to the delight of our fellow-townspeople.' But this ceremony is a ceremony peculiar to citizens. Slaves also grow up, but there is no ceremony to mark a formal change in status: 'Please give my regards to Alexis, an excellent boy – unless he has become a young man in my absence; for that is what he seemed to be doing.'[8]

But some of these letters include the kinds of comments about children we would never find in formal literature. There is an interesting light cast on the anguish caused to children when their parents divorced, as happened so frequently in Rome in this period: when Quintus junior read a letter mentioning his parents' divorce, 'I saw that the boy was astonishingly upset. He came to me in tears to complain. Does this surprise you? I have seen how admirable his family loyalty, sweetness and sense of responsibility are. . .'. The divorce did not take place; but another letter five years later shows that Quintus felt he had to take sides (with his mother) in the continuing conflict between his parents.[9]

Cicero mentions things that he remembers from his own childhood and youth – such as that when he was a youngster, the old men then always used to say that everything had gone to the

dogs, just as he was doing now.[10] In contrast with the high regard
for school lessons found in biography, Cicero recalls his displeasure
as a schoolboy at the sudden arrival of the master – 'Look out! Get
your hands off the writing tablet! Here's teacher, sooner than we
had hoped! There'll be a beating for Cato's team!'.[11] One of
Cicero's most lasting memories of his childhood was reading a line
from Homer's *Iliad* which, he claims, inspired him for the rest of
his life: 'From my childhood I loved that phrase, "Always to be the
best and to excel over all others"'; in a letter to Atticus in
November 54 BC, he regrets that the monopolisation of political
power by Caesar, Pompey and Crassus prevents him from living
up to that fundamental aim of every participant in the competitive
public life of a classical city.[12]

Cicero had achieved that childhood ambition of becoming
famous and powerful largely as a result of his scholarly ability,
expressed in practice in his primacy as an orator. It is not
surprising that education, and in particular the education of his
own son and of his nephew, should loom large in his letters. There
are several references to his interest in the activities of Dionysius,
the teacher looking after his son.[13] Other remarks refer to Cicero's
interest in his sons' rhetorical studies: in July 50, he had visited
Rhodes 'for the sake of the boys', i.e. to inspect the available
rhetoric schools, and he several times expresses his pleasure in
their progress in writing Greek, and reports one of the tutor's
reservations (*adhuc* – 'so far, so good'). But although the boys were
sent to study with the best teachers in Greece, Cicero as a Roman
father still feels that teaching is ultimately the *paterfamilias*' personal
responsibility: his treatise on moral philosophy, *De Officiis* (*On
Duties*; long known in English as *Tully's Offices*), was not just
dedicated to, but intended for, his adolescent son Marcus, and
Cicero explicitly tells Atticus, 'Who can teach this better than a
father his son?'[14]

That Cicero was even more concerned with the education of his
family's children than the average Roman *paterfamilias* is hardly
surprising. Another trait that will not have been typical of
economically less well-cushioned households was his sheer pleasure
in the companionship they provided. They represented much more
than a promise of security for his own old age. In January 60, he
tells Atticus that his 'limited leisure is spent with my wife and my
little daughter and honey-sweet Cicero'; there are similar com-

ments about his baby grandson Lentulus. Several letters end with an expression of his affection for his young nephew Quintus: 'We seem like gods to him.' He takes steps to see that the children will not get hurt by a wall on his estate which is in danger of collapsing: 'there is nothing I want less than for Pomponia and the little boy to go in fear of that wall falling down on them'.[15]

A considerable number of letters to Atticus end with an explicit greeting to Atticus' wife Pilia and daughter Caecilia Attica. The great majority of these greetings are as conventional as the words 'Love to . . .' at the end of letters today; greetings to or from a correspondent's children take their place at the end of a letter just as, and just after, those to or from a wife do. Similar conventional greetings to the addressee's wife and children occur at the end of some of the private letters dating to the early second century AD found at Vindolanda, near Hadrian's Wall. Occasional deviations from the standard conventional greeting show that a powerful Roman politician like Cicero was not oblivious to the feelings of his or his friends' children. He is

> terribly worried by our Attica's state of health, and even afraid that someone may have been at fault. But her *paedagogus*' sense of responsibility and the doctor's concern and the efficiency of the entire household in every respect prevent me from suspecting any such thing. So take care: I can do no more.

Other letters end with greetings to 'that most beautiful little girl, Caecilia' or 'little Attica'. Cicero excuses himself for not having visited little Attica: 'I want to send a kiss to my absent Attica. I was that delighted by the greetings she sent me through you.' 'Give my greetings to Pilia and to Attica, my delight and my love.' 'I want you to give Attica a kiss in my name, since she is such a cheerful little girl: the best thing in children.'[16]

Sometimes the greetings are in the name of Cicero junior. In one or two of these letters we may even detect the words – and the posturing – of a 6-year-old child: at the end of a letter dated April 59, 'Terentia gives you her greetings' is followed by the Greek sentence: 'And little Cicero salutes Titus the Athenian', which we may well suspect was added by young Marcus himself. The next letter, sent soon after, also ends with a Greek phrase: 'And Cicero the philosopher salutes Titus the politician.' (Perhaps the inversion of the theme that it was little Cicero's father who was the politician, while Atticus was a follower of the Epicureans, is too sophisticated to ascribe to a 6-year-old.) A letter sent a little later in the same month ends: '[Terentia] and [italicised words in Greek] *Cicero, the most aristocratic boy*, send their greetings.' Eight years later, in June 51, young Marcus was less exuberant: 'My Cicero – such a modest and sweet boy – sends his greetings.'[17]

PLINY THE YOUNGER

Cicero's correspondence shows that Roman parents had a much wider range of feelings about their children than the classical literary genres give expression to. The collection of Pliny the Younger's letters, made about a century and a half after Cicero's, contains letters which were clearly written or revised with a view to publication. Although these letters are by and large less immediate than Cicero's, they contain a very similar range of attitudes and feelings.

There is a strong bias in favour of literary interests: Pliny's own position, like those of all non-Christian epistolographers, was won largely through his rhetorical ability, and that suggests that he put an even higher value on education than did elite society in general. We may be entitled to wonder whether the pleasure Pliny expresses at returning to school and 'reliving that wonderful time' was widely experienced by his contemporaries (or for that matter by Pliny himself when he had been a schoolboy). Several letters confirm the impression that for Pliny the most important thing for a boy was to undergo the literary education provided by the *grammaticus* and the rhetor. Pliny is concerned to find a morally irreproachable teacher of rhetoric for the son of Corellia Hispulla; up to that level, the boy's education had been within the household. He writes to Tacitus to tell him about his decision to endow a school at Comum, so that local boys will no longer have to be sent to Milan; it is not clear whether this refers to grammatical or rhetorical training. As an experienced barrister, Pliny feels entitled to criticise an inherited educational system which made children begin by learning the most difficult literary text, Homer. When Pliny praises a certain Euphrates because he has 'three children – two of them boys – whom he is educating most carefully', he is expressing his approval of the Syrian philosopher's interest in education as much as his readiness to shoulder the burden of rearing three children.[18]

These comments are partly the result of Pliny's personal interests. But there are also traces of the conflicting attitudes of a wider society. The sharp distinction which the republic made between child and adult is still clear, although from time to time we see in these letters that Pliny could not ignore the fact that he was living in a world where citizen status was becoming increasingly less important. When Pliny gives examples of socially important rituals, the donning of the *toga virilis* is still at the head of the list, before betrothals and weddings. He uses this basic Roman concept whether he is talking of Roman citizens or not – for instance, when describing similar public occasions in the Greek province of Bithynia to Trajan, or even when talking of slaves. Although the comparable public ritual which recognised that a slave had become a responsible person in his own right was the quite different one of manumission, Pliny took it for granted that there was an age below which people were children and ought not to be treated as adults: when two of his *nomenclatores* were hired as claqueurs for three denarii each, what appalled Pliny most was that they were of an age to know better: 'They might recently have put on the toga.' The donning of the toga was still the symbol of achieving adulthood and responsibility.[19]

For Pliny, as for Cicero, childhood, adulthood, and old age are three separate grades with their own appropriate qualities. Pliny praises Fuscus Salinator as 'straightforward as a child, friendly as a young man, serious as an old man'. Consequently he is highly selective in what he reveals about his own childhood. He claims to have enjoyed school (2,18.1, see p. 89 above), and he also pushes interest in literary studies back into his childhood. He had composed a tragedy in Greek at the age of 14. Children put in few appearances in the anecdotes Pliny narrates in his letters. During the eruption of Vesuvius, children scream (as do women, while the men shout: as we would expect in any rhetorical description of a disaster). In Bithynia, foundling children become a matter of administrative concern. But the only letter in which we find children at play is the description of the tame dolphin which swam with the children of Hippo in North Africa – a prodigy which brought such an influx of distinguished tourists into the town that the authorities secretly killed the poor beast.[20]

We will find plenty of support in Pliny for the view that children are uninteresting in themselves, and that the unpleasant effort of raising children is undertaken primarily as an investment in the family's future. Reporting a speech he made to the town council of Comum praising his *alimenta* scheme, Pliny says that a particularly difficult point was having to ask people to undertake the labour of raising children. Asinius Rufus, like the philosopher Euphrates, is praised for having several children. It is a waste if children die before their parents. Their existence gives a sense of security both to individuals and to a whole family: that Corellius Rufus 'died leaving his children behind' is right and proper, while the death of Silius Italicus' younger son as a child was the one exception to the poet's otherwise happy life. When Pliny reports to his wife's grandfather that the girl has had a miscarriage, he seems to express more sympathy for the old man's disappointment than for the fact that his wife had nearly died, and he feels the need to reassure his grandfather-in-law that he will continue to try to provide him with great-grandchildren. But before jumping to the conclusion that Pliny saw his wife primarily as a childbearing machine, we should we should take into account the following letter, where he writes to her aunt expressing his relief at his wife's recovery – though here too, writing to a female, he explicitly assumes that the aunt keenly hopes for a grandchild for her dead brother.[21]

The deaths of the two Helvidiae in childbirth are a tragedy to their father – a single son is now left to uphold the family. But we would be wrong to see this as unqualified selfishness on the part of an older generation. Pliny pauses to express his grief at the plight of the children, orphaned at birth. Caecina Paetus, the conspirator against Claudius, and his wife Arria are recorded as having loved their son as more than just an investment in the future of the family.[22]

A more complex case is that of the child of the successful orator Regulus. Amongst the hostile gossip Pliny reports against his professional arch-rival is the accusation that he was prepared to take a false oath by his own son's life. Pliny grudgingly describes the boy as 'intellectually able, but unreliable'. Did Regulus care for his son so little as to expose him to the anger of the gods, and if so, was this in any sense typical? When the boy died, there was a great display of grief at the funeral, which included the slaughter of all the boy's pets. Pliny attacks Regulus' immoderate grief as well as the pretence of love with which his parents spoilt him. All of this is Pliny's hostile interpretation, rhetorically coloured. More interesting are the ways in which Regulus is said to have tried to overcome the fact that his son was a mere child. The first approach is cultural: Regulus commissions statues and portraits of the boy, and composes a biography of him which he asks to be publicly recited in every city in Italy. Pliny has little sympathy for such an attempt to assign significance to the life of a child. The other way to abolish the distinction between child and man was economic: Regulus had wanted the boy to be able to inherit his mother's estate. This he could not do as a *filiusfamilias*: hence he had been emancipated from his father's *potestas* – which was the reason, Pliny insinuates, why his parents had to spoil him, or buy him.[23]

There are one or two other occasions in Pliny's letters where we can sense a tendency to break down the distinction between child and adult. There is the anxiety to ensure that a property owner should fulfil his obligations of disbursing largesse no matter how young he may be: Pliny himself was adopted as *patronus* of Tifernum Tiberinum 'when I was almost still a boy'. We learn incidentally that a boy might accompany his father on a visit to pay his respects to the local city *patronus*. In Bithynia, he feels that, notwithstanding the clearly defined age requirements laid down by Pompey's provincial charter, it would be better for children with inherited wealth to sit in town councils than for mature men with no money. Political and social power, and the responsibilities of friendship and patronage that they entailed, had always to some extent been inherited; increasingly they were perceived as more important than any formal restraints imposed by age-grades.[24]

A letter reporting the death of his friend Fundanus' younger daughter illustrates the desire to maximise the 'adult' qualities of a child. There is the *mors immatura* motif – the girl was aged 13, and about to be married; the preparations for marriage have turned into those for a funeral. Pliny says that *pietas* for his daughter has driven out all other feelings from the father's mind (referring to the self-control in the face of personal tragedy which a Roman would expect from a philosopher). While Pliny acclaims her adult virtues, he does not ignore that she was still a child: 'No girl was ever more playful, more lovable . . . she had the prudence of an old lady, the bearing of a matron, yet kept a girl's sweetness and the modesty of an unmarried woman.' He praises her affection for her father and his friends:

How she used to hang from her father's neck! How lovingly and
modestly she embraced us as her father's friends! How she used
to love her nurses, *paedagogi*, and teachers as was appropriate to
the status of each of them! With how much effort and intelligence did she use to read! How rarely and carefully would
she play! With what self-control, patience, and constancy did she
bear her final illness! She encouraged the physicians, exhorted
her sister and her father, and kept herself going through the
strength of her spirit when the power of her body had deserted
her.[25]

This passage is of course a rhetorical set-piece, and surely
written with Quintilian's remarks about the deaths of his own two
precocious sons in mind (see Chapter 5 below). But no matter how
rhetorical the presentation, there is no lack of emotion at the girl's
death, as Pliny's emphasis on the girl's affection for her family and
servants shows. The sorrow is as much for the loss of her child-like
qualities as for her potential as a scholar, her self-restraint in
playing, or her respect for her elders. Pliny's personal preference
for literary studies may have led him to put little emphasis on play,
but it did not blind him to the fact that this 13-year-old was a
child, and enjoyed behaving as a child, even though – in
accordance with the *puer senex* motif which we will meet again – her
childish play and study were performed in a serious, adult way.

FRONTO

The correspondence of the North African born rhetoric teacher
Marcus Cornelius Fronto dates to the generation after that of Pliny
the Younger. Fronto counted amongst his pupils the future
emperor Marcus Aurelius, together with his adoptive brother and
co-emperor, Lucius Verus. He continued to advise both of them on
questions of vocabulary and other matters relating to imperial
speech-making up to the time of his death in *c*. AD 166. We would
expect a professional teacher to put even more stress on the value
of education in turning a child into a worthwhile member of the
community than we found in Pliny; and we might also expect that
a man who spent his life setting and marking exercises on the
selection of appropriate maxims for use in speeches[26] would write
letters full of commonplace assumptions. It is therefore remarkable
that while the *Reflections* which his pupil Marcus Aurelius compiled

for his own meditation are so full of traditional commonplace attitudes towards children and childhood, the correspondence between Marcus and his teacher Fronto reveals a great deal of affection towards young children.

Not that the traditional view of children as foolish and mindless is entirely absent. If a guest at a dinner party made an exhibition of himself by performing a spectacular juggling trick when eating an olive instead of getting on with the meal in a decent fashion, that is the sort of thing that children will take delight in. When Marcus, aged about 20, gives Fronto some semi-classified information about the links between the emperor's court and a man Fronto is about to prosecute (Herodes Atticus), he begs not to be judged as 'an insolent little boy'. Fronto realises that this is political and not rhetorical advice, and hastens to assure him that 'your advice is in no way childish or rash'. The *pietas* which a son owes his father, natural or adoptive, continues to be an important theme. Referring to his enemy Herodes, Fronto calls him 'an impious son forgetful of his father's wishes'.[27]

Children are needed as an investment for the future, both by the Roman state and by individual families. Fronto notes the emperor's concern that Italians should have more children because they are needed by the state, especially for fighting. For a family, childlessness is a disaster. In a highly rhetorical letter of commendation to Antoninus Pius on behalf of the Greek historian Appian, Fronto argues that a childless man deserves to be consoled. On the other hand we also hear that the political privileges for those who had several children continued to be awarded in accordance with Augustan legislation.[28]

A child ought to follow in his father's footsteps; Marcus must show himself worthy of his father the emperor. It is a matter of especial delight if children in some way look like their father:

To my lord Antoninus Augustus [Marcus' formal title]: I have seen your little chicks, the most welcome thing I will ever see in my life; they are so like you that nothing can be similarly similar. . . . I saw a likeness of you not just face to face but in several places, when I turned to my right and when I turned to my left. Thanks to the gods, they have a healthy colour, and powerful voices. One of them was holding a piece of nice white bread, as a royal monarch should, the other cheap black bread, as one would expect from the son of a philosopher. I pray the gods that he who sowed such seed be safe, and that the seed be kept safe, and that the stock from which similar children may come be kept safe. Somehow or other, even while I heard their little voices so sweet and charming, I recognised the smooth and attractive tones of your own speech in the little piping of each of them.

The sheer impudence of this piece of flattery may offend modern sensibilities; and Fronto's premises are traditional – the sons of a king and of a philosopher are expected to behave in royal and in philosophical fashion, and their appearance and the tone of their voices must copy their father's. Their physical appearance ought to be perfect, and they have to be under the special protection of the gods. As we have seen in Chapter 2, these are all standard themes from panegyric. Nevertheless the way in which Fronto develops these themes in his letter reveals a much greater willingness to describe what young children are like ('powerful voices'), and the vocabulary he uses (e.g. diminutives) suggests that he expected his reader to have a much more positive interest than we have found in most earlier literature.[29]

Fronto develops the commonplace that parents are happy when their children look like them in another way. Just as the child should look like his physical parents, so the rhetorical style of a pupil should copy that of his teacher. 'Just as with parents, when they discern their own facial features in the appearance of their children, so it is with me when I see signs of my particular teaching in your speeches: "Latona delighted in her heart".' The idea that the teacher is like a parent to his pupil is of some importance in Fronto's remarks about education. He refers to his own teacher Athenodotus as *magister et parens*, and is at pains to point out that the affections of a rhetorician for his pupil remain throughout life, unlike those of nurses and alphabet-teachers, who are often jealous at losing the affection of their wards when they grow up and leave them. He says, as a joke, that he competes with Marcus' mother for the student's love.[30]

Particularly interesting for future usage (especially by Christian teachers) is that this father–son relationship leads Fronto to address a student as 'my son', or more formally, to a magistrate who was probably also a member of the imperial family, 'My Lord, dearest son'. In general, the modes of address we find in Fronto's correspondence point forward to those used in late antiquity, by pagans and by Christians. For Fronto, the title 'Lord' for a member of the imperial family has become standard, even when a boy in his teens is being addressed. Marcus is referred to as 'My lord' in a letter to a third party; and of course the emperor Verus refers to Marcus as 'The Lord my Brother'. Marcus speaks of both his natural and his adoptive mother as 'my Lady'. Marcus' father is 'my Lord'. Fronto naturally refers to Marcus' mother as 'my Lady'. But even Fronto's own son-in-law can be addressed as 'My Lord'. Social equals are twice addressed as 'my brother'. Both are in letters of commendation to provincial governors.[31]

In other respects the conventionality of the themes that Fronto's letters of commendation contain makes them indistinguishable from those of Pliny. One such theme is that the writer has known his protégé since childhood.[32] The importance of education is of course taken for granted by Fronto; if anything, we should be surprised that it is made explicit on comparatively few occasions, for example in a letter to Lucius Verus (whose reputation for culture was not great according to the ancient biographical tradition). Fronto tells him in no uncertain terms: 'It was certainly not the circus and the gladiator's breastplate, Emperor, that imbued you with knowledge of warfare from your earliest childhood, but books and the study of letters.' Marcus himself – whose *Reflections* show little evidence that he cared to recall his childhood – refers to a school text, Hesiod's *Theogony*: 'I remember that once when I was at the schoolteacher's, I read . . .'.[33]

While there are comparatively few references to schooling in Fronto's letters, that other major reality for children of ancient times, vulnerability to illness and death, looms large. We hear of Marcus' concern at his wife's impending confinement, though he seems to be even more concerned at his mother's illness. He mentions the diarrhoea, fever, and emaciation of 'our little girl Faustina, who has given us enough to do'. Fear that the evening breeze might do them harm stops Marcus from allowing his little girls to be taken out of the palace in the late afternoon. The emperor thinks it worthwhile to inform Fronto that one of his daughters has recovered sufficiently to get out of bed and run around her bedroom, or that one of his sons is coughing less frequently. When one of Fronto's own children has a cough, Fronto hopes that better weather and more feeding by the nurse will cure him, 'Since all medicines and all remedies for children's throats are to be found in milk'. Nevertheless the emperor seems to have lost this girl, like four other children, in each case apparently before the next was born.[34]

Consolation on the death of children remains a standard epistolary theme. The commonplaces may be conventional – that an educated father should not resent unexpected misfortune; that he is not too old to have further children; that there are other persons in the world on whom one may bestow one's affections (this in a letter consoling Herodes: the emperor is meant). When a 3-year-old grandson, whom he had never seen, dies far away on the German frontier, Fronto speculates whether his soul might have been 'liberated' from the miseries of this world. He is sceptical. 'If the immortality of the soul should ever be proved, that will be a theme for philosophers to argue about: it will not be an answer to the grief felt by parents.' Nevertheless we have already moved a long way from the classical world's lack of interest in children when we find that Fronto should think of applying the stock theme that 'those whom the gods love, die young' to a *child*, rather than just a young adult.[35]

The dividing line between the child and the adult is no longer as clear-cut as it had still been to Pliny. Fronto's vocabulary is revealing. While he uses words like *puer* in negative contexts (above), there are many occasions where he reveals his delight at children, and the words used to refer to them there may be neutral, or – more usually – diminutives of endearment. A daughter is a *filiola*, little boys or girls are *parvolus* or *parvola* (from *parvus*, 'small'). There is even a diminutive for a 'little lady', *domnula*. They may be 'chicks', *pullus/pulla*. That particular metaphor may even be extended to calling the imperial palace a 'nest': 'In so far as everyone in our little nest has understanding, he offers up prayers for you.' Children are recorded not just as the object of interest, but as themselves interested in adults. Marcus sends Fronto a kiss for his daughter, which he passes on with pleasure; and also tells Fronto that his little children (as well as his wife) send their greetings.[36]

That a child should be kissed may be simply a matter of formality; but that Fronto and Marcus should care about what their children themselves think, and report about their behaviour, is a significant development. Marcus does not just report that his daughter is feeling better, but that she is able to run about the room.[37] Fronto begins a letter to his son-in-law with a conventional prayer that his household will be blessed with many children similar to their father. But he goes on to show that he has carefully watched the behaviour of the two grandchildren:

> Every day there is argument and litigation with that little boy, who is your Victorinus as well as my Fronto. You never ask for a backhander from anyone for any court appearance or speech; but the one word your little Fronto continually and repeatedly gives mouth to is 'Give me' [Lat. *da*]. I hand over whatever I can, bits of paper or writing tablets; those are the things I would like him to keep asking for. But he does show some signs of his grandfather's character as well. He is particularly greedy for grapes. That was the first solid food he sucked down, and almost the whole day long he kept licking at a grape or kissing it with his lips or biting it with his gums or playing with it. He is also particularly keen on little birds: he loves young chicks, pigeons and sparrows. I have often heard from those who were once my own tutors or teachers that right from my earliest childhood, I too was enthralled by the same birds.[38]

The passage shows the degree to which a young child can have an individual personality in his grandfather's eyes, even if that personality to a great extent reproduces that of the grandfather. Some children have become persons, even if 'little ones'. But a small girl (of the appropriate social class) is not just a 'little lady': she is 'a grave lady of old-fashioned virtue', who may reject Fronto's offer to kiss her hands and her feet once she hears that he loves her father Marcus more than herself – in which case, says Fronto, he would rather kiss her tiny hands and fat little feet than the imperial neck and chaste and merry face.[39]

The emperor's little girls, whose hands and feet Fronto so loves to kiss, are respectable 'matrons': that looks forward to the theme of the 'old child', the *puer senex*, which was to become a favourite with Christians.[40] But Marcus Aurelius too has broken the bounds of childhood: his wisdom and his rhetorical ability had always been ahead of his age. The emperor's virtues had been formed by nature before he had had any training: that was of course a panegyrical commonplace. 'Before you had grown up sufficiently to be schooled you were already perfect and complete in every skill; you were a complete man [or: a Stoic philosopher] before you reached puberty, you were skilled in rhetoric before you put on the adult toga.'[41]

Not just imperial virtues, but something more concrete, imperial eloquence (transmitted of course by Fronto), was present in Marcus before he was an adult, and before he had become a citizen. The categories of republican age-grades have been transcended, in a way in which they very definitely had not been transcended in Marcus' *Reflections* (Chapter 1 above). They were not yet obsolete: putting on the *toga virilis* could still be referred to as something real in the second century, and ordinary Romans did not all share the qualities which made Marcus, as a future emperor, exceptional enough to deserve praise. A young prince might act in ways which had traditionally been reserved to mature adult citizens. The correspondence between Fronto and Marcus on the trial of Herodes Atticus is instructive. Marcus had pointed out to Fronto that Atticus had been brought up in the household of his grandfather Calvisius. Fronto had been unaware of this connection between the man he was about to prosecute and the imperial family, and reassured Marcus that the latter's advice was neither childish nor misplaced. But he went further: Marcus 'excelled old men in their prudence'. His advice was that of a hoary and respected elder: Fronto realised that it was his own attitude that was childish. That was when Marcus was about 20, and Fronto twenty years his senior. Fronto later recalled the excellence of the emperor's judgement and of his oratory when he was 'scarcely more than a boy'.[42]

The question that arises is whether Fronto's development of the commonplaces of rhetorical panegyric to the effect that kings had performed marvels as children, in conjunction with the real honour and influence exercised by those children marked out to succeed to the principate, were just literary conceits or actually influenced the attitude of those who listened to them. Fronto goes so far in flattering Marcus that he says that to enjoy Marcus' presence, his conversation, and his letters, he would even be willing to become a boy again.[43] On one level, that was just a flattering variation on the theme that nothing would make a man want to be a child again (cf. Cicero, *On Old Age* 83, p. 27 above). But to express the wish to be a child again would not have made any sense to a Roman audience in Cicero's day: Fronto thought that it would make sense to the readers of his own age.

CYPRIAN OF CARTHAGE

Like Fronto, Cyprian was a wealthy and eloquent North African. If he had not chosen the Christian path, he would have been in no way inferior to Fronto in terms of secular honour and success. Instead of consul, he became bishop of Carthage in 248; and in 258, he won the greatest of Christian honours, the martyr's crown, during the persecution of Valerian I.[44]

The letters of a Christian bishop are in many ways not comparable with the social correspondence of pagan writers: a bishop must exhort his addressees, and many such letters may better be compared to the moral essays of Hellenistic philosophers written in epistolary form – those of Epictetus, or St Paul, or their Latin equivalents, such as Seneca's *Letters to Lucilius*. But a bishop was also giving his flock advice about practical situations, and this allows us to learn something from his letters about his, and their, attitude to children.

As we would expect from a trained orator, many classical *topoi* occur. Women and children are weak, spiritually as well as physically. In a vitriolic attack on Felicissimus, accused of starting a schism, every commonplace of rhetorical invective about the social responsibilities of adult males is brought into play: 'He has taken away the property of orphans and defrauded widows. . . . His father starved to death in the street and he did not even bury him. . . . He kicked his pregnant wife in the stomach and by inducing an abortion killed the fetus.'[45]

We have seen that the metaphor of family relations occurs as a mode of address in Fronto's correspondence. In the letters of Christians, that metaphor is systematically applied and extended. The secular family gives way to a metaphorical family, with God as the father, the Church as mother, and baptism as generation. A schismatic community, a false Church, becomes a step-mother, *noverca*. The visible head of a Church, the bishop, has all the authority of a Roman father. Those who cause schism 'part the sheep from their shepherd, and sons from their parent'. A bishop addresses other bishops, including the pope, as brothers. The clergy are also brothers, even when lapsed. The martyrs are referred to as lords, a confessor (one who admitted to a court that he was a Christian, but was not executed) is addressed as *domine frater*, 'Lord brother'. Even lay people are brothers and sisters –

and a woman who denied Christ in time of persecution is nevertheless still a sister. In fact all Christians throughout the world make up a brotherhood.[46]

In Cyprian's eyes, the wealth or status of one's secular family is of no importance compared with this Christian family. Instead of civic office holding and honours, a Christian respects the glory of the martyrs. Celerinus' grandmother, paternal uncle, and maternal uncle had been martyred: Cyprian refers to these '*exempla* within your own household ... the status of your family, its inherited nobility'. That honour was not reserved to persons who had reached a particular age. The 'illustrious youth' Aurelius had twice confessed to being a Christian, 'approved of by the Lord, dear to God, still young in years, but praiseworthy in his virtue and faith. He may be lowly in terms of his age, but he is great in honour'.[47]

The equality of all in the eyes of God is radically interpreted: on one occasion, God used a young boy as a medium, to warn bishop Cyprian of his obligations. That may be a case of the survival of pre-Christian views of children as 'marginal' and therefore mediators between the human and divine worlds (cf. Chapter 6 below). But Cyprian repeatedly insists that children are equal members of the Christian community. 'So that none should be lacking from your glorious number, so that every sex and age should be held in honour among you, God's regard has associated even children with you in the glory of being Confessors', and he compares these child confessors with Daniel, or with Ananias, Azarias, and Misael, the three youths in the fiery furnace, or the children of Bethlehem slain at Herod's orders: 'an age-group not yet ready for military service was found suitable for the crown [sc. of martyrdom]. Innocent children were killed because of His name, so that it would be clear that those who are killed for Christ are innocent'.[48]

The baptism of the new-born infant is the clearest indication of that equality of child and adult in the eyes of Christians. Some third-century African Christians had grave reservations about this. One Fidus appealed to Old Testament circumcision rules to argue that no child should be baptised before the eighth day, the day on which pagan Romans assigned a child a name. Perhaps more crucially, he argued that babies vomited and defecated during the ceremony. How could such a being be given the Kiss of Peace?

Cyprian's reply to Fidus' arguments represents the views of

sixty-six North African bishops gathered in council, and then as now represents the consensus of Catholic Christianity. If babies are filthy, then Christians should be put off very much more by the uncleanness of adult sinners. 'The child who has just been born has no sin, except that having been born in the flesh as a descendant of Adam he carries the contagion of inherited death from the moment of birth.' 'No-one agrees with your view of what should be done; rather, it is the judgement of all of us that the mercy and grace of God must be denied to no person who has been born . . . who has once been formed in the womb by God's hands.' Cyprian cites the Old Testament story of Elisaeus and the widow's child to argue that 'Our trust in the Divine Scriptures makes it clear to us that God's gift is equally available to everyone, whether a child or an adult'.[49]

In secular terms, of course, people grow up; but there are no distinctions before God. It would not have occurred to any pagan that 'When children scream and cry from the very moment of their birth, what else is it that they are doing but praying to God?'.[50]

AUGUSTINE

It was another North African bishop, Augustine of Hippo, who worked out the implications of the Christian view that all children had equal access to God's grace, and an equal need for that grace, through baptism, because of the sin inherited from Adam. Like Cyprian's letters two centuries earlier, most of Augustine's surviving letters are pastoral rather than social, written to give practical advice while he was bishop of Hippo (from 396 until his death in 430).[51]

Like Cyprian, Augustine makes ample use of the metaphor of Christians as a family, with the Church as mother: just as the earthly mother suffered 'ten months during which you burdened her womb, then the pain of childbirth, then the hard work of bringing you up', so the Church 'conceived you from Christ, gave you birth in the blood of the martyrs, brought you into everlasting light, gave you the milk of faith, preparing more solid food, which you cannot take yet since you are still small and without teeth'.[52]

Bishops, even the rival Donatist bishops, are addressed as *domine frater*, 'Lord brother'. Secular terms of respect appear alongside the simple Christian terms: Pope Innocent is 'The most blessed and honourable Lord, the holy brother'. While the clergy are brothers, laymen are sons, even where they hold high office: a proconsul of Africa, a governor of Numidia. Most strikingly, the emperor Theodosius and his sons address Augustine respectfully as 'Dearest and most beloved father'. It is not easy to distinguish between a purely Christian system of modes of address and the secular terms of respect for social equals that we have already seen in Fronto's letters from the second century. When a pagan intellectual writes to Augustine criticising Christianity, he nevertheless addresses him as *domine pater percolende*, 'My highly respected Lord Father'.[53]

But there are instances where secular relationships are radically contrasted with those of a new, Christian order: when a former proconsul of Africa converted his own father to Christianity, 'I see that your father, of honourable equestrian rank, was conceived by you in the lap of our mother the Church.' The convert is seen as a child: 'Exercise control over this little boy crawling on the ground, teach him to walk in your footsteps from the moment his soul is born', Paulinus writes to Augustine. Augustine has been responsible for Licentius' secular upbringing, and is now his Christian educator as well:

> The piety of Augustine, who bore you in his lap when you were tiny, educated you with the first milk of secular learning as a child, and now gives you milk and nurses you for the Lord with spiritual breasts. He sees that while you are now an adult according to the body, you are spiritually still a child wailing in your cradle, one who cannot yet speak the words of God, hardly walking your first steps in Christ, creeping along with tottering steps, needing Augustine's teaching to control that reeling little boy, like the hands of a mother or the arm of a nurse.[54]

Naturally, the child continues to be seen as vulnerable, both in spiritual metaphor and in reality. Augustine lists the little pains that afflict children – illness, hunger, thirst, physical and mental disabilities – as well as the more terrible things that can happen to babies and affect their spiritual as well as their physical survival:

> One child is born from parents who are Believers, who are delighted to raise him. But the mother or the nurse may suffocate him in her sleep; so he may have no share in the faith of his family. Another child is born as the result of sacrilegious

fornication. Out of fear, his mother cruelly exposes him, he is picked up as a result of the humanity and piety of others, baptised because of their Christian concern for him and becomes a member of the Eternal Kingdom.[55]

The story illustrates the inscrutability of the working of God's grace. That God should have a special concern for the weak was not new: 'The Lord God consoles the afflicted, nourishes the little ones, looks after the sick.' Nor was it an innovation that, in the words of the psalmist, 'even children praise the Lord'. But that implied a status for children which was unthinkable in the classical city. Pagans could not accept that in the infant Jesus 'God lay hidden within the body of a wailing child'.[56]

There were of course practical problems concerning children, but the appropriateness of infant baptism is taken for granted by Augustine. If the child is too young to answer the question 'Does he believe in God?' then those who bring him to the ceremony must answer for him. They are not necessarily the parents; masters might bring the children of their slaves, and exposed infants 'are frequently picked up by nuns'. It is not the child's faith, which cannot yet be said to exist, but the sacrament itself that makes a believer. It cannot be claimed that little children have the intellectual capacity to 'recognise God', just because they leap in the womb like John the Baptist (Luke 1:44): even animals 'exult' if the Holy Spirit moves them. In the same way children who scream and wave their arms about during the baptismal ceremony are not engaged in exercising free will.[57]

Augustine notes that superstitious parents may have their children baptised for theologically dubious reasons, e.g. as protection against physical illnesses. There are other problems: what happens if someone baptised as a child grows up to become an apostate? What happens when parents give a child who has already been baptised into the protection of an idol? He tells the tale of a little girl whose parents fled their home in time of disorder, leaving her to her nurse, who dedicated her to the protection of demons. When the little girl was subsequently taken to Mass, she vomited up the Eucharist. Thus God could show through the non-rational behaviour of a child how those who were supposed to look after her had sinned both against her and against themselves.[58]

Augustine's major problem with regard to infant baptism was

his controversy with the followers of Pelagius, a theologian of British origin who argued along traditional Roman lines that men achieve salvation largely as a result of their own spiritual *virtus*. Children, according to their view, did not have the capacity to perform deeds that were either good or bad; hence they had no need for forgiveness of sin, and no need for baptism. Augustine accused them of inventing a 'third place' apart from heaven and hell for unbaptised but innocent children. The baptism of children was not something superfluous. Every child was stained with original sin, the sin inherited from Adam.[59]

One of the consequences of the Christian belief that even the youngest child might achieve salvation was that Augustine did not feel worried that so many potential adults died as children. For the pagan, premature death was a disaster because the child's life was wasted (see Chapter 1 above); for Augustine, a child who died prematurely might have had as complete a life as a centenarian. He compares life-spans with musical intervals, or the hairs on one's head. Some are short, some are long, both may be perfect and complete. In any case, he points out, children themselves are unequal: some are bright, others so stupid that they cannot learn the alphabet.[60]

The very vocabulary used by Augustine to talk about children shows that his contemporaries no longer saw them as a separate age grade, but as persons who happened to be younger than adults. *Parvuli*, 'little ones', used by Fronto on those occasions when he wanted to express particular delight at children, has become standard, replacing *liberi*. When Augustine passes his greetings on to a child – which is not often, understandably enough considering the nature of pastoral correspondence – he expresses the hope that 'your little man will grow up in accordance with the teaching of the Lord'.[61]

Much has been made of the link between the Augustinian belief in Original Sin and the practice of beating children. As we have seen, beating children was taken for granted in Graeco-Roman antiquity. What Augustine did was provide a new rationale for the practice: children should be beaten, not as a sign that they were not fully adult, but because they needed coercive punishment in *exactly the same way* as adults. The state's right to punish must be exercised for the good of the criminal: it is no different from the 'severity of a good father', even though the state's exercise of that right may on occasion result in unnecessary harm: 'What if a child runs off out of fear of a well-intended beating from his father, falls over and dies?' The father's right and duty to beat his children 'is a form of coercion granted by parents themselves to those who teach skills, and is often applied by bishops in their judgements' (sc. as a penance).

> If as small children, or even as rather bigger ones, we had
> successfully begged our parents or schoolteachers not to beat us,
> which of us would have grown up as a tolerable adult? Which of
> us would ever have learnt anything? These things are done out of
> forethought, not cruelty.[62]

Augustine's reminiscences of the beatings he underwent in his own childhood have a rather different flavour when he talks about them in the *Confessions*, though the theological point he makes there is the same (Chapter 6 below). His letters say little about his own schooldays: he talks of the literary characters he had to study, Aeneas, Medea, and Chremes and Parmeno from Terence's *Brothers*, and about how as a child he imagined what the Mediterranean Sea looked like by comparing it with a local pond.[63]

Augustine's radical rejection of the social relationships and values of the secular world implied a critical attitude to the secular skills, proficiency in which had led to his own rise to fame. While children were to be taken seriously, rhetoric was now something 'childish', and in the course of an exchange of letters with the other great Christian intellectual of the age, Jerome, the two exchange warnings about 'puerile boasting of the sort that young men entering public life used to indulge in, when they would accuse some famous man in order to win a reputation for themselves'.[64] Letter 101 is a particularly acute analysis of the shortcomings of the secular city and its culture – he is 'not fed by literature, which those who are slaves of various vices describe as "free" [i.e. the *artes liberales*, the literary education expected of an adult citizen], but by the bread of the Eucharist'; and he goes on to talk of 'fables, the lies told by orators'.

SYMMACHUS

For Augustine's older contemporary, the pagan Symmachus, there is no such rejection of the inherited, secular social world and its culture. As in the earlier letters of Cicero or Fronto, or Pliny on whom he consciously modelled himself, social occasions like birthdays, betrothals, and weddings are prominent.[65] So are references to the gladiatorial or wild-beast spectacles which brought a great public figure glory, as on the occasion of his son's quaestorship in AD 394 and praetorship in 401. But in one crucial respect these occasions differed from those of the first century: Quintus Fabius Memmius Symmachus was a boy of 8 or 9 when he held the quaestorship. Office holding, the provision of spectacles and other *munera*, and the glory and honour that arose from them, were now no longer associated with politicians who had won elections, but with wealthy families; and those families might be represented by children. There are many letters referring to the way in which *gratia*, the obligations of friendship and political support, ran in families. What is strikingly absent is any reference to the donning of the *toga virilis* as a social ceremony. That that ceremony was ignored by Cyprian and Augustine need not surprise us; it is significant that it no longer means anything to the pagan and secular Symmachus. Just as for Christians, so also for pagans, there was no longer any formal dividing line between children and adults.[66]

Some things had not changed: there are worries about the imminent confinement of his brother's wife, and the illnesses of his own children. A parent's pleasure at the birth of a child soon gives way to concern. The health of his little niece Galla worries him. On rare occasions, he asks for his greetings to be passed on to his grandchildren.[67]

What interests him especially is the school literature course.

Now that my son is beginning to learn Greek, I have been accompanying him in his studies for a second time, as though I were the same age. For the obligation to ensure that our children find pleasure in literature as well as labour bids us to become children again. As far as you are concerned, you have harvested, not just sown: your young man is such an accomplished speaker – as I found out when I spoke to him – that he seems to be treading hard on the heels of his father. You will be very fortunate, my friend, if he beats you. My own teaching is still concerned with creating a plant.

For the pagan child, there was no easy road to salvation through baptism: a parent could only be reassured, *beatus*, about his son's future if he achieved learning. 'May you be well,' he writes to his teenage son, 'and become rich beyond your years with the dowry of literature.'[68]

Of course the hard work of study should alternate with games. Symmachus recommends to the teenage consuls of AD 395, Olybrius and Probinus, that they should go hunting: reading should not be interrupted by playing with dice or football or the Greek hoop or Greek gymnastics. And he remembers the holidays which were clearly an important feature of his own schooldays, especially the feast of Minerva, goddess of wisdom.[69]

The differences between Symmachus and Augustine should not obscure some interesting similarities; they were, after all, living in the same Roman world, which had been undergoing the same social changes since the classical period. There is the tendency we have already seen in Fronto to apply words referring to family relationships as modes of address: Ausonius (a Christian) calls him 'My Lord and son, Symmachus'; a *vir laudabilis* is addressed as 'Brother', a senator as 'My son Caecilianus, most glorious man' ('V[ir] C[larissimus]', the standard title of a member of the senatorial order). And while Symmachus does not refer to children as *parvuli* as Augustine does, there is an interesting shift in the meaning of the word *infantia*. No longer does it refer to an age-grade; Symmachus uses it in what was its original sense, to mean 'speechlessness' – the quality of not being eloquent, or simply of not having got round to writing a letter. If Augustine had followed Fronto in turning children into 'little adults', Symmachus had at least abolished infancy.[70]

NOTES

1 Edition: D. R. Shackleton-Bailey, *The Correspondence of Cicero* (Cambridge, 1965–77; the English translations also in the Penguin Classics series, 1978).
2 *Ad Att.* 10,18.1, 'perimbecillum'; cf. 1,2.1; 1,10.5.
3 *Ad Quintum Fratrem* 2,9(8).1; 3,6.2; *Ad Att.* 4,7.1–3; 12,6; 14; 23; 33; 13,12; 13,13.3; 13,51.2; 16,14.4.
4 *Ad Att.* 14,21.3; 15,4.2; cf. 16,8.1.
5 *Ad Fam.* 3,10.9; cf. 2,13.2 etc.; *Ad Quintum Fratrem* 1,3.
6 *Ad Fam.* 5,16.3f.; cf. 2,16.5.
7 *Ad Att.* 5,17.3; 7,13.3; 7,19; 10,11.4.

8 *Ad Att.* 6,1.12; 6,2.2; 9,19.1 (cf. 9,6.1; 9,17.1); 7,7.7.

9 *Ad Att.* 6,3.8; cf. 6,2.2; 6,7.1; 6,13.38.

10 *Ad Fam.* 2,16.6 (May 49): 'Sed ego fortasse vaticinor et haec omnia meliores habebunt exitus. Recordor enim desperationes eorum qui senes erant adulescente me. eos ego fortasse nunc imitor et utor aetatis vitio.'

11 *Ad Fam.* 7,25: to M. Fabius Gallus (August 45): Cicero is talking about Caesar's schoolmasterly approach to senatorial opponents: 'Sed heus tu, manum de tabula! magister adest citius quam putaremus. vereor ne in catomum [= Gk ΚΑΤ' ΩΜΟΥΣ] Catonianas.' *Catomum*, from the Greek for 'onto the shoulders', refers to the way a child was held over another's shoulders to be beaten. Cf. plate 4.

12 *Ad Quintum Fratrem* 3,5.4: 'Illud vero quod a puero adamaram, ΠΟΛΛΟΝ ΑΡΙΣΤΕΥΕΙΝ ΚΑΙ ΥΠΕΙΡΟΧΟΝ ΕΜΜΕΝΑΙ ΑΛΛΩΝ, totum occidisse.'

13 *Ad Att.* 4,15.10; 6,1.12; 8,4 (February 49).

14 *Ad Att.* 6, 7; 15, 16; 15, 13a (October 44): 'qua de re enim potius pater filio?'

15 *Ad Att.* 1,18.1; cf. 5,19.2; 7,2.4; 12,28.3; 12,18a; 12,30.1; 11,2.1 (December 60); 2,4.7 (April 59).

16 *Ad Att.* 12,33.2 (March 45); 6,4.3; cf. 6,1.22; 6,2.10; 6,3.10; 'puellae Atticulae': 6,5.4; 16,3.6 (17 July 44); 'deliciis atque amoribus meis': 16,6.4, 25 July 44; 16,11.8, 5 November 44.

17 *Ad.Att.* 6,8.5; 2,9.4; 2,12.4; 2,15.4; 5,9.3.

18 Pliny, *Letters* 2,18.1; 3,3; 4,13; 2,14.2; 1,10.8. The references which follow are also to Pliny's *Letters*.

19 1,9.2; 10,116.1; 2,14.6: 'Habent sane aetatem eorum qui nuper togas sumpserunt.'

20 6,26.1: 'puer simplicitate, comitate iuvenis, senex gravitate'; cf. Aulus Gellius on Servius Tullius' tripartite division, Chapter 4 below; 7,4.2; 4,13; 6,20.14; 9,33.

21 1,8.11: 'ut vero aliquis libenter educationes taedium laboremque suscipiat'; 4,15.3 (with the rhetorical *topos* of legacy hunting); 3,3.6; 1,12.11; 3,7.2; 8,10; 8,11.

22 4,21.3.

23 2,20.5; 4,2.1; 4,2.3: 'Habebat puer mannulos multos et iunctos et solutos, habebat canes maiores minoresque, habebat luscinias psittacos merulas: omnes Regulus circa rogum trucidavit'; 4,7.2; 'mancipatum': 4,2.2.

24 4,1.4; 4,13; 10,79.3: 'Sit aliquanto melius honestorum hominum liberos, quam e plebe in curiam admitti'.

25 5,16: 'Qua puella nihil umquam festivius amabilius . . . et iam illi anilis prudentia, matronalis gravitas erat et tamen suavitas puellaris cum virginali verecundia. Ut illa patris cervicibus inhaerebat! Ut nos amicos paternos amanter et modeste complectebatur! ut nutrices, ut paedagogos, ut praeceptores pro suo quemque officio diligebat! Quam studiose, quam intellegenter lectitabat! Ut parce custodite ludebat! Qua illa temperantia, qua patientia, qua etiam constantia novissimam

valetudinem tulit! Medicis obsequabatur, sororem patrem adhortabatur ipsamque se destitutam corporis viribus vigore animi sustinebat.'

26 E.g. Haines I, 12, to Marcus. The standard edition is by M. P. J. van den Hout (Leiden, 1954); C.R.Haines's Loeb (1919) is more accessible. Cf. E. Champlin, *Fronto and Antonine Rome* (Cambridge, Mass. 1980).

27 Haines II, 102 f.; Haines I, 60 ff.

28 Haines II, 112; Haines I, 264; 236.

29 Haines I, 112; Haines II, 118 f.

30 Haines II, 36 (the reference is to Homer, *Odyssey* 6,106); Haines I, 204; Haines II, 124; Haines I, 84; cf. 114. Elsewhere the relationship between teacher and pupil is expressed in the language of Platonic homosexual *eros*, though this is partially to provide the student with an exercise in Attic Greek: Haines I, 20ff.

31 Volumnius Quadratus: Haines I, 308; Arrius Antoninus: Haines II, 176; Haines I, 12; Haines II, 98; 294; Haines I, 16; 154; 84, etc.; Haines II, 170; 240 (Caelius Optatus); 90 (Passienus Rufus).

32 On petitions, cf. Champlin, ch.3.

33 Haines I, 238; Haines II, 150; 146; Haines I, 94: 'olim apud magistrum'.

34 Haines I, 246; 202: 'parvola nostra Faustina, pro qua satis egimus'; 300: 'propter aurae rigorem'; Haines II, 18; 32; 42; 222.

35 Haines I, 168 f.; 162; Haines II, 226; 'si maxime esse animas immortales constet, erit hoc philosophis disserendi argumentum, non parentibus desiderandi remedium'; ibid.: 'quanto natu minor . . . tanto beatior et dis acceptior existimandus est, ocius corporis malis exutus, ocius ad honores liberae animae usurpandos excitus'.

36 *Infans*, Haines I, 250: delight at seeing Marcus' daughter, which makes him imagine that he is looking at Marcus and his wife Faustina as they had been as children; 202; 224; 234; 212; Haines II, 18; Haines I, 2, etc.; Haines II, 32; 42; 118; 32: 'Quantum quisque in nidulo nostro iam sapit, tantum pro te precatur'; Haines I, 154; 234.

37 Haines I, 232; 244; etc.; Haines II, 18: 'Parvolam melius valere et intra cubiculum discurrere'.

38 Haines II, 172: 'Cum isto quidem sive Victorino nostro sive Frontone cotidianae mihi lites et iurgia intercedunt. Cum tu nullam umquam mercedem ullius rei agendae dicendaeve a quoquam postularis, Fronto iste nullum verbum prius neque frequentius congarrit quam hoc: Da. [We may note that Roman children had certain advantages when beginning to utter syllables.] Ego contra quod possum, aut chartulas ei aut tabellas porrigo, quarum rerum petitorem eum esse cupio. Nonnulla tamen et aviti ingenii signa ostendit. Uvarum avidissimus est; primum denique hunc cibum degluttivit, nec cessavit per totos paene dies aut lingua lambere uvam aut labris saviari ac gingivis lacessere ac ludificari. Avicularum etiam cupidissimus est; pullis gallinarum columbarum passerum oblectatur, quo studio me a prima

infantia devinctum fuisse saepe audivi ex eis qui mihi educatores aut magistri fuerunt.' (The boy was to hold the consulship in AD 199, his brother in the following year.)

39 Haines I, 208: 'gravis et prisca femina'; 'manus parvolas plantasque illas pinguiculas'.

40 C. Gnilka, *Aetas Spiritualis: die Ueberwindung der natürlichen Altersstufen als Ideal frühchristlichen Lebens* (Bonn, 1972). For the *'puer senex' topos* in Pliny, see pp.1 f. and notes 20 and 25 above.

41 Haines I, 244; 104; cf. 122; 72: 'ad omnes virtutes natus es prius quam institutus. nam prius quam tibi aetas institutioni sufficiens adolesceret, iam tu perfectus atque omnibus bonis artibus absolutus, ante pubertatem vir bonus, ante togam virilem dicendi peritus'.

42 Haines I, 62; Haines II, 38.

43 Haines II, 34: 'eique ego rei, si fieri posset, repuerascere opto'.

44 For Pontius the Deacon's *Life and Passion of Saint Cyprian*, *PL* 3,1541 ff., see p. 199 below.

45 All references are to the *Letters*, ed. Bayard (Paris, 1925) or *CSEL* 3; several volumes of G. W. Clarke's new edition have appeared. 4,2.1: 'sexus infirmus et aetas adhuc lubrica'; 52 (similar charges are levelled against the tyrants Nero and Domitian).

46 74; 15,2.2; 16,3.1; 47: 'Ad matrem suam, id est ecclesiam catholicam'; *noverca*: 59,13.2; 41: 'id est a pastore oves separare, et filios a parente secernere'; pope: 44–5; priests, deacons, *plebs universa*: 38; cf. 5,2.1; 18; 31; 32. Martyrs: 21,2.1. Lapsed: 17; 21,2.1. *Fraternitas* of all Christians: 75,10.3.

47 39: Celerinus: 'domesticis exemplis . . . familiae dignitas et generosa nobilitas'. Aurelius, 38,1.2: 'inlustris adulescens, a Domino iam probatus et Deo carus est, in annis adhuc novellus, sed in virtutis ac fidei laude provectus. Minor in aetatis suae indole, sed maior in honore'. If this is the same *adulescens Aurelius* as in 27,1, he was not yet able to read, though Cyprian ordained him a *lector*.

48 Child medium, 16.4.1: 'per dies quoque impletur apud nos Spiritu sancto puerorum innocens aetas, quae in ecstasi videt oculis et audit et loquitur ea quibus nos Dominus monere et instruere dignatur'. Confessors and Holy Innocents: 6,3.1; cf. 58,5.1; 61,2.1, 67,8.2.

49 64,2.1: '. . . infans, qui recens natus nihil peccavit, nisi quod secundum Adam carnaliter natus contagium mortis antiquae prima nativitate contraxit . . .; In hoc enim quod tu putabis esse faciendum nemo consensit, sed universi potius iudicavimus nulli hominum nato misericordiam Dei et gratiam denegandum . . . qui semel in utero Dei manibus formatus est'. 64,3.1: 'Esse denique apud omnes sive infantes sive maiores natu unam divini muneris aequalitatem declarat nobis.'

50 64,6.2: 'infantes . . . quod in primo statim nativitatis suae ortu plorantes ac flentes nihil aliud faciunt quam deprecantur?'

51 Scholarship on St Augustine is enormous. Two excellent introductions are: P.Brown, *Augustine of Hippo* (London, 1967); H. Chadwick,

Augustine (Oxford, 1986). For Augustine as a source for social history, B. D. Shaw, 'The family in late antiquity: the experience of Augustine', *Past and Present* 115 (1987), 3 ff.

52 All references are to the *Letters*, *PL* 33. 130,31; 153 init.; 243,7–8.

53 23; Pope Innocent: 'Domino beatissimo et honorandissimo sancto fratri': 175; 116; 86; 185. Emperor: 201.

54 112,3; cf. 85: Paulinus: 25,3; Licentius: 32,4.

55 166,16; 194,32.

56 69.1; 93,50, quoting Psalm 112.1–3; 135–7: 'intra corpusculum vagientis infantiae latet'.

57 186,11; 187,22; 187,25.

58 98,5; 149,22; 98.

59 182, 184; 156; 166,3; cf.175 etc.; 217,16.

60 166,13.

61 20,3, an early letter (AD 380). Cf. 99,3 (408/9).

62 153,16: 'quid si filius timens patris pia verbera, praecipitio pereat?' 133: 'qui modus coercitionis a magistris artium liberalium et ab ipsis parentibus, et saepe etiam in iudiciis solet ab episcopis adhiberi'. 104: 'si quoties parvuli, vel etiam grandiusculi, veniam peccantes deprecati sumus, toties a parentibus vel magistris accepissemus, quis nostrum tolerandus crevisset? quis aliquid utile didicisset? providenter ista, non crudeliter fiunt'.

63 7,3.6.

64 118, 'puerilium rerum'; 82,2, 'puerilis iactantiae'; 72, 'certare pueriliter'; 68,2: 'puerilis est iactantiae, quod olim adulescentuli facere consueverant, accusando illustres viros, suo nomini famam quaerere' – a reference to the *tirocinium fori.*

65 Symmachus *Letters*: in *MGHAA* VI (ed. Seeck). Birthday parties: 6,37; presents: 1,9, 6,79–80; betrothals: 9,39–43; weddings: 9,7, 9,106 f., 9,127–8, 9,133.

66 Quaestorship: 2,78; praetorship: 7,76,2.78; 9,17–25. Inherited status and obligations: 3,3; 9,34, 9,48, 7,88; 2,91; 7,116; 7,126.

67 2,22; 3,34; 2,47 and 2,48; cf. 7,78, when his son was about 12 years old, and 8,58–9; 6,32; 6,40.

68 3,20, 'Dum filius meus Graecis litteris initiatur, ego me denuo studiis eius velut aequalis adiunxi. repuerascere [cf. Fronto, Haines II, 34; p. 99 above] enim nos iubet pietas, ut litterarum dulcedinem liberis nostris labor participatus insinuet. Tuae res non in germine, sed in fruge sunt: cuius eloquentissimus iuvenis, ut fando conperi, proximis facundiae calcibus urguet parentum. O te beatum, amice, si vinceris. Nostra adhuc institutio molitur florem creare, nec imperari potest unico labor. Itaque inter metum meum et diligentiam, lentus pignoris nostri profectus adolescti.' 7,9 (AD 399/402): 'ut bene valeas et supra annos tuos litterarum dote ditescas'.

69 5,67–8. Cf. Ausonius on young Gratian's extra-curricular interests, p. 68 above. Minerva: 5,85.

70 *Infantia*: 1,1; 1,14; 3,1; 5,86.

Chapter Four

CITIZENSHIP AND OFFICE HOLDING

People change as they grow older. It is convenient to divide life up into different phases. But whatever divisions we choose to emphasise, these divisions are not 'natural'. Different societies arrange the human life-span into different divisions, depending on their needs; indeed the same society often uses quite different divisions in different contexts, for different purposes.

In classical Rome, the principal divisions were clear:

> In the first book of his histories, Tubero writes that King Servius Tullius, when he instituted the standard five classes of junior and senior citizens for census purposes, considered those who were under the age of seventeen to be children. From the seventeenth year, he listed those who were already suitable to serve the state as soldiers, and called these 'juniors' up to their forty-sixth year, and then 'seniors'. I have made a note of this so that the distinctions made by the judgement and customs of our ancestors according to that census of the most wise King Servius Tullius between childhood, active manhood, and old age [*pueritia, iuventa, senecta*] should be clear.[1]

The reason for the choice of the seventeenth year rather than 7, or 14, or 18, or 21, represents no problem. From the fourth century BC on, the Roman republic was a community militarised to an unparalleled degree, and what made a young male count (literally, in the census) was his ability to fight in the legions. It was from that ability to fight that the individual citizen's rights were derived, such as the right to appeal to a court of law:

> The Praetor begins with those who are entirely prevented from litigating. The edict lists childhood, and chance afflictions [e.g.

113

deafness on the part of the prospective litigant]. It mentions
childhood, since he denies the right to institute legal proceedings
to anyone younger than seventeen, who has not fully completed
his seventeenth year; since that is the age which is thought
appropriate for entry to public life (that was the age, or a little
older, at which the younger Nerva is said to have given legal
opinions publicly).[2]

The Romans recognised that there could be many other ways of
dividing the 'ages of man'. Roman law distinguished children
below 7 years of age as not yet able to answer for their actions
(technically *infantes*), and girls and boys below 12 and 14
respectively as not yet capable of undertaking the responsibilities of
marriage – or of committing adultery. Greek philosophical and
astrological speculation supplied other possible divisions, into four
or seven 'ages of man'.[3] But the crucial division between child and
adult was at 17: the age at which a male could learn to fight.

The ceremony of putting on the adult toga at about 16 was the
formal preliminary to full citizenship. It was followed by a year's
preparation for service, *tirocinium*.

> *Tiro* is the word for boys who are powerful, and chosen for
> military service and able to bear arms. For they are selected not
> just from the register of births, but on the grounds of their
> appearance and physical strength. Hence the name *tiro*; they do
> not become soldiers until after they have taken the oath.

Despite the pressures a military state like Rome was under to
maximise its manpower, the exceptions to the rule that no one
under the age of 17 should serve in the army were rare. The
reforming tribune Gaius Gracchus in 122 BC insisted that no one
should be conscripted below that age.[4]

The practicalities of the conscription procedure meant that the
community needed to know who was 'adult' before he reached his
seventeenth birthday; the boy's name had to be included in the
census lists well before that point. Consequently it was the
registration of a boy's name in the census lists that became the
ceremonial occasion which marked the end of childhood for males.
It involved giving up the *bulla*, the amulet worn round the neck to
mark children of citizen status, and the donning of the *toga virilis* or
toga pura. Young males would then prepare for the life of a full

citizen during their *tirocinium*, through military exercises and by learning about political and forensic life (*tirocinium fori*) before going off on military service or making their first law-court speech at about the age of 17; Cicero describes this 'tirocinium of the forum', contrasted with 'military tirocinium', in his speech *In Defence of Caelius* of 56 BC. Putting on the all-white *toga virilis* instead of the child's toga *praetexta* with its red border symbolised the citizen's right to appear in public. 'The toga is the dress which we wear in the forum', we are told by the grammarian Nonius. Those who had been exiled from Rome were consequently denied the right to wear a toga.[5] Nonius goes on to quote Varro to the effect that until the third or second century BC, the toga had been worn by everyone, women as well as men: at that stage – perhaps as a result of the imperial republic's increasing emphasis on the masculine activity of warfare – *matronae* began to wear the gown, the *stola*, although the toga continued to be worn by girls on ceremonial occasions (as well as by prostitutes). We may note the legal terms *investis/vesticeps* for child and man: the child is 'undressed' and the adult 'wears a dress' in the sense of the toga.[6]

With the establishment of the principate, military service ceased to be the automatic duty of every young citizen, and became something very much more professional. But the toga continued to be the symbol of non-military public service, the 'military service of the forum' (soldiers wore a cloak). The mid-first century *Laus Pisonis* praises an aristocrat's 'military service wearing the toga', *togata militia*. Tertullian, fulminating against the wickedness of lawyers at the beginning of the third century AD, can still say that 'togas have harmed the State more than breastplates'.[7]

The red margin of the *toga praetexta* worn by children was a symbol of the marginality of those who wore it: potentially, but not yet actually, citizens. It is not surprising that it was worn by adults in certain circumstances: as a symbol of the ambivalence of the wearer, it had a religious force. Hence it was worn by magistrates who at their sacrifices mediated between the Roman people and their gods, as well as by various, but not all, orders of priests (the sacerdotes, pontifices, epulones, and decemviri sacris faciundis). Colonial charters make it clear that the *praetexta* was worn by such officials in Roman colonies as well as the capital.[8]

Just as marriage was the most important social event of a woman's life, so was the exchange of the child's toga for the adult's for a male citizen; we have noted references to this ceremony in the letters of Cicero and of Pliny.[9] It was associated with the feast of free citizens, the *Liberalia*, held on 17 March, though Cicero's remarks make it clear that it did not have to take place on that day; there are references to other times of the year. The fifth-century AD commentator on Vergil, Servius, says that the *bulla* might be dedicated in the Capitol, the temple of the Roman state; hence the phrase *Ad Capitolium ire*, 'going to the Capitol', meant the same as putting on the *toga virilis*. Other references suggest that the *bulla* was rather dedicated to the *lares*, the gods associated with entering or leaving the household or a particular status within it. Wearing a *bulla* indicated citizen status: Suetonius tells of a trader who gave young slaves the *bulla* to wear to avoid paying the import duties levied on slaves. Giving up the *bulla* was a public sign that the young man could now be considered responsible: Juvenal calls an old man who behaves irresponsibly 'worthy of wearing a *bulla*'.[10] More important than surrendering the *bulla* was the real reason why a boy was taken up to the Capitol: his name was registered in the list of citizens in the *tabularium*, the state record office housed in the temple of Saturn on the south-east side of the Capitol. (Similar record offices existed in citizen communities outside the capital; copies were sent to the *tabularium* at Rome.)[11] The reason for registering the boy's name was that he could be conscripted for military service, as well as enjoying the positive rights of citizenship, as soon as he reached the age of 17; but it was not the military oath, but the act of registration, that gave the boy an identity of his own. 'Scaevola [the eminent lawyer: consul 95 BC] tells us that it used to be the custom for boys not to use their personal name (*praenomen*) before they put on the adult toga, and for girls not before they were married.' What marriage did for a girl, the adult toga did for a boy: it turned them into adults with an individual personality. If his parents intended him for a career of public service, then this was the time 'to abandon the friendships of childhood' for more serious political alliances.[12]

The donning of the *toga virilis* is associated by some scholars with another ceremony, the *depositio barbae*, shaving of the first beard and dedication of the hair to the Greek god Apollo after the toga-ceremony. Those who have shaved their beards in this way are sometimes contrasted with children, but normally the shaving off of the first beard seems to have taken place several years later. This

1 and 2. From the *Ara Pacis* (Altar of Peace) at Rome, showing procession of Augustus' family which took place on July 4th, 13 BC.

1. A boy (thought to be Augustus' grandson Lucius, born 17 BC) seeks adult attention.

2. Three grandchildren of Mark Antony and Augustus' sister Octavia. On the left, Germanicus, born 15 BC; the other two, the eldest son and daughter of the elder Antonia, have left no traces in the literary record, and probably died in their teens (cf. p.16, n.22).

3. Antonine Column, Rome (commemorating the German wars of Marcus Aurelius, AD 167–179): an illustration of the most frequent occasion on which children (with women) appear in classical literature – as prisoners of war (cf. p.20).

4. School scene from Herculaneum; on the right, *katomismos* (the beating of a pupil hoisted onto a fellow-pupil's shoulders). Cf. p.28 ff.; p.87, n.11.

5. Bronze As, AD 22/23 (Rome). Tiberius advertises the birth of his twin grandchildren (p.35).

6. Aureus, AD 69 (Rome). Vitellius' son and daughter, with legend LIBERI IMP GERM AUG.

8. Aureus, AD 175 (Rome).
One of a series in which
Marcus Aurelius advertised
Commodus as heir
apparent. Legends:
Obverse: COMMODO
CAES AVG FIL GERM.
Reverse: PRINC IUVENT. (cf. p.125).

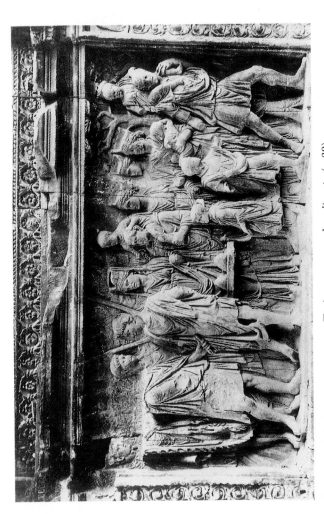

7. Arch of Trajan, Beneventum: Trajan oversees the *alimenta* (p.38).

9. Aureus, AD 201 (Rome). Septimius Severus advertises his son Caracalla as co-emperor. Legend: IMPP INVICTI PII AUGG. (p.126).

10. Aureus, AD 203 (Rome). Severus advertises Geta as *Princeps Iuventutis*. Obverse: GETA CAES PONT COS; reverse: PRINC IUVENT COS. (p.126).

11. Denarius, AD 217 (Rome and Antioch). Macrinus' nine-year-old son Diadumenian as Caesar (M OPEL ANT DIADUMENIAN CAES). On the reverse: military standards with the legend PRINC IUVENTUTIS. (p.126).

12. Sestertius, AD 223 (Rome). The fourteen year old Alexander Severus.

13. Bronze medallion of Gordian III (reigned AD 238–44), aged twelve or thirteen.

14. Follis, AD 310/11 (Rome). Maxentius honours his deceased son Romulus as a god.

15. Aureus, Trier: the progeny of the emperor Constantine. Obverse: FL IUL CRISPUS NOB CAES. Crispus is not yet described as consul (AD 317), therefore presumably under the age of nine. Reverse: Constantine, Fausta and Crispus. Legend: FELIX PROGENIES CONSTANTINI AUG.

16. Fausta nurses two sons of Constantine, Constantine II and Constantius II (both were born in 317: Constantine was probably not her son). Legend: 'The well-being of the state', SALUS REIPUBLICAE.

17. Sarcophagus of a child, Museo Torlonia, Rome. On l., birth and study; in c., death of parent (?); r., apotheosis in a horse-drawn toy chariot (cf. p.146).

18. Childhood sarcophagus, Louvre. L. to r.: nursing scene, with father looking on; father or tutor holding child; boy driving toy chariot; and reciting a poem to his father or teacher.

19. Sarcophagus from Ostia, Vatican Museum. On l., child being nursed and washed, with the three fates behind; r., child being drawn in chariot by a sheep (cf. p.146).

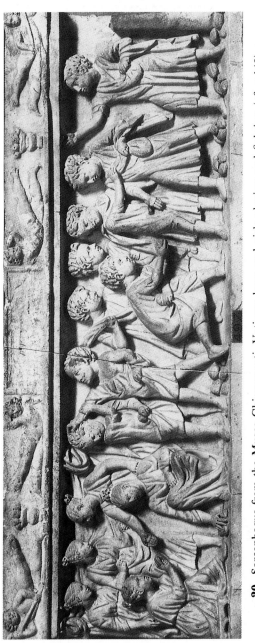

20. Sarcophagus from the Museo Chiaramonti, Vatican: boys and girls playing and fighting (cf. p.149).

21. Statue, probably of Nero, still a child
(note the bulla: p.116), delivers a speech.
Louve.

22. Tombstone of the ten-year-old Avita. To the left, a pet dog, on the right a reading desk. The Greek text reads: 'Avita lived for ten years and two months. Farewell' (cf. p.169).

was fundamentally a Greek tradition, with no formal significance for Romans. Octavian did not shave off his beard until he was 23, in 39 BC, according to Cassius Dio. Nero was 21; he organised a Greek athletic competition, the Juvenalia or Youth Games, to mark the occasion in AD 59. One exception was Caligula, who 'was summoned to Capri by Tiberius at the age of nineteen, and on one and the same day donned the toga and deposited his beard, without any of the honours which accompanied the *tirocinium* of his brothers'. This was because the donning of the toga ought to have taken place some years before; Caligula was too old now to undergo a *tirocinium*.[13]

For the sons of the wealthy, senators and equestrians, Augustus had remodelled the *tirocinium* into something akin to the Greek *Ephebeia*, the two years of public training and military service which an Athenian youth underwent before being recognised as a full citizen. For those who had donned the toga and not yet started their military service at 17, he organised a programme of pre-military physical exercises and participation at public ceremonies. This institution, known as the *Juventus*, was copied by many cities in Italy and the Latin half of the empire.[14] The highly visible nature of this revised *tirocinium* meant that it was advantageous for the political elite to have their sons belong to it for several years. The result was a tendency for children whose families played an important role in public life to put the *toga virilis* on at an ever earlier age; that was particularly true of the children of the Caesars themselves. This did not mean that full citizenship was achieved earlier; but by lengthening the ambivalent, marginal period between childhood and adulthood, it was one factor that obscured the clear distinction between the child or youth who was not yet a soldier and the full citizen who was.

As we have seen, the boy who had not yet donned the toga was only potentially a citizen. Consequently there could be no question of his holding any republican magistracy: 'Women are excluded from all civil and public offices; hence they cannot sit on juries or hold any magistracy or bring actions in court or act on someone else's behalf or act as procurators. *In the same way* children ought not to hold any civil office.' That was the republican principle. No child could be consul, just as no woman could. Unsubstantiated stories about the infringement of this principle emphasised the illegality of the regime of the triumvirs: in 38 BC, someone was elected to the quaestorship the day before he was enrolled as a *tiro*.[15]

The principle should have applied equally to the office of emperor, a position which included a package of magisterial powers bestowed by the Roman people in a law passed on the recommendation of the Senate. It was in fact long adhered to: the succession to Tiberius in AD 37 by Caligula rather than the *puer* Tiberius Gemellus, or to Claudius by Nero rather than the *puer* Britannicus in AD 54, are good examples. But that principle became increasingly inoperative. When the *Digest* was compiled in the sixth century AD, Ulpian's clear ruling was cited under the title 'various rules of ancient law': and even in Ulpian's own day, the early third century AD, the rule was apparently not always being observed – otherwise he would not have written that 'children *ought* not to hold any civil office'. The process by which it had come about that this distinction between child and adult ceased to matter to Roman social organisation was a complicated one.

Categorising people by age is essential to the fair and equal distribution of offices in a republic: one of the principles of a city-state, whether in antiquity or medieval Europe, is that there should be equal chances for those of equal status. There may be other principles which conflict with this. In Rome, it was strongly felt that precedence should be given to those who had *virtus*; and because *virtus* could be inherited from successful ancestors, a very young man might lay claim to *virtus* on the grounds of heredity, even though he had had little chance to prove it in practice. It was in the interests of the majority of senators to control any such claims to precocious virtue: any young *nobilis* who won office earlier than usual (whether by favour or intrigue, or as the result of a perfectly fair popular election) would be taking away an honour that would otherwise have gone to a senator of 'average' ability. This proved to be a particular problem during periods when there was high mortality among middle-aged politicians, resulting in pressure from sons to inherit their fathers' positions of leadership well before the traditional age. The most notable such period – making allowance for the fact that our information depends to a great extent on the accident of the survival of Livy's account for the years 218–167 BC – was the aftermath of the Second Punic War, in which Hannibal had inflicted massive casualties on Romans of all classes.

The majority of senators had a vested interest in resisting any erosion of the principle of equal access to office. The result was legislation, stating what the required age was for holding particular magistracies, in the form of the *Lex Villia Annalis* of 180 BC, which prescribed ten years' military service before anyone could hold the first curule magistracy, the quaestorship. The *Lex Villia* was reinforced by further legislation over the next century.[16] Sulla revised all these regulations during his dictatorship in 81–79 BC: no one could hold the quaestorship before the age of 30, the praetorship before 39, or the consulship before 42. But there were always pressures to allow for exceptions; we may recall that within ten years of Sulla's reforms, his supporter Pompey blackmailed the Senate into allowing him to stand for the consulship before the proper time.

Despite Augustus' restoration of the republican age requirements after the confusion of the civil wars (with remission for patricians and for the fathers of three children), the gradual abandonment of these clear age-grades for the holding of public office is a striking feature of the principate. It was one of the processes which led directly to changing perceptions of childhood. Although no single explanation for this abandonment should be held to be exclusively valid, some explanations may be rejected. Philosophical ideas of Greek origin suggesting that human life should be divided up in more complicated ways than the three simple stages of Servius Tullius appear in literature, but there is no reason to assume that they affected the realities of Roman public life. Pythagoreans proposed dividing life up into four stages, sometimes connected with the four humours. Varro proposed five divisions, each of fifteen years. There were also seven-year cycles advocated by astrologers.[17] But these were philosophical ideas toyed with by intellectuals; they perhaps led to interesting speculation about the 'ideal' age, but had no application to real life. It is difficult to believe that any of them led people to believe that some other division was more important than that between the child and the adult capable of bearing arms.

There were other, more real pressures acting to obviate the distinction between child and adult. We may start at the top. The Caesars had inherited from their republican predecessors the desire of a politically powerful family to express that power publicly and visibly by dispensing it from the strict rules of the *cursus honorum* regarding age qualifications for holding office. The Senate's grant to Octavian of a dispensation allowing him to hold office ten years before the required age, and his subsequent seizure of the consulship at the age of 19, were exceptions resulting from the violence of civil war; but these acts did also express the uniqueness of Octavian's position as Caesar's adopted son.

The imperial power was a complex thing: an expression of one commander's superior military force, but also an agglomeration of republican constitutional powers voted by the Roman people. But there was another element, no less important because it was based on a social relationship not recognised in our own society. Because the household of Caesar was the largest and wealthiest in the Roman world, the emperor was the greatest of patrons: everyone who played a role in public life did so because of the emperor's support. In return, every Roman owed loyalty, not just to the emperor, but to his household: it soon became the Divine Household. Oaths of loyalty were taken, not just to the current emperor, but 'to his wife, his children, and his clan', or 'also to his sons and to his whole household'.[18] This personal, social relationship between patron and client meant that while the emperor's children could not hold public office until they were adults, they were none the less public figures, and as future patrons it was in the interests of their 'clients' – i.e. of anyone in the empire who played a role in public life – to show them honour.

It was also in the interests of the current emperor to avoid conflict by demonstrating that there was one, or preferably more than one, potential successor to head the *domus Caesaris* should he die. There were several traditional methods by which members of the imperial family could be marked out even before they had donned the adult toga. One such occasion was the greatest of Roman public ceremonies, the triumph; it had always been traditional that a *triumphator*, re-enacting the role of the ancient Roman kings, was accompanied by the children of his household.[19]

There was nothing innovatory about Octavian's showing his nephew and intended successor Marcellus off to the Roman people during his triumph over Egypt in 29 BC: Marcellus, aged 13, rode on the right-hand trace-horse, Octavian's step-son Tiberius, half a year younger, on the left. On 26 May AD 17, Tiberius' adopted son and intended successor Germanicus triumphed over Germany; his four sons rode in the chariot with him. The eldest, Nero, had been born in AD 6 or a year later, Drusus in *c.* AD 8, and Caius – later the emperor Caligula – on 31 August AD 12.[20] It continued to be a normal feature of triumphs that an emperor who had the good fortune to have young children would have them with him: in AD 166, Marcus Aurelius' sons took part in his triumph over Parthia. The eldest, Commodus, whose twin brother had already died, had been born on 31 August, 161; Marcus Annius Verus was just 3 or 4 years old (born in 162 or 163, since he himself died aged 7 in 169).[21]

The Roman people, or, more importantly, the army, might be given a donative to mark the occasion when a young prince was first paraded before them: in 8 BC, Augustus' grandson Gaius, born in 20 BC and adopted into the Julian family at the age of 2 or 3, accompanied him to Gaul to be presented to the legions. Augustus gave them a donative because 'for the first time they had Gaius taking part in their exercises with them'. Marcus Aurelius gave his soldiers a donative in Commodus' name while his son was still *praetextatus*, wearing the child's toga.[22]

Like the sons of other noble families, the children of the Caesars would be selected as team-leaders in the 'Troy game', an archaic ritual revived by Augustus. In 13 BC, the junior team was led by the young Caius, aged 6 or 7. Augustus' unfortunate grandson Agrippa Postumus, never allowed public office, nevertheless played in the Troy game in AD 2, aged 10. And there was a famous occasion in AD 47 when the two groups were led by the emperor Claudius' son Britannicus, aged 6, and the 9-year-old Domitius Ahenobarbus, the later Nero (in the minds of many, with a better claim to the succession). Children of the imperial family were paraded on other religious occasions, such as that immortalised on Augustus' *Ara pacis*.[23]

Children might be invited to make a public speech at a relative's funeral. At the age of 12, the future Augustus delivered a speech at the funeral of his aunt Julia: this was before Caesar had returned from Gaul to seize power. As we have seen, the tendency to minimise the age of a precocious divine child led Nicolaus of Damascus to say he was only 9. Tiberius praised his father at his funeral when he was 8; this was entirely in accordance with republican precedent, and neither Tiberius nor his deceased father were 'Caesars'. Caligula gave the funeral speech at Livia's death in AD 29. This was two years before he was given the *toga virilis*.[24]

Again in accordance with republican precedent, children might also preside at funeral games for a relative. In 7 BC, Augustus' grandson Caius, born in 20 BC, presided at the votive games held in honour of his father Agrippa. Claudius had not yet donned the adult toga when together with his elder brother Germanicus, he presided over gladiatorial games in honour of his father Drusus.[25]

It was with regard to priesthoods that the republican principle that children could hold no office was most liable to be breached. Livy tells us that, in the aftermath of the Hannibalic War, the dearth of young patricians even led to a priesthood being bestowed upon a *praetextatus*. Imperial princes were often appointed to one or more priesthoods at the earliest acceptable age: and for most priesthoods, that meant immediately after the boy had donned the adult toga. Octavian (born in August 63 BC) had put on the toga on 18 October 49 BC, and became a pontifex in the following year, in the place of L. Domitius Ahenobarbus, who had died at the battle of Pharsalus. Marcellus' *depositio barbae*, and therefore presumably of the child's toga, took place shortly after Augustus and he had returned from Spain in 25 BC; he was made a pontifex in 24 BC. Caligula was made a pontifex in 31, the year he received the toga.[26]

The *Fratres Arvales*, 'Arval Brethren', may have been an exception; they were re-instituted by Augustus with the specific purpose of praying for (all) the members of the imperial household, and some junior princes seem to have become members even before they had taken the adult toga, although it is not clear that their role was other than ancillary. Tiberius Gemellus had apparently been an Arval Brother at his death even though he had not taken the *toga virilis* when Tiberius died. The short-lived emperor Vitellius made his son an Arval Brother on his seventh birthday. The *Salii* too had always been younger men. Hadrian appointed Marcus Aurelius to the relatively unimportant Salian priesthood when he was only 8; Claudius had appointed a possible successor, Lucius Junius Silanus, to this college at the age of 11.[27]

A young prince who stood in line of succession to the emperor was often marked out by being given the honorific post of *princeps iuventutis*, leader of the six special equestrian centuries (whose members might be up to 35 years old). But like a priesthood or the city prefecture, this was an honour that could not be awarded until after the prince had put on the *toga virilis*. Tiberius' son Drusus was made *princeps iuventutis* soon after his father had been adopted by Augustus in AD 4, as a sign that he too was in the line of succession; but he was then 17 or 18, and had put on the adult toga in AD 2. Only in the third century did this principle come to be ignored, as with other civil offices.

Another honorific post suitable for a future prince was that of prefect of the city during the absence of the consuls at the Latin Festival on the Alban Mount, *praefectus urbi feriarum latinarum causa*. Octavian was selected for this honour by Julius Caesar in early 47 BC, when he was aged 15 – but he already had the adult toga. Because this archaic office was purely honorific, it may have been one for which exceptions were made: Cassius Dio tells us that in 23 BC 'Two persons acted as Prefects for each day of the feriae, and one of them had not even attained the status of a youth' (MEIPAKIA: a *tiro*?). But Cassius Dio may have made a mistake. Germanicus' second son Drusus was born *c.* AD 8; he was given the toga in 23, at the early age of 14, on the same day as his elder brother, and appointed *praefectus* in 25. Marcus Aurelius, born 26 April 121, donned the toga at the age of 15; he became *praefectus* in 137.[28]

During the republic, exceptions had occasionally been made to the rules regarding the age of candidates for magistracies. The Caesars were an exceptional family in the republic as restored by Augustus, and the Senate and people were regularly prepared to grant exceptions (normally of five years) from the normal requirement. In AD 6 such dispensation was given to Drusus' son Germanicus, born 24 May 15 BC, allowing him to hold a quaestorship in AD 7, when he was 20. His son Nero requested similar dispensation in AD 20; another son, Caligula, was granted the privilege before becoming quaestor in AD 33.[29]

But granting certain individuals dispensation from the rules is not the same as abandoning the republican principle. During the first two centuries of the principate, there was no question of anyone holding public office – including the imperial office – before he had put on the adult toga. Cassius Dio describes (in Greek terms) how, in 6 BC,

Gaius and Lucius were being flattered by everyone at Rome . . . the People had elected Gaius to a consulship before he was yet an ephebe [i.e. *tiro*]. Augustus was angered by this, and prayed that the need should not arise for someone to become consul, like himself, when less than twenty years of age.

For the time being, Gaius was given a priesthood, and allowed to be present at sessions of the Senate. But on the following New Year's Day (5 BC), at the age of 14, he donned the adult toga; Augustus assumed a consulship for the first time in 18 years to maximise the impact. But Gaius was not elected to hold public office as a child: once he had donned the toga, the Senate could recommend that he hold a consulship when he reached an appropriate age: 'Out of respect for me, the Roman Senate and People designated Gaius and Lucius Caesar as consuls when they were fourteen years old, that they should hold that office after five years.' It was not until the following year that the young prince was first recorded as having exercised his right to speak in a senatorial debate. In 2 BC, the younger brother Lucius was 14, given the adult toga – Augustus assumed his thirteenth and last consulship for the occasion – and received the same privileges. An inscription from Rome is dedicated: 'By the Senate to Lucius Caesar, son of Augustus, grandson of the god [Caesar], *princeps iuventutis*, designated consul when he was fourteen years old, augur.'[30] Until well into the third century AD, a consulship simply could not be held by a minor.

The same applied to the imperial office itself. When Tiberius' will was opened in AD 37, it was found that he had made his grandson by adoption, Caligula, heir equally with his natural grandson Tiberius Gemellus; but Caligula had donned the toga in AD 31 (aged 18), while Gemellus, probably aged 16, had not: Caligula was justified in saying, as reported by Philo: 'you see yourselves that he is still just a boy and requires guardians, schoolmasters and tutors'. The imperial power could be voted only to Caligula. Exactly the same situation applied when Claudius died in AD 54: his adopted son Nero had been given the toga in 52, at the age of 14; his natural son Britannicus, born 12 February 41, had not. But he would soon be 14: there were rumours that Claudius was planning to institute him, rather than the adopted Nero, as his successor. 'Agrippina, fearing that Britannicus, once an adult, might inherit his father's office, wanted to prevent this by stealing the empire for her own son; so according to report, she had Claudius killed.' Although Tacitus' account of Nero's acclamation suggests that some praetorians wanted Britannicus rather than Nero as Claudius' successor, that was out of the question: Britannicus was still a child.[31]

As the second century progresses, there are already signs that an emperor may be so keen to show that his son will succeed him that respect for the republican distinction between child and citizen begins to disappear. A new departure was to declare a prince 'Caesar'; the complex pattern of families related to the imperial house during the period of the misleadingly so-called 'adoptive' emperors (Trajan to Marcus Aurelius) could have the effect that an emperor himself might be adopted into the household of the Caesars by his predecessor, while his own son remained a member of another family. Marcus Aurelius proclaimed two of his sons, Commodus (*31 August 161) and Marcus Annius Verus, 'Caesars' on 12 October 166. On 15 October 172, he gave the 11-year-old Commodus the additional title 'Germanicus'. In 175, aged 13, he was almost old enough to don the *toga virilis* (other members of the second-century imperial family such as Lucius Verus and Marcus himself are known to have donned the toga at the age of 15); on 20 January he was co-opted to all priesthoods and made *princeps iuventutis*. On 19 May, still a boy, he went to join his father on campaign in what is now Bavaria; instead of ceremonially putting on his adult toga on the Capitol at Rome, he was simply declared to have come of age on 7 July 175. After two successful campaigning seasons, he was proclaimed *imperator* and returned to Rome to celebrate a triumph given in his own name over the Germans and Sarmatians on 23 December 176. In the following year he held his first consulship and was given the titles *Augustus* and *Pater Patriae* by the Senate.

Nothing had yet happened to contradict the principle that children could hold no magistracy. The critical change followed the second 'year of four emperors' in AD 192–3: the existence of several rival claimants for the imperial office at the same time made each of them concerned to show that, if he died, the succession should and would pass to his son (rather than to one of the other candidates).[32] It was in order to counter the claims of Clodius Albinus that Septimius Severus emphasised the existence of his sons, Marcus Aurelius Antoninus Bassianus, known to us as Caracalla, born 4 April 188 (possibly 186), and P. Septimius Geta, born 27 May 189.[33] When Severus became emperor in 193, he did not immediately make his sons members of the Caesarean household. Caracalla was adopted as a 'Caesar', changing his name to Marcus Aurelius Antoninus, and therefore a potential successor, after a military victory on the Danube in 196; in fact this was largely a political move, a signal to the rival emperor Clodius Albinus that Severus was no longer interested in co-operating with him (Albinus was defeated and killed in the following year). From this point, inscriptions regularly call the 8- (possibly 10-) year-old *imperator destinatus*, 'emperor-designate'.[34] His position was confirmed by the Senate at Rome, and he was elected *princeps iuventutis*, and to a number of priesthoods. In 198, the boy accompanied his father on an expedition against Parthia; he was acclaimed Augustus, and given the *tribunicia potestas* of an emperor. On the same occasion, his younger brother Geta was adopted a Caesar.

A 10-year-old was now officially joint emperor with his father. A letter written by the boy survives, replying to the city of Aphrodisias for its congratulations on his appointment. There is no reason to assume that he did not write it himself.[35] But Caracalla held no actual magistracy until after he had taken the adult toga: that happened at Antioch in 201, and only then was it thought appropriate for him to be designated consul for the following year.[36]

His brother Geta has no public role on inscriptions as late as that commemorating the Secular Games held in 204 (he is simply *nobilissimus Caesar*); that would have been the year when he was given the adult toga, and in 205 he held his first consulship, together with his brother (who was holding it for the second time). Only late in 209, when Severus was preparing to leave Italy for an expedition in northern Britain, was the 20-year-old Geta proclaimed co-Augustus.

The precedent of proclaiming a 10-year-old as Augustus was soon to be followed by Macrinus, who as praetorian prefect was the first non-senator to claim the imperial office after the assassination of Caracalla in April 217. Macrinus' 9-year-old son Diadumenianus became Caesar soon after. But following the proclamation of Elagabalus as legitimate successor to the Severan dynasty in Emesa in April 218, Macrinus responded by making the boy co-Augustus. That act was not enough to ensure the loyalty of Macrinus' soldiers, who went over to Elagabalus.

Elagabalus was himself only 13 or 14. Our sources do not make it clear whether he had donned the *toga virilis* or not; it may be worth recalling that Caracalla's *Constitutio Antoniniana*, which granted citizenship to every free community in the empire in AD 212, had the effect of making the distinction between Roman citizen and non-citizen devoid of much of its importance. Elagabalus immediately claimed all imperial titles, including the consulship, and wrote to the Senate justifying his youth by referring to the precedent of Augustus. The Senate could only confirm his titles, add that of *Pater Patriae* (for a 14-year-old) and co-opt him to all priesthoods (14 July 218).[37]

With Elagabalus' successor Alexander Severus, at 13, we have a clear case of a child as emperor, without any adult (father) as colleague. Alexander had been born on 1 October 208 and adopted by Elagabalus in the Senate on 10 July 221; he was proclaimed a Caesar, and designated consul for the following year. Before Elagabalus' death on 11 March 222, an inscription already proclaims Alexander as *Imperator*. A council of regency was appointed to act on his behalf; no one seems to have asked questions about how a child could be an emperor.

As the third century progressed, the tendency for emperors to appoint their under-age children to high office gathered momentum. The evidence is sparse, and it is unwise to rely too heavily on the testimony of the *Augustan History* and of other later biographical works such as the *Epitome De Caesaribus*. Gordian III (238–44) was acclaimed at the age of 13; as a grandson of Gordian I (reigned 238), he had already been adopted as a Caesar by the emperors Pupienus and Balbinus. The teenage emperor held consulships in 239 and 241.[38]

His successor Philip the Arab was emperor from February AD 244 until September 249; his son, Marcus Julius Severus Philippus, had been born *c.* 237/8. When his father became head the imperial household, the son too became a member of that household, and was correctly designated Caesar; as successor designate, he was also given the title *princeps iuventutis*, although only 5 or 6. On the other hand he was not at first given any magisterial powers; references to *tribunicia potestas* only appeared on coins and inscriptions when he was already designated to hold consular office. That was in July or August 247, after a major military victory over the Carpi on the Danube; apart from granting him tribunician power and a consulship, Philip had his 9-year-old son proclaimed Augustus and Pontifex Maximus.[39]

For the end of the third century, our evidence becomes more full with the 'tetrarchy', Diocletian's attempt to ensure that the imperial office would be held by senior and proven army officers. But the dynastic ambitions of Constantine and Licinius soon gave scope to the appearance of further child-emperors, and the dynasties that succeeded – those of Valentinian and Theodosius – showed that emperors had no inhibitions about making their under-age sons not just emperors, but even consuls. Maxentius, for example, not only deified his son Valerius Romulus after his death in 309 and built a temple for him on the Forum next to the vast basilica soon to be appropriated by Constantine; he had also appointed him to the consulships of 308 and 309. We do not know how old the boy was, but Maxentius himself had only been born in c. 283.[40]

The list of children proclaimed as Augustus or as consul of the Roman people by their soldier-fathers is long:

Flavius Julius Crispus: *c. 307; proclaimed Caesar 317, consul 318, 321, 324.

Licinius the Younger: *313/14; proclaimed Caesar 1 March 317; consul 319.

Constantine II: *1 March 317; proclaimed Caesar with his brother Crispus soon after; consul 320, 321, 324, 329, 331.

Constantius II: *7 August 317; Caesar 8 November 324; consul 326 (and nine times as an adult); Augustus 9 September 337.

Constans: *320/3 (the later date is more likely); proclaimed Caesar, Christmas 333; Augustus, 9 September 337; consul 339, 342, 346.

Gratian: *359; consul 366, 371, 374, 377, 380; Augustus 24 August 367.

Valentinian Galates, son of Valens: *18 January 366; consul 369.

Flavius Valentinian II: *371, Caesar 22 November 375, consul 376.

Arcadius: *c. 377; Augustus 16 January 383; consul 385 (and five more times between 392 and 406); on campaign in 386, winning a triumph on 12 October 386, aged about 9.

Honorius: *9 September 384; consul I 386; Augustus, January 397.

Theodosius II: *10 April 401; Augustus 402, sole ruler in the eastern empire from August 408.

Valens III: *2 July 419; Caesar 3 October 424, consul 425; Augustus 23 October 425.

Under the tetrarchy, it had still been accepted that a boy of 6 or so should be treated as a child who needs to be looked after – as Maxentius had been, as we know from a surviving panegyric delivered on 21 April 289. While orators praised the precociousness of these young princes, as we have seen in Chapter 2, late fourth and early fifth century writers still had reservations about whether a child emperor was a proper thing: the author of the *Augustan History* was explicit about the disasters that might follow.

> May the gods save us from boy-emperors and from proclaiming children 'Fathers of the Community' and from those whose alphabet-teachers have to guide their hands when it comes to signing documents, who are persuaded to make consular appointments by sweets and toys and whatever gives children pleasure.[41]

Even Christian bishops, although convinced of the efficacy of baptism in making a child a full member of the community, could betray similar unease about the practical implications of being ruled by an emperor who was still a child. In his *Consolation on the Death of Valentinian*,[42] St Ambrose made great play with the polarity between juvenile immaturity and some other quality which was required to cancel out that immaturity: the wisdom associated with old age or, in more straightforward terms, Christian belief. Valentinian II had been born in 371, proclaimed Augustus at Aquincum on the Danube in November 375 in order to stop the army from setting up a rival emperor of their own in opposition to Gratian and Valens, and died in mysterious circumstances at Vienne, where he was virtually a prisoner of the generalissimo Arbogast, in May 392. Ambrose emphasises that there are two grounds for grieving at his death: 'lack of years' and 'an old man's wisdom'. 'The premature death of pious emperors' affects the whole Christian Church. While most men abandon the sins of youth when they reach old age, it is rare for someone to accept the heavy yoke imposed by Christian morals while still a youth (§10). Ambrose was faced with a problem in praising Valentinian, since he had not yet actually been baptised: thus he stresses that the young emperor's morals had been as good as those of any perfect member of the Church, and points to his lack of interest in circus games, even on his birthday (§15), to the case of a notorious actress whom he had summoned away from Rome to his own court in order, so Ambrose asserts, to protect the morals of young senators (§17), and especially to his refusal to allow the altar of the pagan goddess Victory to be replaced in the Senate House in Rome (§19 f., 52). Ultimately, Ambrose has to claim that the emperor had intended to be baptised, and that this was good enough. The parallels of Enoch (Genesis 5:24) and King Josias (IV Kings 23) show that God does not necessarily cut short a man's life on earth because of personal wickedness. These parallels with Old Testament kingship and his personal faith are what save Valentinian, in Ambrose's eyes, from succumbing to the weaknesses of youth and inexperience.

The same difficulty, this time about an 11-year-old, occurred with a speech Ambrose gave on the day when the body of Theodosius was sent from Milan on its journey to Constantinople for burial, forty days after the emperor's death on 17 January 395. Ambrose by no means took it for granted that the fact that the young Honorius was the son of the deceased emperor would guarantee that he would be accepted as capable of ruling the western empire at the age of 11. In effect, most of his speech in honour of the dead Theodosius is an appeal to the army to respect the emperor's wish that his son succeed him. But the candidate's youth is a problem:

> Do not take his age into account: a commander attains the age of maturity when he has the trust [*fides*] of his soldiers – for his age is mature when his virtue is so. These two are reciprocal, since an emperor's trust lies in the virtue of his soldiers.[43]

When Theodosius was already an old man, he had been able to lead his troops into battle successfully against the pagans at the Frigidus, because he relied on his faith (*fides*) in God; Ambrose draws a parallel with Abraham and Sarah, the strength of whose faith in God enabled them to have a son even when she was past the age for childbearing. In the same way, Honorius' Christian faith will enable him to overcome his youth. But Ambrose seems to have had his doubts as to whether his audience was likely to be convinced by this theoretical argument. He had to adduce an *exemplum* in the form of a biblical parallel: Honorius at 11 is on the verge of adulthood, older than the famous holy king of Israel, Josias, had been when he re-established the worship of the true God (he had been 8 when he came to the throne: cf. IV Kings 22:1). But Honorius had an enormous advantage over the good kings of Israel – he was the son of a Christian emperor, rather than of an idolatrous fanatic like Josias' father (§15). By the end of the fourth century, an individual child's Christian faith in God could be represented as overcoming the artificial distinction between child and citizen that had so long survived the end of the republic.

While the sons of emperors were liberating themselves from every restriction which the classical period had placed on the participation of children in public life, the sons – and daughters – of other wealthy and powerful men were also freeing themselves from age qualifications. Highest in status were the Senators of Rome. Under the republic, senatorial status had not been inherited: it had to be earned through *virtus*, evidenced by popular election to office coupled with behaviour which satisfied the censors who revised the list every five years. A senator's sons, before they had managed to win election to office themselves, were 'knights' or *equites*, not senators.

The development of a formal hereditary senatorial order was due to Augustus. For purposes of day-to-day administration, Augustus used the Senate to legitimate his policies; hence it was in his interest to enhance its status. This he did in various ways, such as excluding 'unworthy' members (not just political opponents) and ensuring that all senators were extremely wealthy. But he also imposed restrictions on the rights of senators as well as their sons and grandsons to marry wives of low status; and gave senators, with their sons and grandsons, certain privileges such as reserved seats at public spectacles. The result was the creation of a distinct senatorial status-group (*ordo*), entry to which was an accident of birth, unconnected with the ability to win elections. From now, every senator's son was a 'Senator of the Roman People' and could call himself a *clarissimus puer* or, if he had donned the adult toga but held no office yet, *clarissimus iuvenis*. The status applied not just to sons of any age, but to wives and daughters as well: they bore the titles of *clarissima femina* and *clarissima puella*. By the second century AD, tombstones of senators' sons who had died in infancy proclaim their status as a 'C[larissimus] P[uer]': 'Nepotianus C.P. lived for thirteen years two months and twenty-one days.' 'To the Spirits of the Dead: in honour of Lucius Marius Vegetinus Lucanus Tiberenus, C.P., who lived for six months and twenty-one days. Vegetinus the Praetor and Claudia Artemidora, C.F., as parents to their sweetest son.' Daughters too are commemorated: 'Scribonia Maxima C.P. lived for forty-five days.'[44]

The status might even be granted to a child as a reward for his non-senatorial father's loyal service to the emperor: under Antoninus Pius, it was granted to the 4-year-old son of a procurator. As imperial representatives, procurators were in a privileged position: their sons were accorded unofficial titles such as 'most honourable' in inscriptions by Greek cities. Although these persons were often themselves already adults, this is symptomatic of the way in which political power and influence was increasingly recognised as something that was inherited, rather than gained through personal *virtus* or office holding.[45]

Friendships (*amicitiae*) had always to some extent been inherited, as had the patronage relationships between individual Romans and particular cities in Italy or the provinces. But it does not seem that a child, even of the imperial family, might yet become the formal *patronus* of an Italian or provincial city in the first century. Caligula is, however, represented as *duumvir* and *quinquennalis* (equivalent to consul and censor at Rome) of Caesaraugusta (Zaragossa) and Carthago Nova (Carthagena) in Spain on coins which have been dated AD 28/9, i.e. while still a *puer*. If the dating is right, this would have been exceptional: at Pompeii, Caligula was elected a *duumvir* in AD 34, when already adult.[46]

As time went on, the distinction between adult citizens and others became less and less important. Municipal *patroni* were powerful figures (not necessarily originating from within a community) appointed to protect the interests of the city against imperial officials or rival cities. A study of 242 inscriptions referring to municipal patrons from Roman Africa reveals half a dozen women and a number of youths or children, including a C[larissimus] P[uer], two C[larissimae] P[uellae].[47] Women and children were excluded from office holding: but they were not excluded from giving concrete benefits to a community, either by granting money for a new building or games, or by protecting the community against the depredations of imperial officials or rival cities. Hence patronage came to be perceived as something handed down within a family. 'They elected him and his children and his descendants as patrons for themselves and their children and their descendants' says an inscription from Zama Regia dated to AD 322. A fourth-century inscription from Veltona in Italy mentions boys made *patroni* because their father was.[48]

The reasons why the children of emperors, senators, and imperial procurators were being given privileges while they were still children were often specific to these particular groups. But there was a much wider tendency throughout the Mediterranean world during this period to emphasise the hereditary nature of political and social privilege, at the expense of the classical distinction between the child and the adult citizen. Quite simply, the Pax Romana, Roman rule over the Mediterranean world, by abolishing warfare, meant that the ability to fight ceased to be a precondition for being a person of value to the community. During the republic, a Roman citizen had been a male old enough to have had his name entered on the list of potential conscripts in the *tabularium* on the Capitol, or in his municipality; from the time of Augustus on, all persons of citizen birth, male and female, had to be registered within thirty days of birth.[49] Adolescents, women, even young children, could now be perceived as persons who could in one of a number of different ways contribute to their city despite the fact that they could not bear arms. They might show conspicuous ability in the skills required of a citizen (for instance, the rhetorical ability looked for in an ambassador); by being in possession of inherited political or social influence with the powers that be; or simply by being rich enough to contribute the semi-voluntary gifts (*munera* or liturgies) that were essential to the functioning of the ancient city.

It is not surprising, therefore, that membership of the equestrian order – loosely, 'the rich' – also became hereditary, though the process was far more gradual than it had been for the Senate. It was only ever formally recognised for the holders of certain equestrian posts in the imperial service: Marcus Aurelius decreed that the descendants of *eminentissimi* and *perfectissimi*, down to their great-grandchildren, were to be freed from any 'plebeian penalties' that might be imposed by the courts. As time went on, the lower rank of *egregii* seems to have been included in this privilege.[50] Formally, a young man still had to be adlected into the centuries of the equestrian *ordo* to become an equestrian; but inscriptions show that children might now be so adlected: 'Tiberius Claudius

Secundinus, died aged 9 years 9 months 18 days; held the Public Horse'; 'To Annius Julianus, Roman Knight, who lived for three years nine months and eight hours'.[51] By the third and fourth centuries AD, we find that, whatever the formal position, equestrian titles were given to children in much the same way that senatorial titles were. Several epitaphs mention a *puer egregius*.[52] Like the wives of senators, women who were related to equestrians also claimed that status: E[gregia] F[emina].[53]

In the cases of senators and equestrians, the conflation of child and adult was to the advantage of the wealthy. But it might also be to the advantage of the community as a whole. While participation in public life in the ancient city gave the successful honour and glory (two words derived from Latin; cf. ΤΙΜΗ AND ΔΟΞΑ in Greek), in return they had to provide their community with 'gifts' or 'services' (Lat. *munera*, Gk ΛΕΙΤΟΥΡΓΙΑΙ, whence our word for the divine service). This exchange of honour in return for spending one's wealth freely ('liberally', as expected of a free citizen) was essential to the functioning of the classical city. Public buildings such as baths, porticoes, aqueducts, temples, the upkeep of the city walls, public feasts and shows, were all *munera* provided by wealthy citizens in return for honour. In a material form, that honour was expressed through the award of statues and honorific inscriptions such as survive in large numbers from almost every Greek and Roman city.[54]

A wealthy family owed the city *munera*. What if the head of that family was a minor? As long as the ability to perform military service remained the crucial criterion for separating the men from the boys, he could play no role in civic life – and could not be expected to provide *munera*. But during the second and third centuries AD, the situation changed. The concentration of wealth in ever fewer families throughout the Roman empire meant that an ever greater proportion of existing resources was diverted to the capital cities of Rome and, from the fourth century, Constantinople, or to the imperial residences (and the army). The result was that the functioning of this classical system of *munera* and liturgies began to break down. Office holding became less and less voluntary; the *Theodosian Code* reveals the extent to which emperors throughout the fourth century (and earlier) felt obliged to save civic institutions by forcing the wealthy (and the not so wealthy) to serve as magistrates and councillors. It is not surprising therefore that there was a strong temptation for cities to tap resources which legally belonged to children. By the fourth century, minors belonging to powerful families are frequently found as Roman praetors or quaestors, providing the Roman people with some of their games out of their family property; we have seen examples in Claudian's panegyrics and Symmachus' letters. A fifth-century inscription honours 'Flavius Valerius Theopompus Romanus, C.P., born a patrician; Quaestor-candidate-designate; his parents, to their dearest son'. Theopompus was not just a *clarissimus puer* and a patrician from birth: he had also been designated to the quaestorship, the expenses for which would of course be paid by his father.[55]

Some children might apparently be appointed to quaestorships without their knowledge, or at least in their absence, and then fined for failing to fulfil their obligations. Constantine disapproved of this abuse: on 9 March 320 (or 329), he wrote to the urban prefect Aelianus:

> Since we have been persuaded by the reverent voices of the Most August Senate, we decree that quaestors shall enjoy the same privileges as consuls and praetors, viz. if anyone under sixteen is nominated in his absence . . . he will not be fined if he does not attend the games.

Another rescript in the *Theodosian Code*, dated 6 March 327, similarly makes it clear that the pressure now was on wealthy families to provide gifts, and the emperor sometimes had to intervene to protect young aristocrats from being forced in their absence to provide games and races: minors under 20 who live in the provinces should not be liable to provide *munera* for the Roman circus and theatre.[56]

The rescript does not refer to the highest office of state, the consulship. We have enough information about the consuls to be able to say that until well into the fifth century, no children seem to have been appointed to that office except for members of the imperial family. The appointment of the teenage consuls of 396, Olybrius and Probinus, was without precedent (and, as we have seen, the immediate result of Theodosius' need to conciliate the pagan Senate after the defeat of Eugenius in the previous year). In almost every case where inscriptional or literary evidence gives us further information about a senator or soldier's career, the consulship appears as the latest, as well as the greatest, position held; e.g. Stilicho, consul in AD 400: 'From his earliest age, through the stages of honourable military service, he was raised up to the pinnacle of everlasting glory and association with royalty.'[57] One consul noted that his career up to the consulship lasted 33 years.[58] As a rule, even men of noble family like Caius Ceionius Rufius Volusianus, consul in 314, cannot have been appointed before their early thirties.

But where the provision of *munera* was involved, we find office holding by children well before the fourth century in both Greek and Latin cities outside Rome. Instances of honours for the sons of freedmen are a special case, and have been well documented; what happened here was that an ex-slave, no matter how wealthy, could hold no civic magistracies (Augustus introduced a priesthood, the *seviri Augustales*, especially to enable them to play a role in public religious life). If they were to be able to contribute to the well-being of their community, the money they spent would have to be spent, not in their own name, but in that of their sons; and the community would have to honour, not the freedman, but his son, even where that son was still a child.[59]

The same applied where the money legally belonged to a minor, but was spent in his name by his mother: an inscription from Pompeii honours N. Pepidius Celsinus, son of Corellia Celsa, who was enrolled as a decurion (city councillor) at the age of 6 for rebuilding the Temple of Isis after it had been damaged in the earthquake of AD 63; it was of course his mother, not the boy, who was the devotee of Isis and who arranged for the rebuilding. We may assume that something similar lay behind the appointment of Cnaeus Cornelius Pulcher, a child of 4, as *Agoranomos* and *gymnasiarch* (magistrate responsible for public places, including the corn supply, and for providing the running-costs of the gymnasium) at Epidaurus.[60]

But it was not only the sons of freedmen or rich orphans who were being elected to municipal office and to membership of city councils throughout the empire. Just as in Rome, a rich man might be happy to provide a further round of *munera* for his town, in return for honour and glory for his small son. An inscription from Amiternum in Italy honours a man who provided the city with one of its last gladiatorial spectacles; in return, his son was given a magistracy. As governor of Bithynia, Pliny noted that young men under 30 were sitting as councillors, notwithstanding the provisions of Pompey's provincial charter. In Pliny's opinion, it was much better that rich young men should be elected, rather than persons qualified by age but without the means. Inscriptions confirm that membership of municipal councils was becoming hereditary, and that the formal provisions of the law barring men under 25 from holding municipal office were increasingly being ignored.[61]

At Ostia, the post of first praetor was held by a boy who died at the age of 4 years, 7 months, and 17 days; another inscription commemorates a 'Roman knight, Town councillor, Second Praetor, who lived to the age of twelve'. At Aricia, a member of the town council died, 'having held every office', at the age of 12. A boy in his fourteenth year had been awarded the status of *duumvir* of Barcelona in the early second century. Particularly interesting is the *Album* or official register of the town council of Canusium (Canossa), now in Florence. In AD 223, there were thirty-one senatorial patrons, eight equestrian patrons, and a hundred city councillors of various rank. But there were also twenty-five 'boys', *praetextati*, some of them the sons of men who were themselves on the city council.[62]

The *Theodosian Code* is full of regulations about age of entry to municipal councils, making membership and the *munera* involved depend upon heredity. This should not be taken as a sign that Christian late antiquity was a static, bureaucratic world which frowned on social mobility, but rather of the government's concern for the survival of the city and its culture. The tendency now was no longer for cities to *allow*, but to *force* the children of rich families to undertake offices. In 331, Constantine enacted:

> Since some decurions of various cities have without inhibition
> summoned minors, who ought to be protected by a public tutor,
> to be members of municipal councils, and it has been claimed
> that young men aged seven or eight have been nominated in this
> way, we decree that absolutely no-one should be nominated as a
> member of a municipal council and forced to perform *munera*
> unless he has entered upon his eighteenth year. From now on all
> such youngsters shall be prohibited from having to perform any
> such service. . . .[63]

The tendency for 'services' to be expected on the basis of heredity also applied to military service. Fourth-century governments repeatedly issued instructions about the age when sons of veterans were liable for conscription. In 326, Constantine required them to enlist between the ages of 20 and 25; if they were unwilling or unsuitable, and had the requisite property, they would be required to perform civic *munera* instead. Other rescripts mention the age of 16 (*c.* 332 and 343), 'the eighteenth year' (331) and 'from the nineteenth year' (*c.* 353).[64] Nevertheless we find children listed as soldiers: in AD 327, Valentinian, Valens, and the 12-year-old Gratian insist that such children deserve no maintenance from public funds:

> Those persons who are enrolled on the official register among the supernumeraries [*accrescentes*, the reserves] shall receive support from their parents until they are thought able to bear arms. Accordingly, further provision for such persons from the imperial fiscus [*annonae*] shall cease.

The problem was not solved: in 394 Theodosius and his sons (themselves aged 16 and 9) instructed the Master of the Offices,

> If anyone begins to perform imperial service while they are children [*infantes vel pueri*], we order them to be enrolled in the lowest rank. In this way they will have the opportunity to win a place for themselves from the time at which they begin to obey orders, and will be able to obtain promotion in our service on the grounds of their own efforts.[65]

Perhaps the most important single factor removing the formal distinction between child and adult citizen was the spread of Roman citizenship to everyone who belonged to any city, Latin or Greek, as a result of Caracalla's *Constitutio Antoniniana* of AD 212. Accounts of Diadumenianus' Elagabalus' and Alexander Severus' acclamation as emperors ignore entirely the question of whether they had donned the adult toga; and from that time on, the characteristically Roman ceremony of replacing the *toga praetexta* with the *toga virilis* loses significance. For Cicero, for Pliny, and even for Tertullian at the beginning of the third century, the donning of the toga had been the example *par excellence* of a social ritual: 'As regards our duties to attend private and public ceremonies, such as the white toga, betrothals, weddings, naming-ceremonies, I do not think that there is any danger of Christians who attend being affected by the breath of idolatry. . . .' It is still 'putting on the Roman toga' that makes a man; and for the early third century jurist Marcian (quoting a rescript of Marcus Aurelius), a Roman citizen.[66] As late as the fifth century, *togati* continues to be the title by which civil as opposed to military officials are known. But for ordinary purposes, the donning of the toga, and with it the distinction between child and citizen, has ceased to matter. It is striking that by the time the *Digest* was compiled in AD 538, the toga was of such insignificance that the word only occurs eight times. For Augustine's parents, it was puberty, not citizen status, that made an adult, in marked contrast to the classical period.[67]

When Isidore of Seville compiled his encyclopaedia in the early seventh century, he clearly assumed that his readers had no idea what a toga looked like: and his account is in the imperfect tense. He thought that 'the *praetexta* is the child's cloak which boys of noble family used to wear up to the age of sixteen as school uniform'. Citizenship plays no part in his description. Childhood has come to be defined, not in the negative terms of the absence of full citizenship, but positively, as the period of learning.[68]

NOTES

1 Aulus Gellius, *Noctes Atticae* 10,28. The jurist Tubero wrote his fourteen-book Roman history around 40 BC; Servius Tullius was the sixth-century king to whom the military reforms which created the levy and the legion were ascribed.

2 Ulpian, *Digest* 3,1.1.3.

3 *Digest* 48,5,14(13),8; Gaius, *Institutes* 1,196; *Digest* 4,4.1. For different divisions of the 'ages of man', cf. n. 17 below.

4 Isidore, *Etymologiae* 9,3.36 f. *praetextati* at Cannae – Val.Max. 7,6.1 and 3,1.1. Pliny *NH* 7,29. Plutarch, *Caius Gracchus* 5.1.

5 Cicero, *De Amicitia* 1.1; *Pro Caelio* 5.11; Nonius 406.14; Pliny, *Letters* 4,11.3.

6 On the toga generally, cf. L. M. Wilson, *The Roman Toga* (Baltimore, Md., 1924); Nonius 540.31 and 541,2; Festus, under 'toga'. Prostitutes continued to wear a *toga meretricia*. Aulus Gellius 5,19.7: 'he who is not *vesticeps* cannot adopt'.

7 *Laus Pisonis* 27 f.; Tertullian, *De Pallio* 5.

8 Cf. the bronze plate inscribed with the law relating to the *Flamen Augustalis* of Narbo, *CIL* XII,6038.

9 Chapter 3 above.

10 Servius, on *Eclogue* 4,50; Propertius 4,1.33; Persius 5.30 ff.; Varro, *Lingua Latina* 7,107; Suetonius, *De Rhetoribus* 1; Juvenal 13,33.

11 Cicero, *Pro Archia* 4,8.
12 Varro, quoted by the anonymous *Auctor de praenominibus*, §3,6: Funaioli, *Grammaticae Romanae Fragmenta* (Leipzig, 1907), 331: 'pueris non prius quam togam virilem sumerent, puellis non ante quam nuberent, praenomina imponi moris fuisse Q.Scaevola auctor est'. Childhood friendships (e.g. with slaves): Cicero, *De Amicitia* 10.33.
13 Juvenal, *Satires* 8,166; Cassius Dio 48,34.3; Crinagoras, in a poem in the *Anthologia Palatina* (6, 161), says that Marcellus has become a man instead of a boy by dedicating his beard to Apollo. Suetonius, *Nero* 12.4; Cassius Dio 61,19.1. Suetonius, *Caligula* 10.
14 M. Della Corte, *Iuventus* (Rome, 1924).
15 Ulpian, *Ad Sabinum*, cited in the *Digest* 50,17.2: 'Feminae ab omnibus officiis civilibus vel publicis remotae sunt et ideo nec iudices esse possunt nec magistratum gerere nec postulare nec pro alio intervenire nec procuratores existere. ITEM impubes omnibus officiis civilibus debet abstinere.' Cassius Dio 48,43.2.
16 A. E. Astin, 'The Lex Annalis before Sulla', *Latomus* 16 (1957), 588 ff., and *Latomus* 17 (1958), 49 ff.
17 E. Eyben, 'Antiquity's view of puberty', *Latomus* 31 (1972), 677–97. Cicero, *De Senectute* 10,33; Seneca, *Letters* 121,15–16; Ovid, *Metamorphoses* 15,19; Censorinus, 14.2; Seneca, *De Beneficiis* 7,1.5.
18 Vow of the people of Narbonne, AD 12/13: *ILS* 112 = Ehrenberg and Jones 100; L. Robert, *Les gladiateurs dans l'orient grecque* (Paris, 1940), no.39, p. 100.
19 L. B. Warren, 'Roman triumphs and Etruscan kings', *JRS* 60 (1970), 49 ff.
20 Marcellus: Suetonius, *Tiberius* 6.4; there was also a *congiarium* in Marcellus' honour: Cassius Dio 51,21.3. Germanicus: Tacitus, *Annals* 2,41.
21 *SHA, Marcus* 12.10, 21.3; *Commodus* 1.2, 10.2; Cassius Dio 72,22.4–6.
22 Cassius Dio 55,6.4. *SHA Commodus* 2.1; confirmed by coins with the legend LIBERALITAS AUG.
23 Tacitus, *Annals* 11,11; Suetonius, Nero 7.Cf. plates 1 and 2.
24 Nicolaus of Damascus §3. Cf. Suetonius, *Augustus* 8; Suetonius, *Tiberius* 6.4; Tacitus, *Annals* 5,1; Suetonius, *Caligula* 10.1.
25 Suetonius, *Claudius* 2.2.
26 Octavian: Nicolaus of Damascus §4, Cicero *Philippics* 5,17, 46, 19.53; Velleius 2,59.3; Marcellus: *Anthologia Palatina* 6,61 (contemporary epigram by Crinagoras of Mytilene); Tacitus, *Annals* 1,3; Suetonius, *Caligula* 10,1 and 12,1; Cassius Dio 58,8.1.
27 Tacitus, *Histories* 2,59.3; Salii: Geiger, Pauly-Wissowa IA.2, 1874 ff.; *SHA Marcus* 4.2.
28 Nicolaus of Damascus, §5. Cassius Dio 53,33.3. Tacitus, *Annals* 4,3. *SHA Marcus* 4.6.
29 Suetonius, *Caligula* 1.1. Tacitus, *Annals* 2,41; Cassius Dio 58,23.1.
30 Cassius Dio 55,9.2; *Res Gestae Divi Augusti* 14: 'Filios meos, quos iuvenes mihi eripuit fortuna, Gaium et Lucium Caesares honoris mei caussa senatus populusque Romanus annum quintum et decimum agentis consules designavit, ut eum magistratum inirent post

quinquennium.' On Herod's will: Josephus, *Antiquities* 17,195, and *Jewish War* 2(25),2.4. Ehrenberg and Jones 65: assigned to 3 BC, but Lucius continued to be aged 14 in the first half of 2 BC. Similar inscriptions have been found elsewhere: *CIL* XI,3040 (from Viterbo); *CIL* VI,900 (Rome); *CIL* III,323 (Nicomedia). There were also coins celebrating the fact that the two young Caesars had put on the citizens' toga (Giard, 1648–66).

31 *Legatio ad Gaium* 4.5 = 26; Josephus, *Antiquities* 20,151; Tacitus, *Annals* 6,9.

32 A. Birley, *Septimius Severus* (London, 1971). Pertinax had rejected the title 'Caesar' for his son in 193: Cassius Dio 73,7.1.

33 Cassius Dio 78,6.5; *SHA Severus and Caracalla*; Cassius Dio 77,2.5.; plates 9 and 10.

34 *ILS* 442, 446, 447; cf. *CIL* VIII,10569 etc.

35 Line 3: EME; J. Reynolds (*Aphrodisias and Rome* (London, 1982), 127) assumes that 'The sentence concerned must be the work of his father or of a secretary'. For another early letter of Caracalla, cf. R. Heberdey, *Forschungen in Ephesus* II, 26.

36 Herodian 3,10.1 f.; *SHA Severus* 16.8; inscriptions describe him as 'TRIB[unicia] POT[estate] IIII DESIGNAT[o] COS.': *CIL* IX,5980 (Capua) and VI,1030.

37 Herodian 5,3 ff.; cf. plate 11; Cassius Dio 78,31; 79,8; 20; *CIL* VI,2001; 2009; 2104 (Arval Brethren).

38 Age 13: Herodian 8,8.8. The *SHA* gives 11 and 16 as alternatives. Cf. plates 12 and 13.

39 *CIL* VII,1178 = *RIB* 2286; Aurelius Victor/*Epitome de Caesaribus*, 28.3.

40 T. D. Barnes, *Constantine and Eusebius* (Cambridge, Mass. 1981), with its companion, *The New Empire of Diocletian and Constantine* (Cambridge, Mass. 1982). Cults had been instituted for the deceased children of emperors as early as the first century: Tacitus, *Annals* 15,23.1 (Nero's 4-month-old daughter Claudia Augusta). Cf. plate 14.

41 *Panegyrici Latini* 10.14.1; *SHA, Tacitus* 6.5: 'dii avertant principes pueros et patres patriae dici inpuberes et quibus ad suscribendum magistri litterari manus teneant, quos ad consulatus dandos dulcia et circuli et quaecumque voluptas puerilis invitet'.

42 *PL* 16.1418 ff.

43 Ambrose, *De Obitu Theodosii* 6 = *PL* 16.1447 ff.

44 R. J. A. Talbert, *The Senate of Imperial Rome* (Princeton, NJ, 1984); *CIL* VI,32022; 1458; 1334. Cf. 1448: set up by a freedwoman 'To Lycia Lorenia Cornelia Crispina, C.P., my most innocent and delightful *patrona*'.

45 'adlecto annorum quattuor in amplissimum ordinem': *CIL* XIII,1808 = *ILS* 1454; G. E. Bean, *Inscriptions of Side* (Ankara, 1965), 26 No.116 = *Année Epigraphique* 1966, 471. On the other hand, the inscription from Burdur which apparently grants the right to use public transport to a procurator's son as early as the reign of Augustus is surely the result of an error of transcription: S. Mitchell, 'Requisitioned transport in the Roman empire', *JRS* 66 (1976), 106 ff.

46 *Prosopographia Imperii Romani ILS* 6396 IV, 170 and 6397.

47 B. H. Warmington, 'The municipal patrons of Roman North Africa', *Papers of the British School at Rome* 22 (1954), 39 ff. No. 56 = R. Cagnat, *Inscriptions Latines d'Afrique* (Paris, 1923), 305, from Siagu; Nos 82 and 83 (= *CIL* VIII, 1181), the two daughters of No. 80.

48 *CIL* VI,1686; *CIL* XI,5170.

49 J. F. Gardner, *Women in Roman Law and Society* (London, 1986), 144 ff.

50 G. Alföldy, 'Die Stellung der Ritter in der Führungsschicht des Imperium Romanum', *Chiron* XI (1981), 169–215 = *Die römische Gesellschaft* (Stuttgart, 1986), 162 ff. On 'plebeian penalties' cf. P. Garnsey, *Social Status and Legal Privilege*, (Oxford, 1970), 241 f.

51 *ILS* 1316, 1317. Some other inscriptions are ambiguous: as G. Alföldy has pointed out, the phrase 'natus eques Romanus' may indicate the child's place of birth in *CIL* VI,1632 = *ILS* 1318; F. Miller, *The Emperor in the Roman World* (London, 1977), 280.

52 *CIL* VI,9241, 1631; X,1815.

53 *CIL* XIII,3454; R. MacMullen, 'Women's power in the principate', *Klio* 68 (1986), 434 ff.

54 A. H. M. Jones, *The Greek City* (Oxford, 1940; repr. paperback, 1981), remains an outstanding description of how the ancient Mediterranean city functioned.

55 *CIL* VI, 31990.

56 *Theodosian Code* 6.4.1 and 2.

57 *CIL* VI,1730–1 = *ILS* 1277–8 ff.

58 Tatianus, consul 391: *ILS* 8844.

59 M. L. Gordon, 'The freedman's son in municipal life', *JRS* 21 (1931) 65–77.

60 *ILS*, 6367; *IG* IV.2, 653.

61 *Année Epigraphique* 1937, no. 119; Pliny, *Letters* 10,79.1 (Augustus had insisted on a minimum age of 22 years); *Digest* 50, 4.8 and 5.2; 17.2; *Lex Malacitana*, *ILS* 6089, §54.

62 Ostia: *ILS* 6143, 6144; Aricia: 'omni munere functus', *CIL* XIV,2170; Barcelona: S. Mariner Bigorra, *Inscripciones Romanas de Barcelona* (Barcelona, 1973), No.47; Canusium: *ILS* 6121. Cf. P. Garnsey, *ANRW* II,1, 229–52.

63 *Theodosian Code* 12,1.19.

64 *Theodosian Code* 7,22.2.1; 7,22.4; 12,1.35; 12,1.19; 18/19; 7,13.1.

65 *Theodosian Code* 7,1.11 (Trier, AD 372). The concern about under-age soldiers was shared by others in late antiquity: *SHA* 20, 28.3.

66 Tertullian, *De idololatria* 16 = *PL* 1,762. He goes on to select the donning of the *toga virilis* as typical of all such ceremonies: 'quia neque vestitutis virilis . . . de alicuius idoli honore descendit'. Marcian, *Digest* 49,14.32: 'accepto usu togae Romanae'.

67 *Theodosian Code* 7,8.10 (AD 413); 6,2.26 (428). Augustine, *Confessions* 4,3: contrast Seneca, *Letters* 1,4.2; Persius, *Satires* 5,30 ff.; Statius, *Silvae* 5,2.61; Apuleius, *Apologia* 87,10 and 98.

68 Isidore, *Etymologiae* 19,24.3–16: 'Praetexta puerile est pallium quo usque ad sedecim annos pueri nobiles sub disciplinae cultu utebantur.'

Chapter Five

LEARNING FOR ADULT LIFE

Republican Rome identified as an adult a man who had put on the *toga virilis*, or a woman who had become a wife. But an adult was also someone who had the skills needed to exercise the adult roles. In propertied households, both men and women needed to know how to read and write to check their accounts, and men needed to know how to be soldiers and, if they wished to play an active role in the public life of their community, how to persuade their fellow citizens as public speakers. As the formal distinctions between child and adult citizen became less and less important during the first three centuries AD, so the ability to assimilate these skills increasingly came to be the criterion which distinguished the child from the adult. Quintilian and Menander's recommendations for the panegyric, as well as surviving collections of letters, show the importance of learning the skills expected of a free man, the *artes liberales*. The child who was precocious as a learner had a good chance of winning recognition as an individual.

In the Roman world, the place where these skills were taught was primarily the household, the *domus*; formal education in schools, an institution borrowed from the Greeks, played a comparatively subsidiary role. For most purposes, a child learnt a skill by watching how it was done. This applied to all *artes*: those which we today classify as 'work skills' as well as 'social' skills or behaviour patterns. The responsibility for teaching children lay with the head of the household, the *paterfamilias*. The household might include other children apart from those of the *paterfamilias* and his wife, natural and adopted: those of his slaves of course, but often also those of his freedmen and freedwomen, and of more distant relatives, dependants, and friends. And given the frequency of remarriage because of death and, at least in the classical period, divorce, the children of several marriages might be brought up under the supervision of the same *paterfamilias*. Consequently the range of individuals towards whom a Roman child might develop 'attachment' for emotional security, and 'affiliation' for company and in order to play, was much wider than the model of a nuclear family might suggest.[1] The more adults a child is in contact with, the easier the 'separation experience' from parents (in our society, at about the age of 3). In a pre-industrial society, the presence of a large number of family members both inside and outside the actual household was especially important in view of the high mortality rate of parents and siblings.

As we have seen from Marcus Aurelius' *Reflections*, wealthy Roman children found 'attachment' and security not just with the mother, but also with the nurse and the 'childminder', the *paedagogus*. The expectation of total loyalty between a child and his *paedagogus* appears in literature as early as Homer.[2] Classical literature assigned a similar role to nurses as the confidantes of women whom they had once looked after. The nurse's loyalty to her mistress often became a theme for tragedy; Phaedra is the classic example. But we should not assume that an adult's respect for the men and women who had looked after him or her in childhood was merely a literary convention. Pliny was prepared to set aside a large sum of money to look after his nurse in her old age.[3]

The circle of adults from whom a baby learnt to speak was therefore comparatively large. This was one reason why ancient writers from Plato to Augustine assumed that language came naturally to children, unlike reading and writing, skills to be learnt from particular teachers. Intellectuals were worried about the effect on children of listening to slave-nurses and childminders who might be of 'barbarian' origin: 'Impressionable and untrained minds are affected by their tales and nonsense.'[4] Childminding was a useful way of employing old and infirm domestics: Pericles is once said to have seen a slave break his leg by falling out of a tree, and commented that he had just become a *paedagogus*. The later emperor Claudius had been entrusted to a retired mule-driver, and the 3-year-old Nero to a dancer and a hairdresser. But we should not be too impressed by the elitist (and sometimes racialist) speculations which led nineteenth-century scholars to worry about the effect of the use of untrained childminders on the children of wealthy Greeks and Romans. Childminding, then as now, required no complicated skills, rather much time and patience (and a minimum of physical fitness). 'The busy old woman will always sit by you; she will tell you lots of little stories', in order to persuade a child to go to sleep. Childminding is also supposed to require an ability to make the child feel secure: we might be more worried by the frequency of references to nurses – and indeed parents – frightening children with threats of monsters and wolves to make them behave.[5]

It was a commonplace to look down on these sub-literary stories, 'such as are told to girls as they are weaving, to lessen the tedium of their work, or to credulous children'. This *topos* went back to Plato's critique of Greek mythology, that the stories told to children gave them entirely false ideas, even when they were presented in a form intended for adult consumption – 'They treat us like children, to whom each tells his own story . . . they press on to the end without caring whether we follow them or are left behind . . .'; 'Falsehood in general passes current among the multitude because they are ignorant of history and believe all they have heard from childhood in choirs and tragedies'.[6] Although no examples of such sub-literary stories survive, we can guess the uncomplicated form that they took from the way Apuleius introduces the story of Psyche in his *Metamorphoses* (4,28.1): 'In a certain city there was a king and a queen. They had three daughters who were very beautiful. . .'.

These stories should be distinguished from animal fables such as Horace's tale of the city mouse and the country mouse, even though that is introduced as 'old women's tales'. These animal fables, says Quintilian, should be learnt by heart, in proper speech. What he was referring to were the collections of fables composed in literary Latin by poets like Phaedrus (and later Avienus) in the tradition of Aesop.[7]

Roman parents and teachers had no qualms that the children of the elite might be infected with seditious ideas by such stories any more than by substandard Latin; the idea that Aesop and his successors expressed the views of the slave-class in these fables is a modern fancy.[8] In fact fables universalise any human experience, and if they were about animals or slaves that was not because those who told them were in some sense advocates of animal or slaves' rights, but because the choice of animals or slaves made it possible (where the story demanded it) to ignore social distinctions, to simplify a story to a level where an audience unaware of the significance of such distinctions could understand the point being made. That is only one reason why the fable was ideal teaching material for small children. Far from being potentially revolutionary, the form of the fable made it authoritarian: the moral at the end of the story has to be accepted, it cannot be argued about, and it is therefore eminently suitable for telling to children without provoking them to ask 'Why?' If the animal fable is associated with slaves and freedmen such as Aesop and Phaedrus, then this is not because these fables preserved the experiences of slaves, but rather because they were characteristically told to children by their *paedagogi*: by men who were often slaves or freedmen, yet had a close and authoritative relationship with their wards. Of course many fables in the literary form in which they appear in the collections preserved are far too complicated to be aimed primarily at children; and we are told that adults too enjoyed listening to fables. One thing that strikes the modern reader is that even in those fables whose plots are quite simple and presumably intended for children, there was no attempt to protect the minds of the young from learning about sex and violence.[9]

The role of animals in these fables alerts us to that fact that, far more than in our own world, children had animals to play with. We recall Pliny's account of Regulus' son: 'The child had lots of ponies, yoked together and single, he had large dogs, little dogs, nightingales, parrots, blackbirds.' The child riding in a scaled-down chariot is a common motif on sarcophagi; as with similar representations of adults riding away in chariots, they probably symbolise the apotheosis of the deceased youngster's soul. But representations of chariots or carts being pulled by sheep (e.g. in scenes from Ostia and in the Vatican and Louvre: plate 19) may well be realistic. There were also toy chariots: Horace mentions one pulled by mice. Lesbia's sparrow and Corinna's parrot show that young adults as well as children had pets. Greek vase-illustrations suggest that pets as exotic as a cheetah might be kept.[10] The terracotta models of cows, horses, deer, goats, and pigs were generally of animals that the child would have had a chance to see: models of lions, tigers, bears, and elephants are conspicuously missing.

The Latin word for play was *ludus*. The same word was applied to adult games, including religious ceremonies; and the word *ludus* was also used for 'school'. The way the word *ludus* applies to all these activities suggests that Romans saw play first and foremost as practice, including our concept of play as 'role-learning'. 'Study should be interrupted with periods of play . . . for many games are quite useful for sharpening children's intellectual capacity, such as when they ask one another riddles.' Play, like school, prepares the child for adult life, mainly by imitation.[11]

Latin writers discussed other ways of interpreting play, including the 'relaxation theory' and the 'surplus energy theory'. Phaedrus' fable of the bow which is always kept taut, and Cicero's account of Roman senators collecting sea-shells, are examples of the former. Cicero sometimes sees play as evidence that children, like some adults, do not have the intellectual or moral capacity to do 'proper' work. Of course games must not be allowed to get out of hand, for children as for adults. The theme that children and adults waste too much time playing is a *topos* found in poets like Ovid as well as teachers like Quintilian. Dice playing was restricted by law to the Saturnalia, a time when 'play' was appropriate to both adults and children. Just as ordinary peasants play football or dice when the weather prevents them from working, and intellectual senators spend their holidays studying literature or mathematics, music or philosophy, so there are appropriate *ludi* to develop the minds of children in the direction of humanity and virtue. 'Building sand-castles, harnessing mice to a chariot, playing 'Odd or Even?', riding on a broomstick' – that was characteristic and acceptable for children. 'Let him who cannot yet love his studies play, so that he will not come to hate them.'[12]

Babies less that 18 months old engage in what child psychologists call 'practice play'. Like babies today, they were attracted by noises, colours, and light. The first toy a child was given was a rattle, *sistrum* or *crepitaculum*. Ancient examples include ones of metal with a handle, or of pottery, with a number of pebbles inside. Others were in the shape of familiar birds: hens and doves. St Jerome noted that children liked shiny stones; the *bulla* that hung around his neck attracted a boy for this reason; for the rich, it might be made of gold.[13] Mobiles had not yet been invented, but where there were no helmets with plumes, babies could always talk to trees whose branches moved in the wind.

By 6 months, the child would be rattling *crepundia*, a line of little playthings dangling from a string. This could be worn across the shoulder, and might include open hands, to avert the Evil Eye. In Roman comedy, these *crepundia* were the standard token by which foundlings could be reunited with their parents.[14]

From 18 months on, after they have begun to speak, children's play becomes symbolic of what they see in the world around them. Obvious examples are playing at 'house', or building sandcastles: 'They pile up sand on the beach in imitation of a house'; Horace mentions how a 3-year-old will have a tantrum when his sandcastle is destroyed.[15] Between 4 and 7, the symbolism becomes 'collective', what is known as socio-dramatic play: children act out the roles of adults. We have seen how much accounts of the childhood of rulers in biography and panegyric made of supposed indications of later adult qualities in the way they behaved as children (Chapter 2 above). But that did not apply only to rulers: Horace makes a dying father say:

> Since the time when I saw that you, Aulus, carrying your dice
> and nuts about in a fold of your tunic, handing them out as
> presents and playing with them, while you, Tiberius, solemnly
> counted them and stored them in secret crannies, I was
> concerned that a different madness might affect each of you [sc.
> that one would grow up to be a spendthrift, the other a miser].[16]

How a child played pointed towards his behaviour as an adult, but not to the extent of determining it. If the child's behaviour suggested moral imperfections, it was not too late for the parents to do something about it, as Quintilian observed. And adults might misunderstand the child's behaviour: Fabius Maximus, the Roman general who wore down Hannibal's army by 'delaying' battle and was therefore called 'Cunctator', was thought to be slow and stupid as a child – but that, says Plutarch, was only an indication that he was going to be a careful and thoughtful adult.[17]

The evidence for the social roles acted out by girls in their play is, not surprisingly, sparse. There are no reminiscences of how girls were prepared in childhood to accept their subservient role as wives. Certain skills were specifically female: even the daughters of the imperial household were taught to spin. Providing sufficient yarn for the needs of the household required an enormous outlay of labour in antiquity, and it may well be said that the female half of the population spent every waking hour spinning so long as they had just one hand free. At Roman weddings, the bride symbolically carried a spindle and distaff.

Marriage was assumed to be what made a girl's childhood meaningful (see pp. 41ff. above). The selective infanticide or exposure of females seems to have resulted in a surplus of males; at any rate it was assumed that all females would marry – the Latin language required no word for 'spinster' (where necessary, *vidua*, 'widow', was used). At all social levels, the first marriage was arranged by the parents, and occurred at an early age. A girl might be betrothed before she could speak: Vipsania Agrippina (the daughter of Agrippa and granddaughter of Atticus) was betrothed to Tiberius before she was 1 year old. While there continued to be no strict minimum age for betrothal, the third-century jurist Modestinus required that 'both sides must understand what is happening, that is, they must be seven years old'.[18]

We may speculate about some of the consequences of early and arranged marriages. Girls had no need to learn courtship techniques; skill in dancing might even suggest immorality. There was generally less call for making children aware of gender distinctions, for instance by making boys and girls wear different clothes. Both normally wore tunics, and on very formal occasions both wore togas (e.g. on Augustus' *Ara Pacis*). There was no hesitation in allowing boys and girls to play together; a sarcophagus in the Vatican shows thirteen children variously playing 'nuts' and fighting. Nine are boys, four girls (Plate 20). Other social distinctions were very much more important than those of gender. We have seen from one of Pliny's letters how, as time went on, a girl could prove her high status through attention to literary studies. For a girl, a scroll might symbolise a more important social distinction than that of gender.[19]

In Rome, as in other cultures, one type of gender-specific toy was the doll. It is interesting that these were not baby-dolls (which first appear in England in the early nineteenth century), but models of young women of marriageable age: the girl was not being prepared for her role as a childminder so much as expected to identify with the ideal of an (attractive) wife. At their marriage, when they were to become 'real' wives, these dolls were solemnly dedicated to Venus.[20] While the literary evidence for dolls is sparse, there is a considerable amount of archaeological support.

Rag dolls have been found from the Roman period from Egypt. Most ancient dolls are of terracotta, some with movable arms and legs, and others painted. Ivory dolls were both high in status, and attractive because shiny. One such was the famous doll belonging to Crepereia: it was 22 centimetres long, and had two gold bracelets and a ring. Another ivory doll was found in the coffin of the late Roman Empress Maria, child-bride of Honorius at the beginning of the fifth century AD. There is no evidence for dolls' houses: and the model furniture found in shrines as dedications to gods seems to have had a different function.[21]

The hall-mark of boys' games was status differentiation: someone would be acclaimed as 'leader' or 'winner', and sometimes someone would be picked out as a 'loser'. Despite the Roman republic's aversion to monarchy, children continued to label their winners as *rex*, 'king': a characteristic chant was *rex eris si recte facies*, 'You will be king if you get it right', and in ball-games the winner was called 'king', the loser 'sheep'. The 'leader' might be selected by tossing a coin: the call was 'Heads or Ships', variously *capita aut navia, caput aut navem*, and we are told that 'generally *navem* is corruptly pronounced *naviam*'.[22]

Then as now, children found the roles of social and political leaders particularly attractive. The large number of references to children acting out 'kings' or, where a republican ideology was paramount, 'judges', is not simply the result of our sources' concentration on the children of the elite; children of all classes found elite roles more interesting, because in any society they are the most visible. Soldiers (indeed any group with special clothing or insignia) are particularly visible; and some Roman parents encouraged their children to play at soldiers by providing them with military uniforms.[23] Civilian officials were just as attractive: 'What children copy – magistracies and the Senate and the *fasces* of office and law-courts – adults play at in all seriousness in the Campus Martius and the Forum and the Senate-House.' As a literary theme, the idea that a future leader is picked as a leader by his playmates goes back to Herodotus' account of Cyrus' childhood. Nero was so frightened when he heard that his step-son Rufrius Crispinus was 'playing at generals', that, according to Suetonius, he found it necessary to have the boy drowned during a fishing trip. Plutarch tells us how justly Cato the Younger behaved when a group of adolescents were abusing their power over smaller boys as 'judges' during a birthday party. Septimius Severus also played at 'judges'.[24]

Well-brought-up Christian children, like their parents, were not interested in such secular office holding. Alexander, bishop of Alexandria, was said to have been strolling along the sea-shore one day when he saw some children playing: they were playing at 'bishops', and the one who had been chosen to be bishop over them was none other than Athanasius, later to be a great theologian. In Syria in the fourth century, children found a new way of dividing up into 'goodies' and 'baddies': they played at 'monks and demons': 'one little girl, dressed in rags, puts her friends into stitches of laughter by exorcising them'.[25]

While children were generally conservative in their choice of leadership roles to play, the 'teams' they divided up into might reflect recent events. One of the omens which presaged Octavian's victory over Cleopatra at Actium was that the children of Rome played at 'Octavians and Antonians'; after a two-day-long battle in the streets, the 'Octavians' won. Later, children replayed the battle: 'Your brother leads the other side, the pond is the Adriatic Sea. . .'. During the Byzantine reconquest of Italy from the Goths in the sixth century AD, the children of Samnite shepherds turned their wrestling matches into a contest between 'Vittigis' and 'Belisarius'.[26]

Horse riding, as always, was a sign of social superiority; children played at riding if they were too young to ride, or without access to the real thing. Horace refers to an old man riding on a broomstick as a sign of second childhood. Socrates was said to have ridden around on a broomstick, to the delight of his small children, and despite the criticism of Alcibiades. We may note that one of the few precise references to a child's age occurs in Galen's recommendation that at the age of 7, make-believe riding could give place to actual riding.[27]

Just as children copied the behaviour of adults in the serious business of politics and soldiering, so they also wished to copy their less serious pastimes. It is not surprising that ancient authors remark (often critically) on children's keenness on chariot racing and gladiatorial contests. Nero, as a little boy, was once too interested in discussing a recent crash by the Blue team (*prasini*) to pay attention to his teacher, and lied that he had been discussing the story of Hector (dragged round Troy in Homer's *Iliad*). There are hints that some parents were as willing to support such interests as to provide their children with toy uniforms. Toy chariots are a standard theme on the sarcophagi of children (see p. 146 above), and Juvenal tells of a doting father who allows his son to play with a uniform of the Greens when he appears at table.[28]

Between the ages of 7 and 12, children move on to a different kind of play, games with rules, which typically involve physical strength, an element of risk or chance, and the development of the intellectual capacities needed to win ('strategy'). Such games include versions of 'Catch' or 'Hide-and-Seek', for which the only evidence from antiquity is in Horace.[29]

There is much more evidence for games developing skill in manipulating objects. A common pastime was catching things in the mouth, with danger of death by choking – Claudius lost one of his sons in this way. Other games of skill involved knucklebones, and nuts, equivalent to our marbles. These games had complicated rules, and it was assumed that they were as suitable for adults as for children; betting might be involved.[30] The anonymous elegiac poem *Nux* lists a number of games of skill involving nuts. The first was to place three nuts close together and then try to throw a fourth nut so as to land on top of the other three without forcing them apart. The second was to roll a nut down a slope so as to hit another. The third was called 'Odd or Even'. One player held a number of nuts in his hand and another had to guess either how many there were, or simply whether they were odd or even in number. The fourth game was rather more complicated: a triangle (hence the game was named after the Greek letter *delta*) was drawn in chalk, containing a number of parallel lines; the nut was thrown into the triangle so as to pass the maximum number of lines without leaving the figure altogether. Finally, there was a 'nux' game which involved throwing a nut into a pot with a narrow neck (*orca*).[31]

In this context we have to list other games of skill and chance, such as 'Ducks and Drakes' mentioned by Minucius Felix, and the ball-games which were played by adults as well as children. Pliny the Younger had two courts, *sphaeristeria*, on his country estate. Different games had rules with varying degrees of complication: 'Datatim ludere' involved two players, 'Trigon' three; 'Harpaston' required snatching the ball from the other players. There are no references to team-games of the English kind. Children would play ball-games of this kind in the street: the *Digest* envisages the possibility of fatal accidents as a result.[32]

Complicated game-rules suggest that 7 to 12 was also the age when children played with tops. Like the ball, the top appears in literature as a symbol of man's fate, tossed about by the gods. Persius had played with one as a boy. But both toys and games might be intended for adults as well as children – like the complicated mechanical toys constructed by Hellenistic engineers.[33]

If 7 was the age when boys would be turning towards these 'adult' games, it was also the time when they would be expected to start on other 'adult' activities, of which the acquisition of literary skills was the most important for free-born children under the empire. The phrase 'Laying aside your nuts' was equivalent to 'going to school'. Martial recommends the reading of Vergil's *Culex* to those who find the *Aeneid* heavy going: 'Here is eloquent Vergil's *Culex*; don't put aside your nuts and read the *Aeneid*.'[34] Toys and games may not have been exclusively the preserve of children, but they were certainly perceived as symbols of childhood. We have seen that girls dedicated their dolls to Venus just before their wedding, while boys gave their *bulla* to their household Lares when they put on the *toga virilis*. The idea of 'putting away childish things' when one became an adult was expressed by St Paul, and is echoed by many dedication-poems in the collection of poems known as the 'Greek' or 'Palatine' Anthology. The list of items a Greek boy might dedicate to Hermes includes bow and arrows, ball, rattle, knucklebones and children's clothes. Galen's remarks about exchanging hobby-horses for real ones suggest that the age of 7 was seen as a suitable point for turning to more serious things: a late poem in the Greek Anthology is a Christian dedication of such toys:

Today, dear God, I am seven years old, and must play no more. Here is my top, my hoop, and my ball: keep them all, my Lord.[35]

If a child was capable of playing adult games from the age of 7, then there were other adult activities that he or she was also now physically strong enough to undertake. Where children were raised in order to provide economic security for their parents, there was no room for any sentimental objections to child labour. From about the age of 7, both slave and free-born children might begin to be taught a specialised skill: what we would describe as 'professional training' would include training in reading, writing, and counting for a substantial proportion of the population (girls as well as boys, slave as well as free), and for free males, the skill of competence in literature: the *artes liberales*. But if a child was unable, or not yet able, to acquire any of these useful *artes*, it was taken for granted that he or she would begin to do whatever 'useful' work he could as soon as he was physically strong and co-ordinated enough to do so, and capable of understanding what it was that was required. That of course applied to children of low social status, slaves and peasants. If the children of the upper classes were not required to work, then that was not because they were too young, but because physical labour would not be expected of persons of their class as adults either.

Explicit references to the kind of work done by children are scarce, but that is as likely to be due to the fact that it was taken for granted as that it was unusual; again, analogy with other pre-industrial societies is instructive.[36] Only in the context of agriculture and, occasionally, training for handicrafts, do we have documentary evidence of the actual ages of individual children involved. Uncertainty about the age of a *puer* poses a major interpretational problem: the word can of course refer to a slave of any age as well as to a child, but many persons of slave status were children, and it is frequently impossible to make more than an informed guess at the age of a slave sent to fetch something or deliver a message. Lawyers' comments suggest that this linguistic ambiguity caused problems in antiquity too: 'A reference to *pueri* can have three meanings. (a) We can call all slaves *pueri*; (b) We may mean boys as opposed to girls; (c) When we refer to children.'[37] Certainly many of the functions performed by slaves as attendants, cleaners, or messengers could be, and were, done by young children.

Children under the age of about 5 years could clearly not be of much help around the house or in the fields, and the *Digest* specifies that a slave under that age should be estimated (for fiscal purposes) as unable to provide labour services of any value, just like a slave who was an invalid. Of course this refers only to their ability to do work; it does not imply that children under that age were valueless – but their value (the price a purchaser would have been prepared to pay for them) would only have been realised once the child had become older. At the age of 10, a slave-child was unquestionably able to provide his owner with some revenue.[38]

Roman agricultural writers took it for granted that children would be engaged in certain unskilled jobs on the land. The exact age of a child agricultural worker did not matter very much, and is rarely referred to. When Columella says that cattle have to be looked after by older men, but *pueri* are able to look after the smaller farm animals, he is not talking about slaves, but children: those who are able to return home to the farmstead each night need not be physically as strong or mature as those who have to stay out on the cattle ranges for long periods. Hence boys, and even girls, can look after those animals that remain based on the farm. The farmyard fowl can easily be looked after by children. Columella recommends that there should be an adult in charge of a maximum of two hundred chickens, but that he should have the assistance of either 'an old woman who is still active or a boy to chase after those birds which go astray, and prevent them from being snatched by thieves or wild animals'. Looking after a couple of goats on the mountainside was an appropriate task for a little girl whose parents were poor.[39]

In the vineyards too there seems to have been work for young children: Columella refers to 'the amount of pruning that one child-hand might do in a day', and although the Latin phrase *puerilis una opera* might mean no more than 'slave', Columella is more likely in the context to mean 'even a child'. At harvest time, the bigger landowners needed as much seasonal labour as they could get. In Roman times, as in the Mediterranean world today, whole families would be hired to help bring in the harvest.[40] An Egyptian papyrus from *c.* AD 100 specifies that children who helped at the olive harvest should be paid up to 4 obols a day, while adult men received a full drachma (6 obols). These harvesters would not just be the children of local peasant families, but also those of village or urban craftsmen, earning the cash which the family would need for those money-payments which had to be made throughout the year until the next harvest-time. One of the Apocryphal Gospels tells how Jesus helped out with the harvest before he was 8 years old, as well as helping (or hindering) his father Joseph in the family carpentry business.[41]

In respect of the training of slaves, as in most matters, the ideal of every Roman household was to be self-sufficient. In his

155

biography of Atticus, Cornelius Nepos bestows especial praise on his subject for not just ensuring that all his slaves were educated, but for having them educated within his own household: 'To train one's slaves by one's own effort rather than by paying someone else is a sign of an industrious character.' We have a considerable amount of epigraphical evidence about the training process for young slaves of the *paedagogium* of the imperial household, including anti-Christian graffiti from the slave-children's classroom.[42]

Only when the *paterfamilias* himself was unable to teach the *ars* which he wanted his child, or his slave, to learn, would he hand the child over to someone who was an expert in that skill; and that applied whether the *ars* was shoemaking or literature. The *Digest* suggests that at Rome masters who intended their slaves to learn a skill would hire them out at about the age of 7 to be apprenticed to free craftsmen, if there was no one who might teach them the required trade within the household. We have references to children being trained as smiths and shoemakers: one legal dispute arose when a shoemaker beat a disobedient slave boy, who had been apprenticed to him, so badly as to cause permanent injury. The course of training might take several years. Lawyers were asked to rule on whether 'hairdressers' mentioned in a will included those girls who had not yet completed the course. For slaves as for other children such basic skills as writing and counting might be taught not within the household, but by payment to a teacher who was an outsider. Teachers could be found to train slaves in some rather curious skills: when Calvisius Sabinus found that he could not buy on the open market a gang of slaves who knew Greek literature off by heart, he had a contractor train a dozen slaves for him.[43]

But the father remained the ideal teacher, and the relationship between a father and his sons was accepted as a paradigm for Roman public life in general.[44] The emperor Augustus claimed not just to be an ideal father to the whole Roman community, *Pater Patriae*, but also to have restored republican ideals of family life to his own household. He did not indeed go so far as to make his daughter look after the imperial goats, or his grandsons help with the olive harvest. But he did make sure that they were trained, within the imperial household, in those *artes* appropriate to their station. 'He had his daughter and granddaughters brought up [the Latin *instituit* means "trained"] in such a way that he even got them accustomed to spinning wool, and forbade them from saying or doing anything that could not be made public and broadcast in the daily records', as Suetonius informs us. But Augustus behaved in an equally authoritarian manner towards the male children of his family. He formally adopted his grandsons Gaius and Lucius Caesar into his own household, and

> he normally taught his grandsons letters, swimming and other elementary skills himself; and he was particularly insistent that they should copy his style of handwriting. Whenever they ate together, the grandchildren would sit at the foot of his couch; and whenever they went on a journey, they would either ride in the carriage before him, or ride on horseback alongside of him.[45]

The skills which the good *paterfamilias* like Augustus taught the children of his household were intended to prepare them for adult life. So long as the classical city maintained its clear distinction between children and adult citizens, these skills in themselves could not turn a boy of citizen birth into an adult; but for those who were not citizens, or for whom citizenship did not matter because they did not have the means to exercise their rights to take part in public life, the effective command of *artes* was what distinguished the adult from the child. Consequently, as the privileges of citizenship gradually became less important over the centuries, the acquisition of *artes* became the crucial step towards acceptance as an adult, not just for slaves but for free children too. The difference was that for the free child – at least, if his family hoped he would be able to take part in public life – the skills in question were not those of the hairdresser and the shoemaker, but the *artes liberales*, the skills expected of a free man.

The Latin word for skill, *ars*, is not used merely of technical or managerial skills which have to be learnt systematically (like the Greek **TEXNH**), but also of social skills, behavioural patterns which are acquired as a result of experience, practice, or systematic learning (as opposed to being innate). Thus the historian Sallust describes bravery in warfare as an *ars*. Acquired moral virtues such as financial integrity and application to hard work are described as *artes* by writers from the republic to late antiquity. The political skills of the powerful are *artes*: Tacitus can say of Nero's ministers Burrus and Seneca that 'they had equal authority based on different *artes*'. Vergil's famous lines predicting that Rome's special *artes* will be to rule the world and to impose the habits of peace on her subjects, in contrast to others who will be famous for the *artes* of rhetoric and sculpture, illustrates how an *ars* could be an acquired pattern of behaviour as much as a specific skill, though it was that too: in Plautine comedy, the most frequently cited *ars* is cooking.[46]

The difference between the Latin word *ars* and the Greek ΤΕΧΝΗ reveals markedly different cultural attitudes to the learning process. The Greek word could never be used to refer to an aspect of behaviour, like the Roman phrase *optimae artes* (perhaps equivalent to 'a person with the best social graces'). A ΤΕΧΝΗ was the skill expected of a particular technical expert, and hence distinct from (and less educationally valuable than) the general knowledge expected from those who wished to play their part as full citizens, the ΕΓΚΥΚΛΙΟΣ ΠΑΙΔΕΙΑ. Although certain activities appropriate to free men, most crucially warfare and the art of rhetoric, were ΤΕΧΝΑΙ, the aim of education (including study of literature) for a future citizen was ΠΑΙΔΕΙΑ. When Greeks used phrases like ΕΛΕΥΘΕΡΙΑΙ ΤΕΧΝΑΙ, 'skills appropriate to a free citizen', they were using ΤΕΧΝΑΙ in a metaphorical sense.[47]

For the Romans, there was no such distinction: rhetoric, soldiering, medicine, architecture – these were all *artes*, and so were the constituents of the secondary education which corresponded to the Greek ΕΓΚΥΚΛΙΟΣ ΠΑΙΔΕΙΑ, the *artes liberales*. In late antiquity, their canonical number was fixed at seven, largely because of the popularity of Martianus Capella's description of them in his book *On the Wedding of Mercury and Philology*.

One of the corollaries of this attitude towards *artes* is that the process of learning is not so much a matter of systematically assimilating theory from someone who is a professional teacher, but rather watching and copying the behaviour of someone who already possesses the *ars*. Hence a deep Roman suspicion of professional teachers: the ideal teacher was the *paterfamilias* or his appointee. It is a commonplace to contrast the Roman method of teaching by *exempla* with the inferior Greek method of teaching by means of *praecepta*: 'We do not learn just with our eyes, but with our ears.'[48] Hence also the reason why the Romans, despite their strong tendency to regulate and systematise behaviour, were surprisingly slow to provide systematic training in the things they were really good at – fighting, architecture, even jurisprudence.

Modern legal historians have shown considerable interest in reconstructing the education of lawyers in Roman times. Nevertheless it must be emphasised that legal teaching remained highly informal until the early principate, and only really became systematised in the second century AD in response to the needs of the increasing numbers of Greeks who were acquiring Roman citizenship and hence needed experts in Roman law.[49] Until that happened, Romans learnt their law by listening to those who were already experts, as Cicero had done. And legal experts, like every other Roman *paterfamilias*, passed their *ars* on to their own sons before anyone else.

Where particular Roman writers did discuss the theory or practice of teaching, as in rhetoric, they generally developed ideas that had appeared in earlier Greek theoretical writings. What was discussed was generally the content of the *ars*, not the process by which it could be learnt. Learning jurisprudence or land surveying, like learning good table manners, was a matter of attending an expert and watching how it was done; and that also applied to learning the alphabet or learning literature. It followed that there was no intrinsic reason why the skill concerned should not be learnt by a child as well as by an adult of whatever age (so long, of course, as the skills which were themselves required to learn the new skill had already been mastered; learning to read had to precede learning literature).

Given the importance of fighting as the one activity that defined the adult male citizen in republican Rome, as in the classical Greek city-states, the absence of any theoretical training in the art of war is perhaps the most striking illustration of this Roman attitude to the learning process. Although by the first century AD individuals seem to have been able to opt out of military service at the cost of losing their chance of political promotion, military service normally continued to be a condition for entry to a political career under the empire as it had been in the time of the republic. The career structure for officers appears to have become more standardised under the early empire. There was a minimum age of 18 years, and inscriptions suggest that from the time of the Flavians on, military tribunes were appointed after they had already served for a year in one of the junior political posts (the *vigintiviri*). Nevertheless it seems that the young officer was still appointed without any formal training; Romans continued to learn the art of war by seeing how it was done as members of the military staff of an experienced general into whose care their father, or one of their father's patrons, had entrusted them.[50]

It has been argued that the existence of a genre of books in Latin on military matters, *de re militari*, shows that there was such formal training. At the risk of digressing, it is worth considering this question in some detail. There were no technical expositions of the subject like those Greek works which from the fourth century BC on had been produced by and for professional soldiers (e.g. Aeneas Tacticus' treatise on the defence of cities). Nor were books considered an acceptable substitute for personal experience, or even a way of systematising the experience gained through personal observation. In his history of the war against Jugurtha, Sallust puts into the mouth of Marius a withering attack on those officers whose knowledge of fighting comes from Greek handbooks instead of practical experience: 'I know some men who after they had been elected consul, started reading accounts of historical events and Greek military handbooks. You may practise a skill after becoming skilful; but in real experience you first have to practise, in order to become skilful.'[51]

Attempts to compile evidence for the use of such textbooks by Romans preparing to lead an army are unconvincing.[52] Cicero includes the reading of Xenophon's *Cyropaedia* and military textbooks by Pyrrhus and one of his generals, Cinna, in a list of the preparations he made for taking command of the province of Cilicia. The context makes it clear that this is meant to be a joke, partly at Cicero's own expense as an inexperienced commander. There does indeed seem to be one occasion where Cicero is serious in recommending the reading of Xenophon's *Cyropaedia*, but that is because it concerns itself with how a ruler ought to behave (morally), not a commander (technically): his brother Quintus ought to study Xenophon, not to become a better soldier, but in order to learn to take more account of *fama* during the remainder of his period as governor of the province of Asia. There is some evidence that inexperienced Roman commanders were anxious to read up on Roman history, as Marius had indicated in his speech. Cicero, for example, says that Lucullus' military successes in the war against Mithridates were particularly remarkable because he had had no previous military experience. But once appointed to command the Roman army in Asia Minor, he lost no time: 'He spent the entire voyage and journey out there partly in talking with experts, partly in reading about military history, so that he left Rome with no military experience but arrived in Asia Minor as a general.'[53]

Roman historical writings naturally contained a great deal of military information, but that did not make them technical treatises. It is not clear that there were any such treatises in the republican period. Cato the Elder wrote about military affairs; the account of this work, referred to as *De re militari*, given by Vegetius suggests that it may have been a pamphlet advocating military reforms rather than a manual of instruction for trainee officers. Vegetius, writing in the first half of the fifth century AD, ascribes to Cato the view that his book would be useful for the republic, since writing preserves for ever experiences which otherwise would survive for no more than one lifetime. But not enough survives of Cato's work to enable us to say for certain whether it was in fact a self-contained pamphlet, or part of the encyclopaedia of essential *artes* which as a good *paterfamilias* he compiled for the benefit of his son. If the latter, then it will have been very much in the tradition of Roman teaching, an example of a father passing on his experience to his son in a series of moral exhortations. Like the approach we find in Cato's other writings, it would have given authoritative information in a series of 'facts', rather than systematically expounding a theory.[54]

Even in the time of the empire, systematic teaching of military expertise remained Greek rather than Latin. In the first century AD, Onasander dedicated an 'Account of Generalship', ΣΤΡΑΤΗΓΙΚΟΣ ΛΟΓΟΣ, to a Roman consular; but Onasander's examples are taken from Greek tradition. There are no references to specifically Roman events or customs – the discussion of omens, for instance, makes no reference to the famous Roman sacred chickens. But from the second century BC on, as Greeks tended to have less and less experience in the practice of warfare because of increasing Roman military control over the Mediterranean, the writings they produced on the subject became increasingly scholarly and pedantic. In the early second century AD, Aelian's discussion contained no references to Rome other than in its preface; most of it was about the working of the phalanx as it had been used by the Macedonians several centuries earlier. The work is dedicated to

Trajan, and Aelian claims that it will be 'useful', ΩΦΕΛΙΜΟΝ. What he means is 'useful' for the grammarian: 'useful' in helping Trajan to understand the literary accounts of the wars of Alexander the Great which that emperor found so fascinating, and to which Aelian refers in his preface. Roman as well as Greek grammarians saw their craft as including the exposition of military passages in both prose and verse authors.[55]

Of Paternus and Catilina, two of the three other Roman writers on warfare mentioned by Vegetius, we know nothing. Frontinus' theoretical treatise on fighting has been lost; but the surviving *Strategemata*, 'On Stratagems', shows that, like other Romans, he was not writing *praecepta*, but compiling inexorable lists of precedents and examples from past history, Greek as well as Roman.

Our survey of Roman treatises on military affairs illustrates a fact of some importance. In the very area in which the Romans excelled, military expertise, there were no systematic training manuals until late antiquity. There is a parallel here with jurisprudence: in both areas, training manuals appear after Greeks begin to enter the imperial service in large numbers as a result of the spread of citizenship in the wake of the *Constitutio Antoniniana* of AD 212. Before this time, the Roman attitude towards military training remained decidedly amateur. Roman officers continued to receive their training as apprentices by seeing how their father or one of his friends did it, and not by systematic instruction – certainly not according to any textbook.

The third century saw both the spread of citizenship and the exclusion of members of the senatorial or landowning classes from military commands in favour of professional soldiers after AD 238. Both factors reinforced the process whereby the *ars* of the soldier ceased to be an essential skill for an adult male. The city *iuventus*-associations disappeared, to survive in frontier regions as courses in military training for the sons of soldiers. Recognition as an adult was no longer associated with the state's need for citizens who could fight; instead, other *artes* – a knowledge of literature (the *artes liberales*), followed by what Livy had called the *artes urbanae*, rhetoric or jurisprudence – were required of those who wished to serve either their local community or the emperor. But they were just as much technical skills as the *ars militaris*. We may note the frequency with which Quintilian applies the same metaphor of military training to his rhetoric course (that Roman poets applied the metaphor to love needs no discussion). And as the privileged status of the citizen became less and less important, so the acquisition of the *artes liberales* came to be the best way in which a child was able to obtain a position in public life. The sooner a child acquired these skills, the sooner would he be recognised as a full, adult, member of his community.[56]

A considerable number of studies of Roman schooling exists.[57] It will suffice to mention some of those aspects which illustrate the Roman empire's changing attitudes to childhood.

We have seen that for Romans learning was a matter of internalising practical skills, *artes*, and the responsibility for this fell on the head of the household, assisted by a wide range of relatives and subordinates. The idea of a 'school' (like the word itself), a formal institution where many children were collected together and taught the same thing, was a creation of the Greek city; its earliest purpose appears to have been to train children to perform hymns as a choir representing the community. (Hence one theory for the origin of the phrase ΕΓΚΥΚΛΙΟΣ ΠΑΙΔΕΙΑ, 'all-round education': it was education for the round circle, ΚΥΚΛΟΣ, in which the chorus performed.)[58] The more democractic a community was, the greater the proportion of children who studied this literary syllabus; a city like Athens needed professional schoolteachers, and by the fifth century BC had developed a three-tier system of education. First the ΓΡΑΜΜΑΤΙΣΤΗΣ taught the skills associated with letters, ΓΡΑΜΜΑΤΑ; then the ΓΡΑΜΜΑΤΙΚΟΣ taught literature; and finally the rhetorician taught the sons of the elite the art of speaking in public.

This educational system and the public teaching that accompanied it were artificial imports to the Roman world. There is no firm evidence of schools in Rome before the late third century BC; Plutarch says that Livius Andronicus, from the Greek city of Tarentum, was the first *grammaticus* at Rome in BC 234.[59] Throughout our period, the rich preferred to have their children taught within their own household, though often in relatively large groups including the children of dependants and friends. The artificial nature of the 'school' is illustrated by the fact that it was called a *ludus*: like games and spectacles, 'school' was contrasted

163

with serious life. But the syllabus, as well as the institution, was artificial: the first subject matter to be taught was not Latin, but Greek literature; the whole idea that children should study academic material rather than practical subjects came from Greece. Indeed as late as Cicero's schooldays in the early first century BC, Roman children had learnt to read from practical texts as well as poetry: the law code of the Twelve Tables. Only in the early empire did schoolteachers develop the Latin literary syllabus centred on the prose authors Cicero and Sallust, and the poets Terence and Vergil. Because both the syllabus, and the school as an institution, were unconnected with Roman social realities, they could exist independently of each other, and at least one – the syllabus – could survive the end of antiquity, and indeed throughout the European Middle Ages.[60]

The skills taught were skills which adults required if they were to be accepted as active citizens rather than uneducated peasants. These skills were enforced upon children according to rules which reflected the priorities of adults, but which children were often incapable of following – as a number of experienced teachers such as Quintilian, Jerome, and Augustine realised. It is logical to think that if a child can master the most difficult problems, he will find everything else easy. If a Latin-speaker masters the Greek alphabet, he will find the Latin alphabet easy. Schoolmasters began by teaching five- or six-year-olds the Greek alphabet; once they had managed that, it was thought, children could apply the same *ars* to learning the Latin alphabet later. As we have seen, it was generally supposed that 7 was the appropriate age to start learning letters; but there was nothing peculiar about much older children, or even adults, attending the school of the *litterator*, like some German hostages in the time of Caligula.[61]

The first thing a child had to learn was the names of the letters, *elementa*, from alpha to omega; then he had to learn them backwards, from omega to alpha. Only after that was he shown what the letters actually looked like. Quintilian and Jerome both remark on the absurdity of this, and recommend the use of 'toy' letters made of ivory, 'and anything else which one can think of which that age finds enjoyable, which it is a pleasure to handle, look at, or say the name of'. The representations of Homer's *Iliad* on stone which have been found from various parts of the Roman world were presumably visual aids for teaching the text.[62] After having learnt to write individual letters, a child would learn to recognise groups of letters, and finally whole words. The theologian Rufinus in the fourth century AD categorises the various ability-groups among schoolchildren as 'abecedarii', 'syllabarii', 'nominarii', and 'calculatores'; the last group were those who had mastered reading and spelling out whole words and were learning the numerical values of letters, addition and subtraction (division and multiplication were so complex in antiquity that they were left to professional *calculatores*).[63]

A child was expected to try to read the most obscure and difficult words first, on the grounds that once his grasp of the *elementa* was good enough for him to make out the meaning of the most difficult words, he would be able to read anything. Having learnt words, he would go on to short sentences, taken from collections of moral maxims such as the *Dicta Catonis*, which survived throughout the Middle Ages, and then short stories, such as Avienus' fourth-century translations from Aesop. One of the most famous of these *chriae*, or exercises, consisted of chanting various variations of the phrase 'Study is hard, but its fruits are sweet' in such a way as to use all cases of the word 'study', singular and plural.[64]

Augustine, when he came to write his *Confessions*, described the enormous difference between the natural curiosity that led a child to want to learn to speak, and the often violent way in which society forced him to acquire the *ars* of letters:

> I was sent to school in order to read. I was too young to
> understand what the purpose of the whole thing was, and
> nevertheless if I was idle at my studies, I was flogged; for that
> was the method favoured by our ancestors. Many who had
> passed through this life before us had built up this stony path for
> me to tread; I was forced to follow, adding to the toil and sorrow
> of the sons of Adam.

Parents and children alike saw that play was preferable to work; yet they forced the little Augustine to learn. 'Even as a boy I did not like lessons and hated being forced to study.' After having learnt to master the alphabet, Augustine went on to do Greek literature, which he hated, which was irrelevant to the Latin world he grew up in, and of which he seems to have remembered absolutely nothing as an adult. He enjoyed Latin literature (primarily Vergil) rather more, perhaps because the stories made sense to a child.[65]

But even at this stage, children were 'taught' rather than 'encouraged to learn'. Literature was a corpus of information which the pupil memorised, often in question-and-answer form. Our word 'catechism' is derived from the Greek for this system of learning by 'echoing back'. Surviving grammatical treatises, especially from the fourth and fifth centuries, give us some idea of how unexciting such teaching must have been. Perhaps the most widely used manual of grammar, Donatus' *Ars Minor*, begins:

'How many parts of speech are there?'
'Eight.'
'Which?'
'Noun, pronoun, verb, adverb, participle, conjunction, preposition, interjection.'
'What is a noun? . . . How many cases does a noun have? . . . What are they?'

It is only fair to say that some catechisms and textbooks contained rather more interesting material, but it is striking that most of these were designed to help Greeks to learn Latin after the spread of Roman citizenship in the east (particularly after the *Constitutio Antoniniana* of 212) created an enormous demand for lawyers and other public officials competent in Latin. These are contained in the collection called the *Hermeneumata Pseudodositheana*. Some of the later examples are intended to help Irish monks learn Latin, but the earliest are for adult Greek-speakers; one is dated to 11 September 207. Although some of the passages which students are required to learn to translate describe events in the day of a Roman schoolboy, others refer to administration and military life; and one is a legal text dealing with manumission – exactly what we would expect for Greeks (whatever their age) hoping for jobs in the imperial service or as lawyers.[66]

This catechetical system of teaching was the recognised way of imparting a TEXNH or *ars* throughout the Roman empire, and it is not surprising that Christians found it as acceptable for teaching catechumens the Apostolic Doctrine as schoolmasters did for teaching Homer or Vergil. Arithmetic was learnt in the same way: Horace refers to Roman schoolchildren learning by heart the jingles about the subdivisions of the coinage, and one of the poems of Ausonius in the fourth century gives us the formulae for calculating the divisions of pounds and ounces. Augustine hated these tables: ' "One and one is two, two and two is four" – how I hated that chant.'[67]

This approach recognised the reality that while a child's central memory increases greatly between 5 and 12, few children can 'organise' the information they have memorised before the age of 7. Before that age, repetition is a useful way of encouraging a child to acquire more information, even if it does not help very much with 'retrieval'. The problem was that recitation continued to be the favoured method even for learning literature at 11 or 12; it will not surprise us that Augustine remembered no Greek, or that it often took five or six years before a child knew how to make use of the alphabet, and another six or seven to memorise Vergil; and graffiti suggest that many schoolchildren never got further than the first three or four books of the *Aeneid*.

Experienced teachers saw that children needed additional incentives to study, if only because they were insufficiently 'rational' to understand what was being done to them. 'When they are small, children are given sweets by their teachers to persuade them to learn the alphabet.' 'Sweets, or brightly coloured flowers, or shiny stones, attract children . . . after her efforts, she should spend some time playing, or be cuddled by her mother . . . then she will learn willingly, and not because she is forced to.'[68] The grammarian Caesius Bassus, in the time of Nero, mentions a puzzle consisting of fourteen differently shaped pieces (twelve triangles, a quadrilateral and a pentagon) which the child could form into a square: the *ostomachion* or *loculus Archimedeus*. Practising with this was held to develop the child's powers of memory; but it could also be used to play with, to create other shapes, e.g. an elephant or a gladiator.[69]

The purpose of the system was to make the child so competent at manipulating the *ars* involved – letters, literature, or rhetoric – that he became as good at it as an adult. We may recall Marcus Aurelius' pride at his ability as an orator, or the boys who recited speeches at the funerals of relatives (see Chapter 2 above). There is a statue in the Louvre showing the boy Nero, still wearing the child's *bulla*, as a successful orator. Precocious success made a man out of a child. This did not apply only to future emperors. Knowledge of the inherited corpus of literature, and the ability to speak in public, were the two administrative skills that were needed to govern both individual cities and the empire as a whole; Cassius Dio, in the early third century AD, includes among the points raised by Maecenas in his programmatic speech on the nature of the principate, the need for the children of senators and equestrians to have a school education.[70]

We have seen the great emphasis on education in the letters of Cicero, Pliny, and Fronto, an emphasis reflected in the frequency of references to schooling in the biographies of emperors and others (Chapters 3 and 2 above). The educated child, especially if he had already assimilated the skills of a public speaker, was well on the way to being taken seriously as an adult. Perhaps the most interesting sign that, in the early empire, education was beginning to be seen as overcoming the limitations of childhood, is that this seems to apply not just to those who as adults were to become successful and eloquent in public life, but also to some boys who never survived to hold public office.

Quintilian describes the deaths of his two sons in a highly rhetorical proemium to the sixth book of the *Institutio Oratoriae*. He states that his purpose in writing down his ideas about oratory had originally been so that, 'If it had been me whom the Fates had snatched away, as would have been just and preferable, my sons could still have benefited from their father's instruction'. Such a handbook was the best legacy he could bequeath to a son 'whose outstanding ability deserved the most diligent support on the part of his father'. It is his son's 'outstanding ability' that the rhetorician is most concerned with. Most of the qualities he remembers about his younger son are equally scholarly – apart from the 5-year-old's pleasant appearance and cheerful chatter (§7), he showed signs of 'those tiny sparks of brilliance, and the possession, even at that age, of a gentle and – I know that the reader will hardly believe this – noble disposition; such a child would have deserved to be loved even if he had belonged to someone else'. A further reason why Quintilian found his death hard to accept was that 'this sweet child preferred me to his nurses, to the grandmother who looked after his upbringing and all the others whom children of that age generally find interesting' (§8).

The death of the elder son at the age of 9 was worse. Unlike the younger, he showed signs 'not of budding, but of complete and well-formed fruit'. Quintilian swears that he had seen in him not just outstanding intellectual virtues, including ('something which teachers can sense') a willing application to work, but honesty, respect, humanity, and generosity as well. The incidental qualities which had to be mentioned in a panegyric were there as well: pleasant and clear speech and the ability to express Greek and Latin literature 'as though they were both native to him'. While these qualities promised to develop in the course of time, the 9-year-old boy's serious application to his work and resistance to grief and fear – as evidenced by the way he bore his illness over a period of eight months – are described as characteristic of an adult (*iam matura*). The eulogy ends with the notion that had he lived, the young Quintilian would have been destined to rise to high office and 'be a candidate for the eloquence of his ancestors'.

Although Quintilian had a professional interest in literary education, we should not imagine that his belief that a child who was precocious at school was already 'mature' was untypical. There is a number of Roman sarcophagi of children showing them being taught literature or declaiming rhetorical exercises.[71] One is that of Quintus Sulpicius Maximus in the Conservatori Museum at Rome; he had died at the age of 11. In AD 94, when he was 8, this boy had submitted a rather unoriginal Greek poem for recitation at Domitian's Capitoline Games. Although he did not win a prize, his parents proudly noted on his tomb that 'he had excited admiration because of his tender years'. In AD 106, a 13-year-old actually won a prize. A sarcophagus in the Louvre shows a young child reciting to his teacher; one in the Vatican has eight children, one of them the deceased holding an oration, the others with various attributes of the seven muses. Since these two sarcophagi are 1.18 and 1.22 metres in length, the two boys are unlikely to have been older than 7 or 8 when they died. Girls as well as boys might be represented on their tombs holding the scholar's scroll. One in the British Museum (in Greek, but bearing the Latin name Avita) shows the 10-year-old with a scroll as well as her pet dog.[72]

Some parents, however, expressed the belief that all this study was simply wasted when a child was snatched away by *mors immatura*: 'What was the point of your enduring the rigours of learning literature and of having read words appropriate to the trumpet of rhetoric if relentless death snatched away your childish years?'[73] A girl too may be described on her tomb as precociously learned (*super annos docta*), as well as attractive (*formosa*). 'Had your life been longer, no girl on earth would have been more learned.'[74] For those children whose parents wanted them to learn in order to attain elite positions within their city or in the imperial service, education was a means of overcoming the limitations of childhood. But for those whose children died before they could put those skills to adult use, death made a nonsense of the parents' wish to see their children as fulfilled persons. Learning could provide no answer to the problem of high infant mortality.

NOTES

1 J. Hallett, *Fathers and Daughters in Roman Society* (Princeton, NJ, 1984); K. R. Bradley, 'Dislocation in the Roman family', *Historical Reflections/Reflexions Historiques* 14. 1 (1987), 33–62; S. Dixon, *The Roman Mother* (London, 1988), Chapter 6 on mother-substitutes.

2 The free-born, even high-born Phoenix, Achilles' *paedagogus*: *Iliad* 9,485–95; other famous examples include Themistocles' Sikinnos in Herodotus 8,75 (and Plutarch, *Themistocles* 12.4). Cf. the description of upbringing of Orestes in Aeschylus' *Choephori* 749–60.

3 Pliny, *Letters* 6,3 cf. J. Vogt, *Ancient Slavery and the Ideal on Man* (Eng.trans., Oxford, 1974), Chapter 5.

4 Tacitus, *Dialogus* 29.1; cf. Aulus Gellius 12,1 (reporting the philosopher Favorinus). Other references in G. Herzog-Hauser, 'Nutrix', Pauly-Wissowa, XVII, 1491 ff.

5 Stobaeus, *Eclogia* 2,233 (ed. Wachsmuth); Suetonius, *Claudius* 2.2; *Nero* 6.3. Poor persons of free status might hire themselves out as child minders: Plutarch, *Moralia* 830ab; Epictetus 3,26.7. Tibullus I,3.84 f.; Avienus, *Fables* 1,1–2:

> Rustica deflentem parvum iuraverat olim,
> ni taceat, rabido quod foret esca lupo.

6 Arnobius, *Adversus Gentes* 5,14; Plato, *Sophist* 242c-243b ('they' refers to Parmenides, the addressee's father); Pausanias 1,3.3, criticising the 'democracy' set up at Athens by Theseus. Cf. Quintilian, *Institutio Oratoriae* 1,8.19.

7 *Satires* 2,6.77 ff.; Quintilian, *Institutio Oratoriae* 1,9.2: 'narrare sermone puro . . . condiscant'.

8 J. Christes, 'Reflexe erlebter Unfreiheit in den Sentenzen des Publilius Syrus und den Fabeln des Phaedrus', *Hermes* 107 (1979), 199–220.

9 Phaedrus 1.18; 2.2; 3.3; 3.11. The same is true of Seneca's *Controversiae*, though these were intended for slightly older children. Anthropologists point out that cultures which stress the link between sex and procreation tend not to protect children from learning about adult sexuality.

10 Pliny, *Letters*, 4,2.3; N. Kampen, *Image and Status: Roman Working Women in Ostia* (Berlin, 1981), figs 4, 7 (chariots), 5 (sheep); Horace, *Satires*

2,3.248. A. Ashmead, 'Greek cats: exotic pets kept by rich youths in fifth century Athens as portrayed on Greek vases', *Expedition* 20 (1987), part 3, 38–47.

11 Quintilian, *Institutio Oratoriae* 1,3.11. On play in Rome generally, cf. Jutta Väterlein, *Roma Ludens. Kinder und Erwachsene beim Spiel im antiken Rom* (Amsterdam, 1976); D'A. W. Thompson, 'Games and playthings', *Greece and Rome* 2 (1933), 71.

12 Phaedrus 3.14:

> Puerorum in turba quidam ludentem Atticus
> Aesopum nucibus cum vidisset, restitit
> et quasi delirum risit. Quod sentit simul
> derisor potius quam deridendus senex,
> arcum retonsum posuit in media via;
> 'heus!' inquit 'Sapiens, expedi quo fecerim.'
> concurrit populus. Ille se torquet diu
> nec quaestionis positae causam intellegit.
> Novissime succumbit. tum victor *sophos*:
> 'cito rumpes arcum semper si tensum habueris;
> at si laxaris cum voles erit utilis.
> Sic lusus animo debent aliquando dari,
> ad cogitandum melior ut redeat tibi.'

Cicero, *De Oratore* 2,22; cf. Quintilian, *Institutio Oratoriae* 1,3.10; Cicero, *De Finibus* 5.55; Cicero, *De Officiis* 1,103: 'ut enim pueris non omnem ludendi licentiam damus, sed eam quae ab honestatis actionibus non sit aliena, sic in ipso ioco aliquod probi ingenii lumen eluceat. Duplex omnino est iocandi genus . . . alter est, si tempore fit, ut si remisso animo, magno homine dignus. . . . Ludendi etiam est quidam modus retinendus, ut ne nimis omnia profundamus elatique voluptate in aliquam turpidinem delabamur. Suppeditant autem et campus noster et studia venandi honesta exempla ludendi'; Ovid, *Tristia* 2,471 f., 483 f.; Quintilian, *Institutio Oratoriae* 1,12.18. Dice: Martial, 5,84.1; cf. Plautus, *Miles* 164 f.; Horace, *Odes* 3,24.58. For Symmachus' advice to steer clear of dice, cf. p. 108 above. Cicero, *De Oratore* 3,58; Horace, *Satires* 2,3.247 ff.:

> aedificare casas, plostello adiungere muris
> ludere par impar, equitare in arundine longo.

Quintilian, *Institutio Oratoriae* 1,1.20.

13 Lucretius 5,229 f.; Daremberg-Saglio, *Dictionnaire des antiquités*, I, 2 1561, and figs 2063, 3064; K. Gröber, *Kinderspielzeug aus alter Zeit* (Berlin, 1928), ill. 20; appendix 5, ill. 4. Jerome, *Letters* 128,1,3; Varro, *Lingua Latina* 7,107; Macrobius, *Saturnalia* 1,6.9.

14 Daremberg-Saglio, *Dictionnaire des antiquités* I, 2 1561 with figs 2065–9; Pliny, *NH* 11,270: 'primus sermo anniculo: set semenstris locutus est Croesi filius et in crepundiis prodigio quo totum id concidit regnum'; Terence, *Eunuch* 753; Plautus, *Cistellaria* 635, *Rudens* 1154 ff.

15 Seneca, *De Constantia Sapientis* 12,2; Horace, *Satires* 2,3.247.

16 Horace, *Satires*, 2,3.171 ff.

17 Quintilian, *Institutio Oratoriae* 1,3.12; cf. 1,3.6; Plutarch, *Fabius* 1.3.

18 Nepos, *Atticus* 19.4; *Digest* 23,1.14; Jerome, *Letters* 128,1.

19 Sallust, *Catiline* 25.2: 'saltare elegantius quam necesse est probae'; Ovid, *Amores* 2,4.25 f.; *Ars Amatoria* 3,311 f.; Pliny, *Letters*. 5,16 (pp. 92 f. above).

20 Persius, *Satires* 2,69 f., with a late Scholiast's comment: 'solebant virgines antequam nuberent quaedam virginitatis suae dona Veneri consecrare'. This pagan custom is also referred to by Lactantius (*Divinae Institutiones* 2,4.13).

21 Examples of painted dolls can be found in the British Museum. A. Reith, 'Die Puppe im Grab der Crepereia', *Atlantis* 33 (1961), 367–9.

22 Horace, *Epistles* 1,1.59; A. Mau, 'Ballspiel', *Pauly-Wissowa* II (1896), 2832–34. Macrobius, *Saturnalia* 1,7.22; *Origo gentis Romanae* 3,5.

23 Martial 14,202, and Juvenal 5,154 (probably a gladiator's armour).

24 Seneca, *De Constantia Sapientis* 12,2: 'Quod illi [=pueri] inter ipsos magistratus gerunt et praetextam fascesque ac tribunal imitantur, hi [adults] eadem in campo foroque et in curia serio ludunt'; Suetonius, *Nero* 35.5: 'privignum Rufrium Crispinum Poppaea natum, impuberem adhuc, quia ferebatur ducatus et imperia ludere, mergendum mari, dum piscaretur, servis ipsius demandavit'; Plutarch, *Cato Maior* 2.5 (their offence was sexual); *SHA*, *Septimius* 10, 1.4.

25 Rufinus, *Historia Ecclesiastica* 10,15; Theodoret, *Historia Religiosa*, *PG* 82, 1284.

26 Cassius Dio 50,8.6; Horace, *Epistles* 1,18.60 ff.:

> . . . nugaris rure paterno
> partitur lintres exercitus, Actia pugna
> te duce per pueros hostili more refertur;
> adversarius est frater, lacus hadria, donec
> alterutrum velox victoria fronde coronet;

Procopius, *Histories* 5,20.1–4.

27 Riding: depicted in A.A.M. van der Heyden and H. H. Scullard (eds), *Atlas of the Classical World*, (London, 1959), 155, ill. 394. Hobby-horses: Daremberg-Saglio, *Dictionnaire des antiquités* III, 2.1358, fig. 4637; Horace, *Satires* 2,3.248 f.; Valerius Maximus 8,8 ext.1; Galen, *De Sanitate Tuenda* 1,8 = Kühn VI,38.

28 Tacitus, *Dialogus* 29.3 ('paene in utero matris'); Suetonius, *Nero* 22.1; Juvenal, *Satires* 5,142 ff.:

> . . . ipse loquaci
> gaudebit nido, viridem thoraca iubebit
> adferri . . . quotiens parasitus venerit infans.

29 Horace, *Ars Poetica* 417: 'occupet extremum scabies', with Scholiast's comment: 'hoc ex lusu puerorum sustulit, qui ludentes solent dicere quisquis ad me novissimus venerit, habeat scabiem'.

30 Suetonius, *Claudius* 27.1; Martial 14,19.
31 Pseudo-Acro's scholion on Horace, *Satires* 2,3.248; *Nux* 79 f. and 81 ff.; Persius, *Satires* 3,48 ff.
32 Minucius Felix, *Octavius* 3.5 f.; Martial 14,47; Pliny, *Letters* 2,17, 12; Martial, 14,48; *Digest* 9,2.11 and 9,2.52.4.
33 Vergil, *Aeneid* 7,378 ff.; Persius, *Satires* 3,48. Toys: Vitruvius 10,7.4: Ctesibius' automata; Gellius, *Noctes Atticae* 10,12.9: Archytas' wooden dove.
34 Seven as age for school: Juvenal, *Satires* 14,10. Persius, *Satires* 1,9 ff.; cf. Martial 14,185:

> accipe facundi Culicem, studiose, Maronis,
>   ne nucibus positis ARMA VIRUMQUE legas.

35 Dedications by girls at marriage to Artemis or Aphrodite: *Anthologia Palatina* 6,60, 133, 206–9, 275 f., 280; by boys to Hermes: 6,282, 309.
36 In his *Italienische Reise*, Goethe lists some of the occupations of children in eighteenth-century Naples: collecting refuse, selling drinking-water, lemonade, pastries and fruit, carrying fish to the shops, collecting shavings, gathering sticks for kindling (Penguin Classics translation, 318). Cf. K. R. Bradley, 'Child labour in the Roman world', *Historical Reflections/Reflexions Historiques* 12 (1985), 311 ff.
37 *Digest* 50,16.204.
38 *Digest* 7,7,6.1; *CJ* 6,43.3.1.
39 Varro, *Res Rusticae*, 2,1.10: 'in fundis non modo pueri sed etiam puellae pascant'; Columella, 8,2.7. Ovid, *Fasti* 4,511:

> Filia parva duas redigebat monte capellas.

40 This was one of the reasons why the Roman elite was so keen to see that a considerable peasant population continued to exist, even during the period when there was no shortage of slave labour: cf. P. D. A. Garnsey, *Non-slave Labour in the Greco-Roman World* (Cambridge, 1980), 34 ff.
41 Columella 11,2.44; Pap. Fayum 91 and 102; Pseudo-Matthew ch.13; in its present Latin form this Gospel only dates back to the eighth or ninth century, but it is based on a much earlier eastern Mediterranean version.
42 Nepos, *Atticus* 13,3 f.: 'pueri litteratissimi . . . neque tamen horum quemquam nisi domi natum domique factum habuit: quod est signum non solum continentiae, sed etiam diligentiae . . . diligentia quam pretio parare non mediocris est industriae. A. D. Booth, 'The schooling of slaves in first-century Rome', *TAPhA* 109 (1979), 11–19; *ILS* 7755.
43 *Digest* 17,1.26.8; Seneca, *Letters* 27,5 f.; J. Vogt, 'Alphabet für Freie und Sklaven', *Rheinisches Museum* 116 (1973), 129–42 = *Sklaverei und Humanität. Ergänzungsheft* (Wiesbaden, 1983), 17–27.
44 Cf. W. K. Lacey, '*Patria Potestas*', in B. Rawson (ed.), *The Family in Ancient Rome* (London, 1986), 121 ff.
45 Suetonius, *Augustus* 64.2 f.

46 Tacitus, *Annals* 6,13.2; Vergil, *Aeneid* 6,851 f.
47 F. Kühnert, *Allgemeinbildung und Fachbildung in der Antike* (Deutsche Akademie der Wissenschaften zu Berlin, Sektion für Altertumswissenschaft 30, 1961).
48 Quintilian, *Institutio Oratoriae* 12,2.30; Seneca, *Letters* 1,6.5: 'longum iter per praecepta. Breve et efficax per exempla'; Pliny, *Letters* 8,14.4: 'non auribus modo verum etiam oculis'.
49 D. Liebs, 'Rechtsschulen und Rechtsunterricht im Prinzipat', *ANRW* II, 15 197 ff.; F. Schulz, *A History of Roman Legal Science* (Oxford, 1946); Kübler, 'Rechtsunterricht', *Pauly-Wissowa*, IA.1,394 ff.
50 Seneca, *ad Marciam de Consolatione* 24.1; Pliny, *Letters* 47, 10; Suetonius, *Tiberius* 9; Pliny, *Letters* 2,31; Cassius Dio 67,11; Aulus Gellius 10,28; Cassius Dio 52,20; Mommsen, *Staatsrecht* II, 203 n.2; G. Alföldy, 'Die Generalität des römischen Heeres', *Römische Heeresgeschichte* (Amsterdam, 1987), 3 ff.
51 Sallust, *Bellum Jugurthinum* 85,12.
52 Cf. Liebenam, *Pauly-Wissowa*, VI, 1679; F. E. Adcock, *The Roman Art of War under the Republic* (Cambridge, Mass., 1940); B. Campbell, 'Teach yourself how to be a general', *JRS* 77 (1987), 13 ff.
53 Cicero, *Ad Fam.* 9,25; *ad Quintum Fratrem* 1,1.23: 60 BC; Cicero, *Contra Academicos* 2,1–2. I see no reason to assume that Brutus was reading a military textbook on the eve of the battle of Philippi: Plutarch, *Brutus* 36.2.
54 Vegetius 2,3; A. E. Astin, *Cato the Censor* (Oxford, 1978).
55 Aelian, *Tactica, prooimion*, 6; Lucius Cincius: Aulus Gellius 16,4 – on political assemblies, the powers of consuls, the duties of lawyers, and archaic words; Aulus Cornelius Celsus: Quintilian, *Institutio Oratoriae* 12, 11.24: 'mediocri vir ingenio'.
56 Livy 9,42.
57 H. Marrou, *Histoire de l'education dans l'antiquité* (Paris, 1948, many editions), remains one of the most interesting. Cf. also S. F. Bonner, *Education in Ancient Rome* (London, 1977).
58 F. Kühnert, *Allgemeinbildung und Fachbildung in der Antike.*
59 Plutarch, *Quaestiones Romanae* 278 E.
60 P. Riché, *Education et Culture dans l'occident Barbare* (Paris, 1962).
61 Seven: Juvenal 14.10 etc.; German hostages of unspecified age learning *e litterario ludo*: Suetonius, *Caligula* 45.
62 Quintilian, *Institutio Oratoriae* 1,1.26. Quintilian's ideas were repeated by Jerome, *Letters* 107,4.2 (most accessible in the Loeb edition by F. A. Wright, 1933); E. Michon, 'Iliacae Tabulae', *Daremberg-Saglio, Dictionnaire des antiquités* III,1.372.
63 Rufinus' translation of Origen, *On Numbers* 27.13; cf. Jerome, *Letters* 128,1.2; T. E. Kinsey, 'Melior the Calculator', *Hermes* 107 (1979), 501.
64 These were maxims used as a basis for grammatical or rhetorical exercises. 'The fruits of learning are sweet' was ascribed to Isocrates: cf. Aphthonius, *Rhetores Graeci* II,23,14 ff.
65 Augustine, *Confessions* 1,9–14.

66 *Corpus Glossariorum Latinorum* III (ed. G. Goetz, Leipzig, 1892). There is also a considerable quantity of teaching material on papyrus from Roman Egypt.

67 Horace, *Ars Poetica* 325 ff.; Ausonius, *Eclogues* 6 ('Technopaignion'), 12; Augustine, *Confessions* 1,13.22.

68 Horace, *Satires* 1,1.25 f.:

> Ut pueris olim dant crustula blandi
> doctores, elementa velint ut discere prima,

and Jerome, *Letters* 128,1.3. Much the same approach had been taken by Quintilian.

69 Caesius Bassus, *de metris* (ed. Keil, *Grammatici Latini* VI, 271 f.): 'solebatque nobis pueris hic loculus ad confirmandam memoriam prodesse plurimum'; Ausonius 17 (*Cento Nuptialis*), ed. Peiper 208: ed. Evelyn White, I, 374, appendix 395 f.: 'harum verticularum variis coagmentis simulantur species mille formarum: helephantus belua aut aper bestia, anser volans et mirmillo in armis, subsidens venator et latrans canis, quin et turris et cantharus et alia huismodi innumerabilium figurarum'.

70 Cassius Dio 52,26.1. Cf. plate 21.

71 H. Marrou, ΜΟΥΣΙΚΟΣ ΑΝΗΡ (Grenoble, 1938). Cf. plates 17 and 18.

72 *ILS* 5177 (Rome):

> Q. Sulpicio Q.f. Cla. Maximo domo Roma vix. ann. XI
> m. V d. XII Hic tertio certaminis lustro inter Graecos
> poetas duos et L professus favorem, quem ob tenaram
> aetatem excitaverat in admirationem ingenio suo perduxit
> et cum honore discessit. Versus extemporales eo subiecti
> sunt, ne parent[es] adfactib[us] suis indulsisse videant.

Cf. *ILS* 5178, L. Valerius Pudens, 'coronatus' in AD 106; Avita: BM Cat. Sculpture 649, plate 22.

73 *ILCV* 727:

> Quid te grammaticae iuvit tolerasse labores
> consona rhetoricae verba legisse tubae
> si mors dura ruens pueriles occupat annos?

74 *CIL* VI,21846; cf. *CIL* VI,18324.5 f. Both are 7-year-olds.

Chapter Six

EQUAL IN THE SIGHT OF GOD

Classical society relegated children, together with women, old men, and slaves, to the margins of community life. While that gave each of these groups an intermediate position between being fully human and being a beast, it might also give them a position intermediate between the human world and that of the gods. In much the same way, barbarian societies might be said by the Romans to have no laws, either because they were sub-human, or because they were 'by nature' so just that they needed no laws to keep them in order.[1]

The relative physical weakness of the child, the old man, and the woman, meant that these three groups were thought to require, or deserve, particular support from the supernatural. We have seen that Pliny listed all sorts of magical remedies meant to give children special protection.[2] Rationalist scholars in the last century sometimes tended to assume that the comparative frequency with which women, slaves, and lower social groups are attested in literature or in inscriptions as appealing to the divine world indicated that such groups had a less rational or 'scientific' attitude to nature, either congenitally or as a result of unequal educational opportunities. Comparative studies by more recent sociologists rather suggest that those groups who appeal to the divine world are just as 'rational' as anyone else. It is because they are excluded from the political process or from social influence that they have no other way to express their concerns than by reference to powers outside the political community, controlled as it usually is by 'rational' adult males. Evidence from the ancient world shows that adult males from the upper classes were as ready as their women or slaves to resort to magic, if they felt that they had no other way to influence events – for instance, if they did not know who it was who had harmed them.[3]

It was this powerlessness that lay behind the assumption that 'marginal' groups were more likely to be in touch with the divine world than were adult male citizens. In the ancient world, as in many other human societies, evil magical practices have been ascribed to women, especially old women like Horace's hag Canidia. The old are thought to be particularly numinous. Hence they also typically have the power to prophesy, like the Sibyl of Cumae.[4] In Greek oracular shrines too the god often spoke through a woman, like the Delphic Pythia. That is no evidence that such cult-practices survived from a mythical matriarchal age when women held power over men; still less that anyone in the classical period thought that women were men's equals. It simply underlines the marginality of women; they are further away from the centre of society than men, and therefore nearer both to heaven and to hell.

Children, too, can be seen as mediators between the social world of adult citizens and the divine; a child's propensity to make statements which an adult would be embarrassed to make, or statements which fall outside the logical context of adult discourse, makes it particularly likely that a society which already believes in prophecy will ascribe inspired insights into the future to children (just as more recent societies have interpreted the same phenomenon as evidence that a child has a 'natural' propensity to tell the straight truth, while adults obfuscate). In the *Aeneid*, when the Trojans have reached the promised land of Italy, it is Aeneas' son Iulus who utters the ominous words, 'Have we been reduced to eating our own tables?', which remind Aeneas that his father Anchises had once promised him that they would reach their goal when they came to the place where hunger would force them to eat the tables as well as the food laid out on them.[5]

The games children naturally play could be seen as ominous (see pp. 150 f. above). Among the list of prodigies that pointed to Octavian's victory over Antony and Cleopatra at the battle of Actium was the battle between children calling themselves 'Octavians' and others calling themselves 'Antonians'; and a Samnite shepherd-boy playing the role of 'Belisarius' ominously defeated his opponent 'Vittigis' during the Byzantine reconquest of Italy in the sixth century.[6]

Some of the anecdotes related in ancient biographies are of the same type. As we have seen, most of the stories told about unexpected sayings by children are ominous only in the sense that they reveal what the child's own character will be when he becomes an adult. But sometimes a child's words tell the future for others; the omen may be good or bad. The daughter of Aemilius Paullus, the Roman general who destroyed the power of Macedonia under King Perseus in 167 BC, owned a pet dog which happened also to be called Perseus. When her father came back home from the Senate session at which war had been declared on Macedon, she ran up to kiss him, and told him that 'our Perseus is dead': that was accepted as a good augury for the outcome of the war. At the outbreak of the war against Hannibal, a six-month-old baby was reported to have shouted 'Victory!' in the Roman forum. On the other hand, when Pompey came back from his great victories in the east to be embroiled in the political conflict which ultimately (albeit many years later) led to his death, his daughter's teacher wanted her to show off what she had just been learning. She recited a line from a (lost) Greek tragedy which went, 'You have come back from war. Better that you had died there'.[7]

A child might also draw attention to a truth that was too embarrassing or too dangerous to be mentioned in public by adults. In 41 BC, Livia very suddenly divorced Claudius Nero, the father of her two sons, and married Octavian.

> A little twittering boy, such as women keep around them to play
> with, generally without any clothes, seeing Livia in one place
> with Caesar, and Nero sitting elsewhere with someone else, went
> up to her and said, 'What are you doing here, my Lady? Your
> husband (pointing at him) is over there'.[8]

A child might be portentous in itself: that was especially true of misshapen births, such as the ones that appear in Livy's history (see p. 38 above). When a child was reported to have been born with three heads at Syracuse shortly before the civil wars of AD 68/9, this was interpreted to foretell the rule of the three emperors Galba, Otho, and Vitellius, none of whom was capable of survival.[9]

The child's 'marginality' gave him magical powers. The ghost of a child who had died prematurely might be invoked to haunt an enemy. It was believed that witches used various parts of a dead child's anatomy when they prepared their concoctions; details are listed on Egyptian magical papyri. It was widely held by Romans that witches would go so far as to kill small children in order to use them for their spells: the epitaph of a slave-boy, not yet 4 years old, from the household of the younger Livia at Rome claims that 'The cruel hand of a witch has snatched me away, while she remains on earth to harm people with her skills. Parents: watch carefully over your children!' This was not an irrational fear restricted to slaves; the idea appears in Cicero, Horace, and Petronius.[10]

One of the more peculiar aspects of this idea of children as not fully belonging to society is that in a number of stories they play the role of the community's executioners. The execution of evil-doers is a 'marginal' activity: it is the point where a civilised community feels it is face-to-face with evil, and where the criminal is between life and death. Romans went a long way in ritualising public executions: by throwing criminals to wild beasts, or making them fight each other as gladiators. As 'marginal' beings, children too may (mythically speaking) be an ideal instrument for that. An ancient fable concerned a schoolteacher of Falerii, who during a siege of his city by the Romans in the fifth century BC kidnapped his pupils and surrendered them to the enemy. The Romans would not tolerate such a mean trick, and handed the schoolteacher over to the same children to be beaten to death. Another story went that when Caligula fell ill, someone was said to have vowed to give his own life should the emperor recover; the emperor recovered, and handed the devotee over to the children (*pueri*, which in the context can hardly refer to slaves) of Rome to be killed. And in the third century AD, the Christian schoolteacher Cassian of Imola was said to have been handed over to his own pagan pupils for execution; they martyred him with their styluses.[11]

Burial customs confirm that, like slaves, 'children and adolescents are seen as people without a full place in the community'. The younger the child, the more 'marginal'; while the laws of the Twelve Tables banned burial within the city wall (the dead were 'outsiders'), children under 40 days of age were normally buried not just inside the city, but under the threshhold or foundations of a wall of the house: at the 'edge' of the house, as they had been at the 'edge' of the household. They were also, unlike adults, buried at night.[12]

It is not therefore surprising that the Romans should have

assigned particular roles to children in some of their religious ceremonies. It was entirely appropriate that when a woman drew lots to ask the gods whether her sweetheart would return safely from a journey, the lots should be interpreted by a child acolyte.[13] The rationale behind this was not primarily, as some have thought, that sexual purity was required at a religious ceremony, and a child could be guaranteed to be pure. It certainly was the case that when adults prepared for a religious ceremony, they were expected to abstain from sex. Sexual intercourse was recognised as part of the normal secular life of an adult male; to abstain from it was a sign that something abnormal was about to happen, namely an attempt to make contact with the divine world. But it is the child's 'marginality', not its supposed lack of interest in sexual gratification, that makes it a suitable participant in religious practices. In that way, a child is akin to the eunuch-priests of Cybele, the great goddess whose worship had been brought to Rome from Asia Minor in 204 BC. Eunuchs were suitable mediators between the Roman state and the divine world, not because they were sexually untainted (hostile comments suggested that they notoriously were not), but because the eunuch is a 'marginal' figure *par excellence*. He is not just an imported foreigner with no social existence in his host community (like a slave), but someone physiologically incapable of ever being linked to anyone within that community; under Roman law, they were even forbidden to adopt. Eunuchs will be boys, individuals with no family ties, for ever.[14] If Roman writers explained that the word *pueri* was derived from *puri*, it was not because they were sexually pure, but because they had no hair on their face or body: 'The boy is so called from his purity, because he is pure, and does not yet have any hair or down on his cheeks'.[15]

An intermediary with the divine world becomes even more sacred if he is marginal in more than one respect. Hence the peculiar figure of the Etruscan dwarf soothsayer Tages, who is at one and the same time a child and an old man. The multiplication of a number of different 'marginalities' in the same context remained as potent a symbol for Christians as it had ever been for pagans: we only have to think of the Christ-child in a manger, honoured by wise old men or kings on the one hand and shepherds on the other, with domestic animals in attendance. He who is both old and young is also divine: the theme is nicely encapsulated in a late Roman epigram addressed to Christ, 'Child, Old Man, born before all ages, co-eval with your Father'; and it becomes widespread in the image of the early medieval monk as a *puer senex* who stands right outside the secular adult community.[16]

Adult sons and unmarried daughters under their father's *potestas* naturally take part in the family cult. Marcus Aurelius told Fronto how he had to assist his father Antoninus Pius. But sons and daughters who were still children had some special roles to play. Ovid describes a family preparing the annual sacrifice to Terminus, the god of boundaries, on 23 February. The peasant woman brings the sacrificial fire from the family hearth in a potsherd, her husband builds it up with bark; the boy holds a basket of corn, and throws three handfuls into the altar-flame. Then the girl puts slices of honeycomb on the flames, and 'others' (in a wealthier household than that romantically described by Ovid, the household slaves) add some wine. The whole family is dressed in white, and keeps sacred silence.[17]

The dividing line between the sacred and the profane in domestic matters is not always easy to distinguish. The proper handling of food and of drinking vessels during their preparation had religious overtones, and the first-century AD agricultural writer Columella tells us that a whole string of Greek, Carthaginian, and Roman predecessors had advised that those who were in charge of the preparation of food ought to be chaste and continent:

> Equipment should only be handled by a child, or at least by someone who is completely restrained in matters of sex. If a man or woman has had intercourse, he or she should wash in a river or in running water before touching the stores. For this reason, they thought that it was essential for this work to be done by a boy or girl, who would distribute each day's supplies.

The store-room, the *penus*, was a sacred place; it was for the children of the household to act as intermediaries between the adult consumers and the gods of the store-room, the *penates* who preserved the harvest produce and protected the household from starvation. According to Servius' fifth-century AD commentary on the *Aeneid*, it was the children who had to announce that the household gods were propitious when the *paterfamilias* offered sacrifice in the course of a meal. This daily ceremony is parodied by Petronius in the *Satyricon*.[18]

It would seem likely that the role of children in the rituals of the

Roman state originated as parallels with their role at the household ceremonies. By the time of Augustus, their participation was also based on another factor, the Greek custom of having the children of the community sing as a chorus at state festivals. (That was of course one element of the origin of the chorus at religious occasions such as dramatic performances, and lay behind the fact that Greek communities had public schools where large numbers of children from different families were taught together.) The Greek influence may have affected the use of children as early as the end of the third century BC: Macrobius, in the early fifth century AD, cites the augur Marcus Laelius as his authority for a story about a *lectisternium*, a public supplication to the gods, carried out during the Second Punic War. The sons of citizens as well as freedmen whose mothers and fathers were both still alive chanted the hymn. The best-known example of such a ceremony is that of the Secular Games instituted by Augustus in 17 BC to usher in a new and more peaceful age after the civil wars had come to an end. Not only does the text of the hymn survive, composed by Horace in sapphic metre (as though it were in imitation of Greek ritual), but we also have an inscription which gives a detailed account of the rituals: 'After the completion of the sacrifice, a hymn was sung by twenty-seven [= 3 x 3 x 3] chosen boys, all with their father and mother still alive, and the same number of girls. This was on the Capitol. The hymn was composed by Q. Horatius Flaccus.'[19]

As late as the third century AD, similar choirs of children from noble Roman households still performed on ceremonial occasions. Cassius Dio refers to them at the deification of the emperor Pertinax by Septimius Severus in AD 193, and Herodian at Septimius' own deification in 211. The Greek word in both cases is ΠΑΙΔΩΝ, which includes girls as well as boys.[20]

These hymn-singing ceremonies were clearly heavily influenced by Greek precedents, and we cannot be certain about whether they were frequent in the republican period, before the systematic 'restoration' of so many cults and priesthoods by Augustus. The same applies to the curious ceremony called the 'Lusus Troiae', the Troy game, in which two groups of boys, one aged 7 to 11 and the other 11 to 14, engaged in a mock battle on horseback.[21] That appears to have been an Augustan innovation, and was not popular with everyone: the noble Messala Corvinus spoke out against this new-fangled nonsense in the Senate after his grandson had fallen off his horse and broken a leg. Some contemporaries were convinced that the Troy game was an ancient Roman ritual; Iulus-Ascanius plays a prominent part in Vergil's account of one in the *Aeneid* (5,545 ff.). There is ground for scepticism. Dionysius of Halicarnassus, in the time of Augustus, describes 'boys of noble households just coming up to manhood' riding in a procession at the opening of the Capitoline Games as early as the fifth century BC; but he explicitly compares them with the ephebes at Greek ceremonies, and the whole purpose of his description is to show how like Greek festivals Roman festivals had always been. At the very least, Augustus was heavily influenced by Greek precedents when he assigned such prominent roles to children in the rituals he reconstituted.

Dionysius' account of how Romulus instituted the *camilli*, boys who assisted certain Roman priests at their sacrifices, is similarly coloured by his desire to prove that the Romans were really Greeks, and that their best institutions were all Greek in origin. Here at least his proofs are so unconvincing that we may be certain that we are dealing with a Roman institution of some antiquity. His account runs as follows:

> Since it was necessary for certain ceremonies to be carried out by women, and others by children both of whose parents were still alive, Romulus ordered the priests' wives to be priestesses in association with their husbands, so that these ceremonies also might be performed in the best way possible. If there was anything which the law of the country forbade men to celebrate, then these women should perform them, and their children should ministrate as necessary. Those who had no children should choose the most attractive boy and the most attractive girl from some other household, tribe by tribe. The boy was to serve the priests until adolescence, the girl for whatever period she should remain unmarried. It is my belief that he borrowed these things also from the customs of the Greeks.[22]

Dionysius goes on to call these child-acolytes *camilli*. It is not evident from our sources whether the word might properly be applied to the child assistants of any Roman priest or college of priests, or just to those of the ancient priest of Jupiter, the Flamen Dialis, and his wife, the Flaminica, as well as the priests of the archaic *curiae* or tribal units.[23] The grammarian Festus tells us that while some authorities restricted the word to the acolytes of the Flamen Dialis and the Flaminica only, others said that 'The ancients called all boys *camilli*, as in the ancient verse in which a father teaches his son farming: 'In the dry dust of winter, in the spring mud: gather the harvest when it is ripe, *camille*.'[24] Some scholars have argued that a verse by the tragedian Pacuvius quoted by Varro suggests that in the second century BC the word *camilla* could apply to any servant girl (though in fact the context of the line appears to be grand and sacred: she is a servant of the gods, *caelitum camilla*).[25] Varro also mentions a *camillus* as attending the archaic form of marriage ceremony called the *confarreatio*. Whatever the categories of boys strictly entitled to be called *camilli*, it is clear from representations of Roman religious ceremonies – including family ceremonies such as weddings – that in the early imperial period child acolytes were present at a wide range of social occasions. They performed the sorts of duties which Columella had referred to in an apparently secular context, namely carrying and holding vessels of food or water at sacrifices, religious processions, and weddings.

One college of priests about which we are particularly well informed because of the survival on marble inscriptions of detailed minutes of their meetings and ceremonies, were the twelve 'Fratres Arvales', the 'Brethren of the Fields', as reconstituted by Augustus to reward his supporters and to serve as a focus of loyalty towards the imperial household.[26] Their records tell us that at sacrifices they were assisted by four 'boys of free birth whose fathers and mothers were still alive', who also seem to have been present at the brethren's ceremonial banquets. Normally these four boys were themselves the sons of serving current brethren. This would confirm Dionysius' story about the Roman priesthood being modelled on the 'secular' family. The priest who conducted ceremonies on behalf of the Roman state was assisted by his 'children' in the same way as the *paterfamilias* when he offered up sacrifices for his household. This does not mean to say that the Romans thought of their community as an extended family, but rather as analogous to a family.[27] Hence colleges of priests like the Arval Brethren or the Luperci represented themselves as 'brothers', as though an artificial family. The Christian metaphor of the Church as a family had one of its roots in pagan cult associations.

Since the low social status of children was connected with their physical weakness and liability to succumb to danger, children were both nearer to the gods, and dearer to them: they needed more divine protection. In each of the crises a child had to face, he required the assistance of a particular divinity. St Augustine, in one of his attacks on pagan polytheism, was scathing when he came to list those divinities who had no other role (and therefore, he implies, no other power) than to protect a foetus and an infant in various different circumstances as it passed through childhood.[28]

In another passage, he rejected the arguments put forward by rationalist pagans in late antiquity to the effect that all the gods and goddesses were really different emanations or aspects of a single supreme Godhead. Again he gives a long list of deities which these intellectuals wish to identify with Jupiter:

> Suppose that he is *Diespater*, who brings children into the light of day; *Mena*, whom the Romans put in charge of women's monthly periods; *Lucina*, who is called on for help in childbirth. He is called *Opis* for helping the new-born by placing them on the surface of the earth; when he opens the infant's mouth for the first time to let him cry, let him be called *Vaticanus*; as *Levana*, he looks after the raising up of the new-born child from the ground; as *Cunina* he is said to guard the child's cradle. They say that one aspect of Jupiter is as the three fates, the *Carmentes*, who decide the new-born child's future; as *Fortuna*, he is invoked as the god of chance. The breast was called 'ruma' in archaic times: as *Rumina*, let him be the god of breast-feeding. In charge of children's drinking-habits, let him be *Potina*, and in charge of their eating, *Educa*. When children are scared, he protects them as *Paventia*. . . .[29]

Augustine is a hostile source, but pagans who were sympathetic to the ancient polytheism confirm the plethora of gods whose assistance was required to protect every aspect of childbirth and of growing up. Aulus Gellius quotes Varro to the effect that the two Fates referred to by Augustine, the Carmentes, were called 'Postverta' and 'Prorsa', the one to look after regular (cephalic) births, the other breech-births.[30]

But in all these cases, classical society saw children as especially associated with the divine world because they were unimportant, not because they were the same as adults: the child may serve as an acolyte just because he is not an adult, he is not really there.

Despite the conclusions reached by some scholars, this seems to be as true of the so-called 'mystery religions' as of the formal cults of Roman families and of the Roman community. There are many references to children participating in the Eleusinian Mysteries, for instance – 'They must dedicate their wreaths and garlands before any of the initiates do so' – but there appears to be only one clear and exceptional case of a child being initiated into it as a full and equal devotee.[31]

Whatever the exact role of children in the various mystery cults, in general the presence of children at the pagan religious ceremonies of Roman families and of the Roman communities was not a sign of the equality of child and adult, but a sign that the child only marginally belonged to the human community. It was because the child 'did not count', was in a sense 'not there' as a citizen, that the child could be used to assist at ceremonies, and that the child's words could be taken as ominous, mediating between the divine world and the human.

Naturally those Romans who were Christians brought something of this attitude with them. We have seen that in time of persecution, Cyprian thought that God spoke to him about his duties as a bishop through the utterances of a child medium. When the Christians of Milan were looking for a bishop in AD 374, it was a child who first chanted 'Ambrose for bishop'; the congregation accepted the omen.[32]

For Christians as for pagans, the 'marginality' of boys made them suitable as servers or acolytes at religious ceremonies, a role that is still given to children today. This development is not at all easy to trace, but it is clear that by the fourth century, the Christian order of 'reader' (*lector*) was increasingly being reserved to children or young men, even – paradoxically – to ones who were too young to read yet. Cyprian appointed as *lector* a young man who had been brave enough to confess his faith during a persecution, but could not read.[33]

There is some evidence for boy *lectores* in the personnel and the liturgy of the church in Rome. The *Liber Pontificalis* supplies much information about individual popes, generally reliable at least from the early fourth century on.[34] The so-called *Gelasian Sacramentary* contains information about the rituals of incorporation within various clerical grades, but unfortunately no texts survive on the rite of ordination of *lectores*. Their tasks were to read the scriptures;

to sing or chant; and to bless the bread and new fruits brought by the congregations as offerings. From the fourth century on, the office normally undertaken by deacons of providing water for washing the priest's or bishop's hands at Mass might be transferred to child lectors.[35] It has been suggested that this was a significant development, for here boys could be seen as not merely acting as servers, but fulfilling a limited sacramental role in the Mass. It is not surprising that the Byzantine emperor should have tried to ban the installation of *lectores* under the age of 18, though without apparent success. But by the tenth century, they had lost this role; partly as a consequence of the great increase in the importance of singing following the Carolingian reforms, the Roman Church introduced a new order of *Psalmistae* (the ancestors of modern church and cathedral choirs) to chant the words of the liturgy. The failure of an order of child *lectores* to survive as an institution resulted in much later misunderstanding of their role: Aquinas thought that they were catechism teachers. Since the tenth century, the role of children in the liturgy of the western churches has been purely ancillary. Children have of course from time to time played important, and sometimes curious, roles in non-liturgical religious ceremonies.[36]

There are occasional references to the functions of these *lectores* in the Church fathers. They are described in a letter on 'the Seven Orders of the Church' ascribed to Jerome; and Augustine refers in a sermon to the Gospel text which has just been read out by a *lector* with his 'childish heart', *corde puerili*. Ennodius tells us that Epiphanius was ordained a *lector* when he was 8. Victor of Vita, in his account of the persecution of Catholic Romans by Arian Vandals in North Africa, says that 'amongst those who were exiled were many *lectores* who were little children'. He also tells an atrocity story about a child lector who was shot, receiving an arrow in the throat as he was about to chant the Easter alleluia verse.[37] The *Liber Pontificalis* tells us that Pope Liberius (352–66) was a *scripturorum lector* as a boy (*parvulus*), and Pope Eugenius (654–7) is described as having been a 'cleric from his cradle', presumably as a lector; but clerics might remain humble *lectores* until well into their twenties. Popes Zosimus (417–18) and Simplicius (468–83) had to remain in the status of lectors until the age of 20 or 30. Fifth- and sixth-century inscriptions, some in atrocious Latin, confirm that there were *lectores* who died at the ages of 20, 25, and even 73; but we also have the epitaph of a boy who 'lived in peace for five years' (i.e. died five years after being baptised). 'Severus, an innocent lector, died aged thirteen'; others were aged 12 and 14. At Lyon, the *lectores* were organised in a school, under the command of a *primicerius*.[38]

The role of children as *lectores* was in the main still ancillary, or 'marginal', as it had been in pagan ceremonies. It is not necessary to accept the view of some scholars, that from the fourth century on these *lectores* took over a sacramental role in the ritual of washing the bishop's hands. But there is a quite different reason for believing that Christians thought that children might have as much of a right to share in the spiritual community as adults.

The outward sign of that membership of the *ecclesia*, the assembly of citizens of the New Jerusalem, was baptism. But in essence, being a Christian meant being 'saved'; and the feature of Christian salvation which distinguished it from what was offered by any pagan cult was the belief in the resurrection of the body. This central feature of Christianity was inherited from Judaism: the prophets' proclamation that just Jews would rise again is echoed by the evangelists.[39] Christians extended baptism, salvation, and resurrection to the gentiles. The New Testament does not make it clear whether this resurrection is due to all who believe (John 6:39 ff.), or to all who participate in the Eucharist (John 6.53). But it is clear that it is a matter of corporate membership of the Church; just as Jews were justified by being part of the People of Israel (and the resurrection was often associated with the resurgence of a Jewish national state), so Christians shared in the resurrection by virtue of belonging to the new, 'True Israel', 'Verus Israel'. Hence it seemed possible to some Christians to incorporate even the dead: the Christians of Corinth, like the Latter Day Saints, baptised deceased relatives. St Perpetua dreamt that she 'saved' the soul of her dead brother.

Belief in the resurrection of the dead raised a series of difficult questions about the nature of the resurrected body, particularly in the case of children who had died before reaching adulthood, or even had died in the womb. Augustine, as one of the most systematic defenders of children's right to baptism, discussed the problem in several sermons and tracts, and admitted that no certainty was possible on some of these questions: thus it was only 'probable' that an aborted foetus would share in the resurrection.

'We do not find these questions defined in the Scriptures.'[40]

The same may be said to apply to the question of the origin of child baptism. There are difficult theological and historiographical issues involved: many scholars interested in the issue over the centuries have been less concerned to reconstruct the practice of the Christian past than to justify their own views about what Christian belief should be in the present. This is true of recent investigations by Lutheran theologians, arguing about whether the Church should be a Church of believers (i.e. adults, since children cannot understand what belief would commit them to), rather than the Church of a Christian people, including its children: the Church in question being primarily the German Lutheran Church, whose claim to be the expression of a Christian nation was thought by some of its theologians to have lost validity as a result of the events of 1933–45.[41] But arguments about the antiquity of child baptism, and the relationship between baptism and confirmation, can be found masking political and doctrinal issues at much earlier times: e.g. during attempts to harmonise Latin Catholic and Greek Orthodox practice in the later Middle Ages, or even in the ninth century.

The arguments in favour of the view that infant baptism was instituted by the Apostles include literary and epigraphic evidence from the first few centuries AD. In a report to Trajan, Pliny the Younger stated that Christians included 'many of every age-group'; Origen's defence of Christianity *Against Celsus* shows that Christians were accused of preaching to the lowest and least rational members of the human race: women, slaves, and children.[42] But Pliny's words are imprecise, and Celsus was clearly using a *topos* which Christians were proud to pick up in their turn: Aristides says that Christians 'instruct their slaves and their children' in the faith, and Irenaeus of Lyon includes 'infants, little children, boys, youths and old men among those who through Him are reborn in God'.[43] The passages opposing infant baptism are few and far between: one favourite is Tertullian, who in one of his radical appeals for a pure Church went so far as to question whether Christians should marry and went on to ask: 'Why should an innocent age scramble to have sin remitted – let them come when they have grown up, when they learn, when they can be taught why they are coming; let them become Christians when they are capable of knowing Christ.' But even in this rhetorical tract he accepts that small children have the right to be baptised if they are in danger of death, and that such a baptism is fully valid.[44]

We know much less about the practice of the various Christian churches in the pre-Constantinian period than we do about the theology. One of the earliest liturgical handbooks, the *Canons of Hippolytus*, is ascribed to the early third century pope, but is for the most part very much later.[45] Canon 21 ordains that, at baptismal ceremonies, 'They shall baptise the little children first. And if they can answer for themselves, let them answer. But if they cannot, let their parents answer, or someone from their household.' It is clear from this that real children are meant – 'child' is not a metaphor for the new-born Christian, as it so often can be in the Fathers. On the other hand, the Canons also say that a convert should normally undergo three years' instruction before baptism; that would indicate that children, or at least infants, were not normally baptised. As late as AD 381, St Gregory of Nazianzen in Asia Minor recommended that the normal age for baptism should be 3, since at that age the child can answer questions and has some understanding.[46]

Christian epitaphs do not resolve the problem. While they make it clear that some very young children were being baptised, those who died were, by definition, in the position of requiring emergency baptism. A mosaic now at Sfax (Tunisia) commemorates 'Quiriacus, well-remembered, who lived for three years and two days, and fell asleep on June 29th' (cover illustration). A third-century inscription commemorates Apronianus, 'Who was greatly loved by his mother; when she saw that he was going to die, she asked the Church to let him leave this world as a believer'. He died aged 1 year 9 months and 5 days. Julia Florentina, aged 18 months and 22 days, was baptised at the second hour of the night and lived for four hours after that, 'so that she was able to accept the Eucharist' (*ita ut consueta repeteret*). Apronianus' mother had to *ask* the Church for him to be baptised; and there are many cases of adult believers who had not yet been baptised in the fourth century AD, including Constantine the Great, or the young Valentinian II whose funeral oration by Ambrose we have looked at (see pp. 129 f. above). It is not persuasive to argue that these non-baptised Christians were a result of the stream of adult converts in the fourth century. That could hardly have been true of the young brother of St Perpetua.[47]

An even less persuasive argument is that early Christians converted, not as individuals, but as families: the Acts of the Apostles
frequently tells us that St Paul baptised someone 'with his whole
household'. This might be taken to include not just women and
slaves, but also children. Yet it is striking that while Paul is
adamant that in Christ there is no distinction by culture, gender,
or social status, he says nothing about Christ overcoming the
difference between child and adult.[48] Jewish precedents do not help
either; while Christian baptism is clearly a development of the
Jewish practice of requiring a ritual purification from proselytes
from the first century BC on, a purification which may sometimes
have enabled the proselyte to dispense with circumcision, the
earliest reference to such baptism being applied to infants is by
Rabbi Huna (*c*. AD 212–97). It would seem that Jews, Christians,
and pagans were all subject to gradually increasing pressures to
recognise children as full members of their communities.[49]

The Christians' emphasis on personal salvation was perhaps
particularly well able to articulate the feeling that individuals,
including children, were freeing themselves from the rules imposed
by membership of the secular city, including the classical
constraints in respect of age-requirements for citizenship and office
holding. It is agreed that, by the fourth century AD, many
churches, both Latin and Greek, incorporated children into the
religious community as soon after birth as was practicable. This
was at odds with the very obvious fact that babies and toddlers
could not be thought to have accepted divine salvation in the same
way as adults. Baptism could not serve a Christian society as a
ritual symbolising the progression from child to adult, leading to
full participation in the community of adults. For the Christian,
every baptised infant already belonged as completely as an adult.
There were of course secular institutions in medieval and early
modern Christian societies which served to make a clear distinction
between children and adults: for women, marriage continued to
have this function (as in many peasant cultures), while there is
evidence from many parts of Europe of youth groups serving to
initiate boys into adult life. The future knight's years of service as
an esquire is an example, and many of the rituals associated with
apprenticeship as preparation for adult life survive.[50]

The idea that every child, so long as he or she was baptised, was
the equal of an adult within the Christian community, runs counter

to experience to such an extent that it provoked the need for a new ritual serving to distinguish those who can from those who cannot give assent to the salvation they have received in baptism. The western Church responded by instituting confirmation as a separate sacrament. The multiplicity of terms used in the New Testament for the rituals incorporating the newly converted into the Christian community assisted this process. Thus Acts of the Apostles 8:12 and 14 could be used to show that, even in the Apostolic age, there existed a distinction between baptism, performed by Philip, and confirmation, performed by the Apostles at Jerusalem; the Apostles Peter and John pray (15), and place their hands on the converts' heads (17) with the effect that they receive the Holy Spirit. Early Church writers make it clear that they see baptism and confirmation as one ritual, with separate elements: the Council of Elvira[51] allows deacons, or any confirmed Christian, to baptise when someone is in danger of death, but 'he must bring him to the bishop so that the sacrament may be completed by the laying-on of hands'. The word 'completed', *perfici*, is the word which from the time of St Ambrose at the end of the fourth century is used to describe confirmation. But until well into the Dark Ages, this confirmation by the bishop took place at the Easter or Pentecost immediately following the baptism, and not during adolescence: 'When the bishop wishes to confirm infants, boys, or others who have been sprinkled with the sacred water of baptism . . .', says the *Liber Pontificalis*. Pope Innocent I, in the fifth century AD, insisted that this confirmation of baptism had to be reserved to bishops, citing the texts in Acts 8.[52] In the east, both parts of the ceremony were administered by ordinary priests, a practice unwillingly recognised as valid in the ninth century by Pope Nicolas I, to avoid argument with the Greeks ('*pacis causa*').

The evidence makes it clear that, whatever the date at which infant baptism became common, Christians in the fourth century AD did not see either baptism or its 'confirmation' by the bishop as in any way connected with a change in status from child to adult. Even if those scholars who deny that infant baptism was the norm are right, it remains the case that by the year 200 at the latest, Christians recognised that, if the necessity arose, even the youngest baby had the right to be accepted as a full member of the Christian community through baptism. And he was accepted, not as an adult before his time, but as the child he was. While St Perpetua was in prison awaiting the crown of martyrdom, she dreamt that she saw her unbaptised 7-year-old brother Dinocrates in purgatory. When she woke up, she prayed for his salvation. Then, in a further dream, she saw him again, now dressed in white and no longer suffering. 'When he had drunk to his satisfaction, he left the water [sc. of baptism] to play, as children do, and enjoy himself; and I woke up. Then I realised that he had been taken away from the punishment [of Hell].'[53] Pagan children could overcome the limitations of their tender years by holding adult offices, or learning adult skills. The Christian child had no need to be precocious: he could win salvation on the same terms as adults without ceasing to be a child, while continuing to play, *more infantium*, 'as children do'.

For the Christian child, winning glory or holding office in the secular community, or being precociously successful in acquiring secular knowledge, was irrelevant to salvation. If these things distracted him from his Christian duties, they were positively deleterious. Only in the fourth century did some Christians come to see that the exercise of secular office holding might be a good thing: that political power, properly exercised, might be used in the service of God.[54] But the secular honour and prestige that motivated the political elites of the classical city – in Christian terms, vain-glory – was something that Christians were agreed ought to be shunned.

The Romans had considered the secular skills of literature and rhetoric as technical skills, *artes* like reading or writing or making shoes. As such, they were morally neutral. So long as they could be put to good use, Christian Greeks and Romans saw no need to reject them – even though they were the inventions of pagans, and were full of stories referring to pagan gods, or demons. Consequently Christians felt able to continue to use the same syllabus even after the end of the Roman empire, and throughout the Middle Ages – in contrast to orthodox Jews and Muslims, whose children learnt their letters from the Bible or the Qur'an.

The writings contained in the New Testament have little to say about the attitude Christians ought to take to the Hellenistic schools of the ΓΡΑΜΜΑΤΙΣΤΗΣ and the ΓΡΑΜΜΑΤΙΚΟΣ in which some at least of the authors and their readers had learnt to read and write their Greek. In Palestine, there appear to have been no formal institutions for teaching children (other than the synagogue services) before the Pharisees set up scripture schools in the the first century BC in order to counter the attractions of the more advanced teaching offered by the Greek grammatical, rhetorical, and philosophical schools in the Hellenistic cities of the east (including many Palestinian cities). These rabbinical schools limited themselves to the study of the sacred scriptures in the sacred language, Hebrew; there were no schools in which Jewish children could learn the skills of reading and writing either Aramaic or the Greek KOINH in a specifically Jewish way.

Although there had been opposition to elements of Greek culture from the beginning of the second century BC on, and such opposition had been an important element in the creation of an independent Jewish state under the Maccabees,[55] the opposition of later rabbinical tradition should not obscure the fact that in the Hellenistic period many Jews, particularly in the Diaspora, were happy to take part in Greek cultural institutions without feeling that such participation tainted them with idolatry. There were not perhaps many Jews who were prepared to go as far as the leaders of the community at Miletus, who had seats inscribed with their titles reserved for them in the civic theatre as a sign that they wished to take part in civic festivals, even though those festivals honoured pagan gods; but there are a number of instances of Jews in the Diaspora enrolling as ephebes and taking part in the activities of the gymnasium. Whatever the high priests at Jerusalem might say, Philo saw no objection to athletics. These Jews did not deny the religion of their fathers: but they saw the religion of their fathers from within the framework of Hellenistic culture. For the writer of the second-century BC *Letter of Aristeas*, or for Philo, Judaism was not opposed to the *paideia* of the Hellenistic world in which they lived: rather, it was a philosophical system like Stoicism or Epicureanism – and because it was superior to any of these systems, it was the perfect completion of a proper *paideia*.

That situation only began to change towards the end of the first century AD.[56] The Roman destruction of Jerusalem in AD 70 led to the end of any political or legislative role for representatives of the Jewish landowning elite through the Sanhedrin. During the following half-century, the Romans (accustomed to accepting the authority of their own experts in religious law, the college of Pontifices) gradually gave more and more authority over questions affecting the behaviour of those who professed to be Jews to the teachers, the rabbis. By late antiquity, the rabbis, through their head the Galilean patriarch to whom the Romans had given the authority to define Jewish custom, had come to monopolise the right to interpret what was and what was not in accordance with Judaism, and to impose their own view of orthodoxy on Jews not just in Palestine, but throughout the Roman empire. During these centuries, Judaism gradually but decisively turned its back on Graeco-Roman culture.

This clear self-demarcation on the part of Judaism post-dates the appearance of Christianity. Just as it is anachronistic to ascribe the later clear rejection of gentile practices to most first-century AD Jews, so it is an oversimplification to cite Christian writers' objections to the *content* of pagan culture as evidence that Greek and Roman Christians rejected the *forms* of classical culture and education. Where elements of secular culture – in particular, the doctrines of pagan philosophers – conflicted with Christian belief, then Christians were adamant. For St Paul – unlike Philo, or the author of the *Letter of Aristeas* – Athens and the New Jerusalem are irreconcilable: but he is talking specifically about the fact that Greek philosophy could make no sense of even the most fundamental Christian principles such as the resurrection; and he warns his correspondents against being influenced by popular versions of Platonic or 'gnostic' philosophy.[57]

Nevertheless there is little to lead us to suppose that Paul required radical changes in the way in which Christians, whether Jews or gentiles, taught their children the skill of letters. Like many of the Christian writers who came after him, he saw no contradiction in quoting from the pagan literature he had learnt at school. In the highly formal address to the Council of the Areopagus at Athens ascribed to him by the Acts of the Apostles (17:28), he cites a line from Aratus (*Phainomena* 5): 'As some of your own poets have said, "We are all his [Zeus'] offspring".' In the letter to Titus (1:12), Paul quotes a line from Epimenides, the first half of which also appears in Callimachus' *Hymn to Zeus*: 'It was a Cretan prophet, one of your own countrymen, who said, "Cretans are always liars, vicious brutes, lazy gluttons".' If Paul's source could be shown to have been Callimachus directly, then it might be significant that a diaspora Jew with religious inclinations remembered statements about Zeus that he had been taught as a schoolboy. It is more likely that maxims such as these were learnt as part of lists like Pseudo-Phocylides or the later Latin *Dicta Catonis*. Such a collection was surely where Paul learnt Menander's line that 'Bad company is the ruin of a good character' (I Corinthians 15:33), or the reminiscence of Isocrates' famous *chria* about the fruits of study being sweet.[58] Such Greek collections of simple maxims for children were not all that different from contemporary Jewish compilations such as the *Wisdom of Solomon* or Ben-Sirach's *Ecclesiasticus*. Paul's clear hostility to Greek philosophy should not therefore be assumed to apply to classical education in general.

While there was a number of Christian thinkers in the Greek world, such as Origen, who tried to represent Christianity as being in accordance with philosophical premises shared with pagans, the lower esteem in which philosophy was held in the Latin half of the empire meant that there was not the same incentive to prove that Christian and pagan thinkers shared common ground. Minucius Felix's Ciceronian dialogue, the *Octavius*, is an exception.[59] Latin Christians preferred to apply Paul's polarity between Christ and Belial to philosophy:

> What has righteousness to do with wickedness? Can light consort with darkness? Can Christ agree with Belial, or a believer join hands [i.e. establish a relationship of trust] with an unbeliever? Can there be a compact between the Temple of God and the idols of the heathen?'
>
> (II Corinthians 6:14 ff.)

If a writer could show that an opponent shared some of his ideas with pagan thinkers, this was clear proof that he was heterodox. The argument appears in Pope Hippolytus' *Refutation of all Heresies*, written in Greek at the beginning of the third century AD, as well as in the contemporary writings of Tertullian, the first Christian writer in Latin of whom substantial works survive.[60]

Tertullian fulminates against *sapientia saecularis*, the wisdom of the secular world, in several of his writings. His tone is quite different from that of the Alexandrian Christians Origen and Clement, who wished to put neo-Platonist ideas to the service of Christ. A much-quoted passage occurs in a work denying the claim of heretics to speak on behalf of true Christianity:

These teachings were invented by men and demons for itching ears by the ingenuity of worldly wisdom; the Lord called it foolishness and has chosen the fools of this world to perplex even philosophy herself. For she is the basis of Worldly Wisdom, a rash expounder of the divine nature and order. And then, the heresies themselves are equipped from the storehouse of philosophy. That is where Valentinus' aeons and infinite forms (whatever that may mean) and human trinity came from – he was a follower of Plato. That is where Marcion's God, who is improved by his inability to be affected, comes from – he was taken over from the Stoics. Even Epicurus is listened to, to prove that the soul dies. . . . What is there in common between Athens and Jerusalem? What is there in common between [Plato's] Academy and the Church? What is there in common between heretics and Christians?

But Tertullian's rejection of pagan philosophy, in highly rhetorical language, does not mean that he considered the *artes* that a child learnt at school equally reprehensible. His argument is contorted, and not easy to follow. The subject matter of literature was of course dangerous; but that did not make the skill itself evil. Because the schoolteacher was involved in the secular world, a Christian who wanted to earn a living teaching this material was naturally compromised: but it did not follow that the children he taught would be.

We should also consider the case of teachers of reading and writing, and also of masters of literature. These people have to talk about the gods of the pagans, and discuss all their titles, genealogies, myths, distinguishing insignia. Then they have to observe the festivals, as the occasions on which they reckon up their fees.

They have to bring their classes along to pagan rituals, and give the children a holiday when pagan officials decide to stage a sacrifice. 'You cannot hold that this is suitable for a Christian teacher unless you consider that it is suitable for a Christian who is not a teacher.'[61]

But teaching must be distinguished from learning: a schoolmaster implicitly accepts pagan rituals by teaching about them. (§10): 'As a result, a basis is established for belief in the demons from the first moment a child learns: ask yourself whether a man who asks pupils questions [*catechizat*] about idols is not committing idolatry.' On the other hand, 'a Christian pupil attending a school will not accept the truth of what he hears about the gods.' Tertullian recommends that children should be taught about God and their Christian faith before anything else, as soon as they can reason. As for the teacher,

> necessity gives him an excuse, since *there is no other way of learning*. But not to teach letters is easier than not to learn them, just as keeping clear of the contamination of pagan ritual which schooling brings is easier for the Christian pupil than for the schoolteacher.

In other words, letters, literature, and rhetoric are necessary skills; if they are properly used, they do not have to be rejected simply because they were invented by pagans.

> It was Mercury who first taught the use of letters; I will admit that they are necessary not just for commercial dealings, but also for our devotion towards God. And if the same individual invented the lyre, I will not deny – when I think of the psalms of David – that he created this invention too for the use of holy men, and that he was serving God.[62]

So long as a child had already been taught to be a firm believer, the acquisition of these literary *artes* could be a positive thing.

Some Christian writers pointed out, in highly rhetorical language, that rhetoric was a dangerous weapon, and that in the wrong hands it did a lot of harm. But that was in the context of the competitive secular community. The Christian was warned not to learn rhetoric, but not so much because rhetoric was itself evil, as because the situations in which it was needed were evil. Some went further: secular skills were not necessary to salvation, and were thus evil in so far as they diverted the Christian from the spiritual exercises that ought to be his primary concern. As Commodian put it in the third century AD:

> Vergil is read, and so are Cicero and Terence. All they produce is what is agreeable – they say nothing about the real issues of life. What use is it to chase pointlessly after worldly things here on earth, to know all about the wealth of kings, or their wars?

And to know the 'raging forum' as a lawyer, to know that one can never be certain that the application of the laws cannot be subverted by bribery. Let him be an advocate, let him be praised as a divine speaker – when he is dead, it will do him no good, if he denied Christ while he was alive.[63]

Secular education, like the secular office holding which it led up to, was ultimately irrelevant. This is the reason why schooling is so rarely referred to in lives of saints. It has been argued that the celibate monastic readership for whom such texts were written had no interest in children. But these monks had themselves learnt letters. It was simply that they did not consider that such learning was relevant to their salvation.

One of the earliest hagiographies is the third-century *Passion of Saints Perpetua and Felicity.*[64] Vivia Perpetua is simply introduced as 'of good family, with an all-round education, and honourably married': the details did not interest the Christian writer or his audience. Similarly Pontius the Deacon, in his *Life and Passion of Saint Cyprian,*[65] explicitly states that he has no interest in the saint's family and education (§2):

Where shall I begin my account? At what point shall I start the account of the good things he had, if not at the beginning of his Faith, his heavenly birth? The things a man of God has done need not be enumerated from any other point than that at which he was born to God. Of course he studied, of course good *artes* imbued his excellent heart, but I shall pass over these. For they are useful only in secular terms.

Because secular education was a matter of acquiring morally neutral skills, there was no contradiction in Christians both using these skills and claiming that they were irrelevant to salvation. Lactantius used the Old Testament metaphor of 'spoiling the Egyptians', using weapons taken from the enemy for the service of God. It is not surprising that the teaching of rhetoric, as well as literature, continued in Italy until the ravages of the Byzantine reconquest in the sixth century AD. The poems and letters of sixth-century Gallic bishops such as Avitus of Vienne and Sidonius Apollinaris show that Christianity did not by any means bring about the end of classical rhetorical culture.[66]

Nor did it mean the end of the classical school syllabus, based on pagan authors. Only during the reign of the emperor Julian the Apostate (AD 361–3), when Christians were banned from teaching literature on the grounds that only pagans could properly teach pagan texts, was there an attempt to provide Christian children with a syllabus based on the Bible: a *grammatikos* called Apollinarius rewrote the Old Testament in Greek verse, while his son of the same name, who was bishop of Laodicea on the coast of Syria, did the same for the New Testament.[67] After Julian's death, such a specifically Christian syllabus was not needed. In both the Greek and the Latin world, Christian children continued to learn the *artes liberales* from pagan material. Although there were suggestions that this would not be suitable for those children dedicated by their parents to the service of God at an early age, there is no evidence that the alternative syllabus based on the Bible which St Jerome drew up for the young nun Laeta was ever actually used by anyone.[68]

There were problems about using pagan texts to teach children belonging to the bishop's household to read and write; but as for Tertullian, what caused concern was not that the material was unsuitable for children to learn from, but that it was unsuitable for clergymen to teach. The problem did not become acute until the post-Roman period: in many western European communities, there no longer was anyone who possessed the *artes liberales* except for the clergy. The Councils of Toledo (527) and Vaison (529) insisted that bishops must make provision for teaching their *lectores* to read. A bishop of Lisieux in the sixth century was delighted when a teacher opened a school in his town, but the *doctor* soon moved on. Often bishops had to teach their young oblates themselves: and when that happened, it was worrying, since bishops were not there to teach secular skills. This is the context of a notorious attack on teaching the *artes liberales* by Gregory I in a letter to Desiderius, the bishop of Vienne.[69] Pope Gregory, himself a highly educated man from a senatorial family, did not question the need for children to learn the skills of reading and writing, even from pagan authors: but he did not want that to become the occupation of bishops. A child's spiritual upbringing had to be kept separate from his acquisition of secular skills.

For the Christian, the answer to the question of what made a child a person, given that adult citizenship was no longer at the centre of social life, could not be inherited wealth or status, nor could it be precocious ability at one's letters. The radical answer was that any distinction imposed by secular society between those who mattered and those who did not, was artificial. The Christian God cared for children, as he did for slaves, women, and barbarians, just as much as for adult males.

It was Augustine who worked out some of the most crucial implications of this. His strong sense of his own imperfection, even as a baptised Christian (and from 395, bishop of Hippo Regius), led him to analyse the secular habits (*consuetudines carnales*) which had gradually moulded his personality since his birth, and which he found so difficult to reform. The result was the *Confessions*, written between AD 397 and 401, the earliest literary work to take the writer's own childhood seriously. In it he traced how God's grace, rather than any human power to act properly, had brought him where he was, and how that grace was as much concerned with a little child as with any adult.[70]

There was no precedent for such a book, no literary genre which would enable the reader to expect any particular approach. Augustine has to explain that his assertions are based on his own observations – which suggests that he thought they might well contradict the presuppositions we have looked at in Chapter 1 about how children behave (1,6). In 1,7 in particular, he notes that observation will reveal how one behaved oneself as a baby: 'Who can remind me? Will it not be the tiniest little baby now, in whom I can see all the things I cannot remember about myself?' – for instance, how a baby screams when it wants milk and is not given any; and how the real reason why no one scolds a baby for this kind of behaviour is that it would be quite useless. It is lack of strength, not lack of will, that makes babies harmless. There is no such thing as a naturally innocent child, as some suppose: we just have to look at the jealousy and envy between babies fed by the same nurse, quite a problem for mothers and nurses. It was the same envy and jealousy as that shown by adults when they competed for prestige and public offices in the secular world.

While Augustine had to observe other babies to describe his *infantia*, he could rely on his own experience to describe *pueritia*. Augustine accepted the Platonic assumption that the faculties of thought and memory potentially existed from birth: speaking is not 'taught' in the sense of being imposed from outside, as writing is, but arises naturally: 'For it was not older people who taught me, teaching me words in some logical order as they later taught the alphabet, but I myself weighed in my memory, with the mind which you, my God, gave me . . .' (1,8). Augustine lists a large number of these *maiores homines* from whom he learnt: nurses, slaves, friends of his own age, later the local *patronus*, as well as his parents.

For all his respect for his mother Monica, Augustine's account leaves us with the impression that his parents' main interest in his progress was according to the values of the secular world: 'My parents did not want to remove me from temptation by arranging a marriage; their only care was that I should learn to make the best possible speech and persuade people through my words' (2,2). They did not want to curb his adolescent affairs:

> She did not care about this, since she was afraid that her hopes for me might be impeded by the shackles of a wife: this hope was not the hope she had through You in the world to come, but her hope in education. Both my parents very much wanted me to study literature; my father, since he did not think about You at all, and what he thought about me was foolish; as for my mother, not only did she think that the normal secular course of studies would not impede me in approaching You, she did not even think about whether or not they would be of any assistance. (2,3)

Augustine thought that other parents had been equally concerned with secular rather than divine criteria. Alypius 'did not abandon the earthly road of a career as a lawyer, which his parents had kept repeating to him' (6,8). When Alypius' mother died, her eldest son Nebridius wanted the funeral to take place at home: a funeral was one of the public spectacles through which a family could advertise how it had risen in the world. Augustine stresses that Monica herself had overcome *ista inanitas*, this nonsense: 'She did not want her body to be sumptuously dressed or buried with spices, nor did she wish for a choice monument or care for the ancestral tomb' (9,11–13).

Specialist *artes* such as knowledge of Christian rituals and prayers (1,9) and writing and literature were learnt from experts. Beating plays a major part in Augustine's memories of his schooldays; he saw little to justify it except tradition. ('This was praised by our ancestors.') He also recalled feeling that parents were imposing a double standard when they disapproved of children playing truant from school: 'I was disobedient, not because there was anything better than what my elders had in mind for me, but simply because I loved games.' Augustine's radical rejection of the secular values places all these *nugae* on the same level. Secular society is irrelevant to real happiness; hence it is absurd that parents should force their children to study so that they may become wealthy and respected adults.

> Parents want their children to achieve the same glory as is given to those who pay for these 'games'. Yet the same parents will have their children beaten if these games get in the way of the studies which will enable them to provide such games.[71]

Status, honour, loss of face, motivate small children in exactly the same way as adults. Augustine's desire to win led him to cheat at games and to quarrel bitterly when he found that his playmates were cheating him (1,19). When as a boy he stole food, or as an adolescent robbed the famous pear-tree, his motives included the fear of losing face among his friends if he did not accept their standards of behaviour. Later in life, Augustine's outstanding rhetorical ability led him to tap other sources of prestige; although as a student at Carthage his position as *maior*, top of the form, stopped him from actually taking part in the vandalism and rioting his fellow students indulged in, he claims that he nevertheless felt some shame at not joining in (3,3). But he still cut lectures, even if he now no longer lied to his parents about this out of the sheer fear of being beaten, as he had as a child (1,16–19). The human shortcomings which made an adult a sinner were no different in a child.

> We may exchange our *paedagogi* and schoolteachers, nuts and footballs and singing-birds for Prefects and kings, for money, land and slaves; but the same desires stay with us through all the stages of our lives, just as severer penalties replace the beating of a schoolmaster. (1,19)

The prizes of adult life as a citizen had as little ultimate value as those of children's games. Christian salvation had replaced glory as a citizen, or brilliance as an orator; and that Christian salvation was just as much available – and just as necessary – for the smallest child as for the most brilliant or powerful adult.

The limitations imposed by our evidence make any general conclusion difficult and dangerous. The vast majority of the population of the Roman empire has left no record of its feelings about children, and we can only assume that its 'peasant' attitudes subsisted basically unchanged alongside the views expressed on its behalf by intellectuals. Our evidence gives us no reason to believe that there was any change in the most important single factor affecting childhood – the high rate of mortality. But there were changes in the way in which people came to terms with that fact. The classical period had done so by excluding children from civic life; Jews and Christians responded by giving not just the youngest child, but even the child in the womb, the same right to a place within the religious community as any adult.

What is not so easy to judge is how this change between classical and late antique attitudes to children was related to the wider social transformation of the Mediterranean world, principally the disappearance of any significant role for the citizen as a member of a distinct status-group. In certain respects religious beliefs directly affected behaviour – for instance, by categorising infanticide as murder. But some of the evidence, such as the tendency for the children of elite families to be granted an ever greater role in public life, and the increasing emphasis on education as the mark of an adult, suggests that there were also respects in which the role of Christianity was rather to give expression to a social process which during the first three centuries was affecting all city-communities within the empire.

NOTES

1 T. E. J. Wiedemann, 'Barbarians in Ammianus Marcellinus', in
 I. S. Moxon (ed.), *Past Perspectives* (Cambridge, 1986), 189 ff.
2 Pliny, *NH* 28,257–9, pp.17 f. above.
3 A. Audollent, *Defixionum Tabellae* (Paris, 1904; repr. Frankfurt, 1967),
 nos 104, 22–37, from Cyprus, relating to litigation.
4 Horace, *Epode* 5. Vergil, *Aeneid* 6. Cf. H. W. Parke, *Sybils and Sibylline
 Prophecy in Classical Antiquity* (London, 1988).
5 *Aeneid* 7,107–134.
6 Cassius Dio 50.8; Procopius, *Histories* 5,20.1–4. Shepherd-boys were
 doubly 'marginal': shepherds lived an asocial life away from cities, at
 the edge of the wild.

7 Plutarch, *Aemilius Paullus* 10,4; the story is also mentioned by Cicero, *De Divinatione* 1,103; 2,83; Livy 21,62.2; Plutarch, *Moralia* 737 B = *Quaestiones Conviviales* 9,1.3.

8 Cassius Dio 48,44.3. For other references to these naked child-slaves, see Chapter 1, n. 51 above.

9 Philostratus, *Life of Apollonius* 5,13.3.

10 Bücheler, *CLE* 987; Cicero, *In Vatinium* 6.14; Horace, *Epodes* 5; Petronius, *Satyricon* 63.8. Cf. Shakespeare, *Macbeth*, Act IV, Scene 1,30: 'Finger of birth-strangled babe'.

11 Livy 5,27.9; Suetonius, *Caligula* 27; Prudentius, 'Passion of Saint Cassian of Forum Cornelii', *Peristephanon* 9 = *PL* 60,432. This is a different kind of story from that which is told by Greek historians, of the children of a community executing the children of a criminal or tyrant while their parents execute the tyrant himself: Herodotus 9,5.3; Polybius 5,56.15.

12 A. J. Bremmer, *The Early Greek Concept of the Soul* (Princeton, NJ, 1983), 99; n.77 for infant burial in Rome. E. Cuq, 'Funus', Daremberg-Saglio, *Dictionnaire des antiquités* II, 1386–1409.

13 Tibullus 1,3.11.

14 Cf. Ovid, *Fasti* 4,226, where the goddess requires 'semper fac puer esse velis'.

15 Isidore, *Etymologies* 11,2.10: 'Puer a puritate vocatus, quia purus est, et necdum lanuginen floremque genarum habens.'

16 Cicero, *De Divinatione* 2,50; *Anthologia Palatina* 1,21: 'ΠΑΙ, ΓΕΡΟΝ, ΑΙΟΝΩΝ ΠΡΟΓΕΝΕΣΤΕΡΟΣ, ΠΑΤΡΟΣ ΟΜΗΛΙΞ'; C. Gnilka, *Aetas Spiritualis: die Ueberwindung der natürlichen Altersstufen als Ideal frühchristlichen Lebens* (Bonn, 1972).

17 Fronto: Haines I, 180; Ovid, *Fasti* 2,645–54; D. P. Harmon, 'The family festivals of Rome', *ANRW* II, 16.2, (1978) 1592 ff.

18 Columella, *Res Rusticae* 12,4.3; Servius, *ad Aen.* 1,730; Petronius, *Satyricon* 60.

19 Macrobius, *Saturnalia* 1,6.14; *CIL* VI,32323 = *ILS* 5050; we also have details of the Secular Games of AD 204: *ILS* 5050a.

20 Cassius Dio 75,4.5; Herodian 4,2.5.

21 Cf., for example, Tacitus, *Annals* 11,11; see p.121 above.

22 Dionysius of Halicarnassus, *Antiquities* 2,22.

23 Macrobius, *Saturnalia* 3,8.7; Plutarch, *Numa* 7.5.

24 Festus p. 82, 16–25 Lindsay.

25 From Pacuvius' *Medo*: Varro, *De Lingua Latina* 7,34; cf. Macrobius, *Saturnalia* 3,8.7.

26 W. Henzen, *Acta Fratrum Arvalium* (Berlin, 1874); Ae. Pasoli, *Acta Fratrum Arvalium* (Bologna, 1950).

27 W. K. Lacey, 'Patria Potestas', in B. Rawson (ed.), *The Family in Ancient Rome* (London and Sydney, 1986), 121–44.

28 Augustine, *City of God* 7,2.

29 Augustine, *City of God* 4,11.

30 *Noctes Atticae* 16,16.4.

31 *IG* III–2,4077; W. Burkert, *Greek Religion* (Oxford, 1985), 309 ff.

M. Nilsson, *The Dionysiac Mysteries of the Hellenistic and Roman Age* (Lund, 1957), believed that children were initiated; but the presence of children at ceremonies, as depicted on Pompeian murals, does not prove that they were present on equal terms with adults.

32 Paulinus the Deacon, *Life of Ambrose* 3 = *PL* 14,31.

33 Cyprian, *Letter* 27.1. See Chapter 3, n.49.

34 L. Duchesne, *Le Liber Pontificalis* (Paris 1886–92).

35 *Quaestiones veteris et novi testamenti* 101.

36 Justinian's attempts to control *lectores: Novellae Justiniani* III,1 etc. Aquinas: *Summa* III Sup.37.2. On the later semi-liturgical roles played by children, see, for example, K. Edwards, *The English Secular Cathedrals in the Middle Ages*; R. C. Trexler, 'Ritual in Florence: adolescence and salvation in the Renaissance' in C. Trinkans (ed.), *The Pursuit of Holiness in Late Medieval and Renaissance Religion* (Leiden, 1974), 200–64.

37 Ps. Jerome, *Epistle* 12.3 = *PL* 30.156; Augustine, *Sermo* 352.1 = *PL* 39.1550; Ennodius, *Vita Epifanii* 8; Victor Vitensis, *De Persecutione Vandalorum* 3,34 = *CSEL* 7.89.

38 *ILCV* 1266, 1267, 1264, 1268 (age 73); 1277 and 1285 (5 years); 1271: 'vixit annos p[lus] m[inus] XII'; 1280: 'Severus lectur ennocens . . . annis tredece'; 1283 (14 years); 1273 (16). Lyon: *ILCV* 1287.

39 Isaiah 66:24; Daniel 12:2; Mishnah, *Sanhedrin* 10 (ed. Danby, pp. 397 f.); Josephus, *Antiquities* 18,1.3(14) and *Against Apion* 2,30(318); Matthew 22:23; Mark 12:18; Luke 20:27; Acts 23:8; Paul, I Corinthians 15:12 ff. For the essentially Jewish rather than pagan origin of Christian baptism, see A. J. M. Wedderburn, *Baptism and Resurrection* (Tübingen, 1987).

40 Augustine, *Sermo* 242, 3.4, and 13: *PL* 38.1140; *Enchiridion* 87, *PL* 40.272 f.

41 Arguments in favour of the proposition that infant baptism is an authentic Christian tradition going back to the time of the Apostles have been stated by J. Jeremias, *Die Kindertaufe in den ersten vier Jahrhunderten* (Göttingen, 1958; Eng. trans., *Infant Baptism in the First Four Centuries*, London, 1960). The case against, argued by followers of Karl Barth's view of the nature of the Christian Church, is represented by K. Aland, *Die Säuglingstaufe im Neuen Testament und in der alten Kirche* (Munich, 1961; Eng. trans., *Did the Early Church Baptize Infants?*, London, 1962); the controversy remains unresolved.

42 Pliny 10,96.2: 'multi omnis aetatis'; Origen, *Contra Celsum* 3,50 and 55.

43 Aristides 15.6; Irenaeus, *Adversus Haereses* 2,22.4b = 33.2.

44 Tertullian, *De Baptismo* 18.

45 Dom Gregory Dix (ed.), *Hippolytus: Apostolic Tradition* (London, 2nd edn, 1968).

46 Hippolytus 42.1. Gregory of Nazianzen, *Oratio* 40 (AD 381) = *PG* 36.400.

47 Apronianus: *ILCV* 1,1343; Julia Florentina (Catania, Sicily, early fourth century): *ILCV* 1,1549; Perpetua: see n. 53 below.

48 Galatians 3:28; I Corinthians 12:13; Colossians 3:11.

49 A pagan reference to baptism for the circumcised: Juvenal, *Satires*

14,104. The ritual baptism of young children (with their father) may be deduced from the Babylonian Talmud: *Yebamot* 47A (cf. M. Simon, *Verus Israel*, Eng. trans. (London, 1985), 484, n.30).

50 A. Varagnac, *Civilisation traditionelle et genres de vie* (Paris, 1948) is a classic.

51 AD 305/6; Canon 38, Mansi 2,12. On the development of confirmation, cf. J. D. C. Fisher, *Christian Initiation: Baptism in the Medieval West* (London, 1965).

52 Innocent I, *Letters* 25.6 = *PL* 20,554. The Council of Trent, in response to Protestant arguments, specified a minimum age of 7 years.

53 *Passio SS Perpetuae et Felicitatis* = *PL* 3,17 ff., 39: 'et satiatus abscessit de aqua ludere more infantium gaudens: et experrecta sum. tunc intellegi translatum eum esse de poena'.

54 Cf. Augustine's *City of God*.

55 V. Tcherikover, *Hellenistic Civilization and the Jews* (New York, 1974), 350 f.; E. Schürer, *The Jewish People in the Time of Christ* (Eng. trans., Edinburgh, 1973). S. Liebermann, *Greek in Jewish Palestine* (New York, 1942), 29, quotes a minority view cited in the Palestinian Talmud: 'A man is permitted to teach his daughter Greek, for it serves her as an ornament.'

56 M. Simon, *Verus Israel*.

57 I Corinthians 1:18 ff.; Colossians 2:8.

58 Hebrews 12:11: cf. p.165 above.

59 Lactantius' attitude is rather more complex; while he wishes to apply worldly *sapientia* to the service of God, and show that Christianity is consonant with all that is best in pagan philosophy, he assumes that his audience will be rightly suspicious of the way pagan philosophers have misused their *sapientia*: *Divinae Institutiones* 1, 1.5; *De Opificio dei* 20,2–5.

60 T. D. Barnes, *Tertullian* (Oxford, 1971).

61 Tertullian, *De Idololatria* = *CSEL* 20.39 ff.; 40,6.9 ff.

62 Tertullian, *De Corona* 8 = *CSEL* 70,168; Mercury is euhemeristically assumed to have been a man.

63 *CSEL* 15,153; 'insanum forum' is a quotation from Vergil, *Georgics* 2,502; the idea of the laws being subverted by bribery comes from Cicero, *De Officiis* 3,118.

64 *PL* 3,17.

65 *PL* 3,1541 ff.

66 J. E. Sandys, *A History of Classical Scholarship* (Cambridge, 3rd edn, 1921); C. N. Cochrane, *Christianity and Classical Culture* (Oxford, 1940); W. Hagendahl, *The Latin Fathers and the Classics* (Göteborg, 1958); P. Riché, *Education et culture dans l'occident barbare* (Paris, 1962).

67 Socrates, *Historia Ecclesiastica* 3,16. The Latin *Cento Probae* was not a serious attempt to replace the syllabus taught by schoolteachers: Isidore, *De viris illustribus* 22.

68 Jerome, *Letters* 107.

69 Gregory of Tours, *Historia Francorum* 6,36; Gregorius Magnus, *Epistles* 11,54 = *PL* 77.1171. Note also Jerome's famous dream in which he worried about being more interested in writing good Ciceronian Latin

than in theology, 'Ciceronianus es, non Christianus': *Letters* 22.30 = *PL* 22.416.
70 There is a Penguin Classics translation of the *Confessions* by R. S. Pine-Coffin (1961). For general introductions to Augustine, cf. Chapter 3,n. 51 above.
71 *Confessions* 1,10: 'Ludos maiorum, quos tamen qui edunt ea dignitate praediti excellunt, ut hoc paene omnes optent parvulis suis, quos tamen caedi libentur patiuntur, si spectaculis talibus inpediantur ab studio, quo eos ad talia edenda cupiunt pervenire.'

BIBLIOGRAPHY

Adcock, F. E., *The Roman Art of War under the Republic* (Cambridge, Mass., 1940).

Aland, K., *Die Säuglingstaufe im Neuen Testament und in der alten Kirche* (Munich, 1961; Eng. trans., *Did the Early Church Baptize Infants?*, London, 1962).

Alföldy, G., 'Die Stellung der Ritter in der Führungsschicht des Imperium Romanum', *Chiron* XI (1981), 169 ff. = *Die römische Gesellschaft* (Stuttgart, 1986), 162 ff.

Alföldy, G., 'Die Generalität des römischen Heeres', *Römische Heeresgeschichte* (Amsterdam, 1987), 3 ff.

Astin, A. E., 'The Lex Annalis before Sulla', *Latomus* 16 (1957), 588 ff.; *Latomus* 17 (1958), 49 ff.

Astin, A. E., *Cato the Censor* (Oxford, 1978).

Audollent, A., *Defixionum Tabellae* (Paris, 1904; repr. Frankfurt, 1967).

Baldwin, B., *Suetonius* (Amsterdam, 1983).

Barnes, T. D., *Tertullian* (Oxford, 1971).

Barnes, T. D., *The New Empire of Diocletian and Constantine* (Cambridge, Mass., 1982).

Bieler, L., ΘΕΙΟΣ ΑΝΗΡ (Vienna, 1935/6).

Birley, A., *Septimius Severus* (London, 1971).

Birley, A., *Marcus Aurelius* (London, 2nd edn, 1987).

Bonner, S. F., *Education in Ancient Rome* (London, 1977).

Booth, A. D., 'The schooling of slaves in first-century Rome', *TAPhA* 109 (1979), 11 ff.

Bradley, K. R., 'Dislocation in the Roman family', *Historical Reflections/ Réflexions Historiques* 14.1 (1987), 33 ff.

Bremmer, A. J., *The Early Greek Concept of the Soul* (Princeton, NJ, 1983).

Brind'Amour, L., and Brind'Amour, P., 'La deuxième Satire de Perse', *Latomus* 30 (1971), 999 ff.

Brind'Amour, L., and Brind'Amour, P., 'Le dies lustricus', *Latomus* 34 (1975), 17 ff.

Brown, P., *Augustine of Hippo* (London, 1967).

Brunt, P. A., *Italian Manpower* (Oxford, 1971).

Brunt, P. A., 'Marcus Aurelius in his Meditations', *Journal of Roman Studies* 64 (1974), 1 ff.

Buecheler, F., (ed.), *Carmina Latina Epigraphica* (Leipzig, 1921).

Burkert, W., *Greek Religion* (Eng. trans., Oxford, 1985).

Cameron, A., *Claudian* (Oxford, 1970).

Cameron, A., and Cameron, A.M., 'Christianity and tradition in the historiography of the Late Empire', *Classical Quarterly* 14 (1964), 316 ff.

Cameron, A. M., and Kuhrt, A., (eds), *Images of Women in Antiquity* (London, 1983).

Chadwick, H., *Augustine* (Oxford, 1986).

Champlin, E., *Fronto and Antonine Rome* (Cambridge, Mass., 1980).

Christes, J., 'Reflexe erlebter Unfreiheit in den Sentenzen des Publilius Syrus und den Fabeln des Phaedrus', *Hermes* 107 (1979), 199 ff.

Clark, G., 'Roman women', *Greece and Rome* 28 (1981), 193 ff.

Clauss, M., 'Probleme der Lebensalterstatistiken aufgrund römischer Grabinschriften', *Chiron* 3 (1973), 395 ff.

Cochrane, C. N., *Christianity and Classical Culture* (Oxford, 1940).

Collingwood, R. G., and Wright, R. P., *Roman Inscriptions in Britain* I (Oxford, 1965).

Cox, P., *Biography in Late Antiquity: A Quest for the Holy Man* (Berkeley, Los Angeles, London, 1983).

Crook, J., *Law and Life of Rome* (London, 1967).

Cuq, E., 'Funus', Daremberg-Saglio, *Dictionnaire des antiquités* II, 2, 1386–1409.

Danforth, L. M., *The Death Rituals of Rural Greece* (Princeton, NJ, 1982).

Della Corte, M., *Iuventus* (Rome, 1924).

de Mause, L., *The History of Childhood* (Chicago, 1974).

Dix, Dom Gregory, (ed.), *Hippolytus: Apostolic Tradition* (London, 2nd edn, 1968).

Dixon, S., *The Roman Mother* (London, 1988).

Dover, K., *Greek Homosexuality* (London, 1978).

Duncan-Jones, R. P., 'Age-rounding, illiteracy, and social differentiation in the Roman empire', *Chiron* 7 (1977), 333 ff.

Engels, D., 'The problem of female infanticide in the Greco-Roman world', *Classical Philology* 75 (1980), 112 ff.

Eyben, E., 'Antiquity's view of puberty', *Latomus* 31 (1972), 677 ff.

Eyben, E., 'Family planning in Graeco-Roman antiquity', *Ancient Society* 11/12 (1980/1), 5 ff.

Fernique, E., 'Crepitaculum', in Daremberg-Saglio, *Dictionnaire des antiquités* I, 2, 1561 ff.

Fisher, J. D. C., *Christian Initiation: Baptism in the Medieval West* (London, 1965).

Frier, B., 'Roman life expectancy: Ulpian's evidence', *Harvard Studies in Classical Philology* 86 (1982), 213 ff.

Frier, B., 'Roman life expectancy: the Pannonian evidence', *Phoenix* 37 (1983), 328 ff.

Gardner, J. F., *Women in Roman Law and Society* (London, 1986).

Garnsey, P., 'Trajan's Alimenta', *Historia* 17 (1968), 367 ff.

Garnsey, P., *Social Status and Legal Privilege in the Roman Empire* (Oxford, 1970).

Garnsey, P., 'Aspects of the decline of the urban aristocracy in the empire', *Aufstieg und Niedergang der römischen Welt* II, 1 (1974), 229 ff.

Garnsey, P. D. A., *Non-slave Labour in the Greco-Roman World* (Cambridge, 1980).

Geiger, F., 'Salii', *Pauly-Wissowa*, IA.2, 1874 ff.

Giard, J.-B., *Catalogue des monnaies de l'empire romain I: Auguste* (Paris, 1976).

Gnilka, C., *Aetas Spiritualis: die Ueberwindung der natürlichen Altersstufen als Ideal frühchristlichen Lebens* (Bonn, 1972).

Goodman, M., *State and Society in Roman Galilee* (Totowa, NJ, 1983).

Gordon, M. L., 'The freedman's son in municipal life', *Journal of Roman Studies*, 4 (1931) 65 ff.

Grant, M., *Gladiators* (London, 1967).

Griessmair, E., *Das Motiv der Mors Immatura in den griechischen metrischen Grabinschriften* (Innsbruck, 1966).

Gröber, K., *Kinderspielzeug aus alter Zeit* (Berlin, 1928).

Gruen, E. S., 'Augustus and the ideology of war and peace', *The Age of Augustus* (Louvain, 1986), 68 ff.

Hagendahl, W., *The Latin Fathers and the Classics* (Göteborg, 1958).

Halfmann, H., *Die Senatoren aus dem östlichen Teil des Imperium Romanum* (Göttingen, 1979).

Hallett, J., *Fathers and Daughters in Roman Society* (Princeton, NJ, 1984).

Hammond, M., 'The composition of the Senate', *Journal of Roman Studies* 47 (1957), 74 ff.

Hands, A. R., *Charities and Social Aid in Greece and Rome* (London, 1968).

Harmon, D. P., 'The family festivals of Rome', *Aufstieg und Niedergang der römischen Welt* II, 16.2 (1978), 1592 ff.

Harris, W. V., 'The theoretical possibility of infanticide in the Greco-Roman World', *Classical Quarterly* 32 (1982), 114 ff.

Herzog-Hauser, G., 'Nutrix', *Pauly-Wissowa*, XVII, 1491 ff.

Heimbecher, W., 'Begriff und literarische Darstellung des Kindes im republikanischen Rom' (diss. Freiburg, 1958).

Hollingsworth, T. H., *Historical Demography* (Ithaca, NY, 1969).

Hopkins, K., 'Contraception in the Roman empire', *Comparative Studies in Society and History* 8 (1965), 124 ff.

Hopkins, K., 'On the probable age-structure of the Roman population', *Population Studies* 20 (1966), 245 ff.

Hopkins, K., *Death and Renewal* (Cambridge, 1983).

Humphreys, S. C., *The Family, Women and Death* (London, 1983).

Jeremias, J., *Die Kindertaufe in den ersten vier Jahrhunderten* (Göttingen, 1958; Eng. trans., *Infant Baptism in the First Four Centuries*, London, 1960).

Jones, A. H. M., *The Greek City* (Oxford, 1940; paperback repr., 1981).

Just, R., 'Freedom, slavery, and the female psyche', *CRUX* (Exeter, 1985), 169 ff.

Kassel, R., *Quomodo quibus locis apud veteres scriptores Graecos infantes atque parvuli pueri inducantur describantur commemorentur* (Würzburg, 1954).

Kepartova, J., 'Kinder in Pompeii', *Klio* 66 (1984), 192 ff.

Kinsey, T. E., 'Melior the Calculator', *Hermes* 107 (1979), 501.

Kübler, B., 'Rechtsunterricht', *Pauly-Wissowa*, IA.1, 394 ff.

Kühnert, F., *Allgemeinbildung und Fachbildung in der Antike* (Deutsche Akademie der Wissenschaften zu Berlin, Sektion für Altertumswissenschaft 30, 1961).

Lacey, W. K., 'Patria Potestas', in B. Rawson (ed.), *The Family in Ancient Rome* (London, 1986), 121 ff.

Lafaye, G., 'Ludi', Daremberg-Saglio, *Dictionnaire des antiquités* III, 2, 1356 ff.

Lafaye, G., 'Pupa', Daremberg-Saglio, *Dictionnaire des antiquités* IV, 1, 768 f.

Laslett, P., and Wall, R., (eds), *Household and Family in Past Time* (Cambridge, 1972).

Lattimore, R., *Themes in Greek and Latin Epitaphs* (Urbana, Ill., 1962).

Leclerc, H., 'Alumni', *Dictionnaire d'archéologie chrétienne et de liturgie* I (Paris, 1907), 1288 ff.

Leo, F., *Die griechisch-römische Biographie* (Leipzig, 1901).

Liebenam, 'Exercitus', *Pauly-Wissowa*, VI, 1589–1679.

Liebs, D., 'Rechtsschulen und Rechtsunterricht im Prinzipat', *Aufstieg und Niedergang der römischen Welt* II, 15 (Berlin/New York, 1976), 197 ff.

Lloyd-Jones, H., *The Justice of Zeus* (Berkeley, Cal., 1971).

Macfarlane, A., *Marriage and Love in England 1300–1840* (Oxford, 1986).

MacMullen, R., 'Social mobility and the Theodosian Code', *Journal of Roman Studies* 54 (1964), 49 ff.

MacMullen, R., 'Women's power in the principate', *Klio* 68 (1986), 434 ff.

Malitz, J., *Die Historien des Poseidonios* (Munich, 1983).

Marrou, H., ΜΟΥΣΙΚΟΣ ΑΝΗΡ (Grenoble, 1938).

Marrou, H., *Histoire de l'education dans l'antiquité* (Paris, 1948; many editions).

Mau, A., 'Ballspiel', *Pauly-Wissowa*, II (1896), 2832 ff.

Michon, E., 'Iliacae Tabulae', Daremberg-Saglio, *Dictionnaire des antiquités* III, 1, 372 ff.

Misch, G., *Geschichte der Autobiographie* (Eng. trans., *A History of Autobiography in Antiquity*, London, 1950).

Mitchell, S., 'Requisitioned transport in the Roman empire', *Journal of Roman Studies* 66 (1976), 106 ff.

Momigliano, A., *The Development of Greek Biography* (Cambridge, 1971).

Moxon, I.S., (ed.), *Past Perspectives* (Cambridge, 1986), 189 ff.

Nash, E., *Pictorial Dictionary of Ancient Rome* I (Tübingen/London, 1961).

Neraudau, J. P., *Etre enfant à Rome* (Paris, 1984).

Newman, G., *Infant Mortality* (London, 1906).

Nicolet, C., *The World of the Citizen in Republican Rome* (Eng. trans., London, 1980).

Nilsson, M. P., *The Dionysiac Mysteries of the Hellenistic and Roman Age* (Lund, 1957).

Pattison, R., *The Child Figure in English Literature* (Athens, Ga., 1978).

Payne, G. H., *The Child in Human Progress* (New York, 1916).

Peek, W., *Griechische Versinschriften* I (Berlin, 1955).

Rawson, B., (ed.), *The Family in Ancient Rome* (London/Sydney, 1986).

Reynolds, J., *Aphrodisias and Rome* (London, 1982).

Riché, P., *Education et culture dans l'occident barbare* (Paris, 1962).

Rossi, L., *Trajan's Column and the Dacian Wars* (Eng. trans., London, 1971).

Saller, R. P., *Personal Patronage under the Early Empire* (Cambridge, 1982).

Saller, R. P., '*Familia, domus* and the Roman conception of the family', *Phoenix* 38 (1984), 336 ff.

Sandys, J. E., *A History of Classical Scholarship* (Cambridge, 3rd edn, 1921).

Schürer, E., *The Jewish People in the Time of Christ* (Eng. trans., Edinburgh, 1973).

Schulz, F., *A History of Roman Legal Science* (Oxford, 1946).

Shaw, B. D., 'Latin funerary epigraphy and family life in the later Roman empire', *Historia* 33 (1984), 457 ff.

Shaw, B. D., 'The family in late antiquity: the experience of Augustine', *Past and Present* 115 (1987), 3 ff.

Simon, M., *Verus Israel* (Eng. trans., London, 1985).

Stone, L., *The Family, Sex, and Marriage in England 1500–1800* (London, 1977).

Syme, R., *Emperors and Biography* (Oxford, 1971).

Syme, R., 'Neglected children on the *Ara Pacis*', *American Journal of Archaeology* 88 (1984), 583 ff.

Talbert, R. J. A., *The Senate of Imperial Rome* (Princeton, NJ, 1984).

Talbert, R. J. A., (ed.), *Atlas of Classical History* (London, 1985).

Tcherikover, V., *Hellenistic Civilization and the Jews* (New York, 1974).

Thompson, D'A. W., 'Games and playthings', *Greece and Rome* 2 (1933), 71 ff.

Toynbee, J. M. C., *Death and Burial in the Roman World* (Ithaca, NY, 1971).

Toynbee, J. M. C., *Animals in Roman Life and Art* (London, 1973).

Varagnac, A., *Civilisation traditionelle et genres de vie* (Paris, 1948).

Väterlein, Jutta, *Roma Ludens. Kinder und Erwachsene beim Spiel im antiken Rom* (Amsterdam, 1976).

Veyne, P., 'La Famille et l'amour sous le haut-empire romain', *Annales* 33.1 (1978), 35 ff.

Veyne, P., 'Homosexuality in ancient Rome', in P. Ariès and A. Bejin (eds), *Western Sexuality* (Eng. trans., Oxford, 1985).

Vogt, J., 'Alphabet für Freie und Sklaven', *Rheinisches Museum* 116 (1973), 129–42 = *Sklaverei und Humanität. Ergänzungsheft* (Wiesbaden, 1983), 17–27.

Vogt, J., *Ancient Slavery and the Ideal of Man* (Eng. trans., Oxford, 1974).

Wallace-Hadrill, A., *Suetonius* (London, 1984).

Warmington, B. H., 'The municipal patrons of Roman North Africa', *Papers of the British School at Rome* 22 (1954), 39 ff.

Warren, L. B., 'Roman triumphs and Etruscan kings', *Journal of Roman Studies* 60 (1970), 49 ff.

Wiedemann, T. E. J., 'Thucydides, women, and the limits of rational analysis', *Greece and Rome* 30.2 (1983), 163 ff.

Wiedemann, T. E. J., 'Barbarians in Ammianus Marcellinus', in I. S. Moxon (ed.), *Past Perspectives* (Cambridge, 1986), 189 ff.

Wiedemann, T. E. J., *Slavery* (Greece and Rome New Surveys in the Classics No. 19, 1987).

Wilson, L. M., *The Roman Toga* (Baltimore, Md, 1924).

Wrigley, E. A., *Population and History* (London, 1969).

INDEX